Presented To:

_____

By:

_____

Date:

_____

God's Little Devotional Journal for Women

Honor Books
Tulsa, Oklahoma

Second Printing

God's Little Devotional Journal for Women
ISBN 1-56292-643-8
Copyright © 2000 by Honor Books
P.O. Box 55388
Tulsa, Oklahoma 74155

God's Little Devotional Journal for Women

Introduction

How much more real your thoughts and dreams become when you jot them down in a journal! Whether you have ever kept a diary or journal in the past, *God's Little Devotional Journal for Women* makes it easy for you to reflect on your daily life. Each day, this beautifully crafted journal brings you an inspirational story to uplift and motivate you. We also have included scriptures, quotes, and relevant writing prompts to help you record your thoughts.

The English poet Lord Byron once wrote, "The journal is a relief. When I am tired . . . out comes this, and down goes everything." Keeping a journal is not hard. You don't have to write pages and pages of prose perfect enough for publication. You only have to be true to yourself. Writing in a journal is therapeutic, and one of its greatest benefits is spiritual growth.

Draw nearer to God and experience His love and grace through the wonderful stories in this journal as you reflect on your spiritual life. At the end of the year, use the extra pages to reflect on how much you've grown in your relationship with God. Read and write with an open heart, and let God speak to you today!

Bending Low

*A wise man will hear and
increase learning, and a man of
understanding will attain wise counsel.*

PROVERBS 1:5

As a young man, Carlos Romulo, the former president of the Philippines, won an oratorical contest in the Manila high school he attended. His father was puzzled, however, when he noticed his son ignoring the congratulations of one of the other contestants. As they left the auditorium, he asked Carlos, "Why didn't you shake hands with Julio?"

"I have no use for Julio," Carlos replied. "He was speaking ill of me before the contest." The father put his arm around his son and said, "Your grandfather used to tell me that the taller the bamboo grows, the lower it bends. Remember that always, my boy. The taller the bamboo grows, the lower it bends."

A woman once advised a new employee: "Fifty percent of the people in this organization will teach you what to do and the other 50 percent what not to do. It's your challenge to figure out which percent goes with which person." Even if someone isn't a good example, we can always learn from that person what not to do.

Everyone has something to teach us—not only those who are experts in their fields or those who just tell us what we want to hear. Every human being is a living encyclopedia of ideas, insights, facts, experiences, and opinions. If we are wise, we will keep our eyes and ears open and learn from everyone around us.

———

*I am defeated, and know it, if I meet
any human being from whom I find
myself unable to learn anything.*

What HAVE
I LEARNED
FROM THOSE
AROUND ME?

Loving the Unlovable

*My son, hear the instruction of
your father, and do not forsake
the law of your mother.*

PROVERBS 1:8

What KEEPS
ME FROM
LOVING AN
UNLOVABLE
PERSON?

---

*A little boy's mother once told him
that it is God who makes people good.
He looked up and replied, "Yes, I know
it is God, but mothers help a lot."*

When both of Susie's parents died, she had no other relatives to care for her, so she was placed into foster care. Eventually, she came to live with the Weavers. Mrs. Weaver found Susie sullen, withdrawn, and uncommunicative. When she asked to see Susie's records, she found that other families agreed. The first foster family wrote, "Susie is a quiet, shy girl." The second family wrote, "She obeys, but she doesn't participate much in the family." *I doubt if Susie will be with us long,* Mrs. Weaver thought. Still, she decided to keep Susie through the Christmas holiday and then talk to her social worker about a transfer to another home.

At Christmas, the Weavers exchanged a number of lovely presents, including gifts for Susie. Then Susie handed Mrs. Weaver a brown paper sack decorated with a rough drawing of a Christmas scene. Inside, she found a rhinestone necklace with a couple of stones missing and a little half-empty bottle of perfume. As Mrs. Weaver put on the necklace and dabbed perfume behind her ear, Susie said, "Mom's necklace looks good on you. You smell good like she did, too." Mrs. Weaver's heart melted. She vowed to renew her efforts to love Susie, and she succeeded. By the following Christmas, Susie had become her adopted daughter.

When we come across someone in need, sometimes our first inclination is to send that person on to someone who can provide the necessary help. Often, however, we may be just whom that person needs. As Mrs. Weaver discovered, when we make the decision to help, God supplies the strength and wisdom we need to make a difference in someone's life.

Helplessness

Blessed are all those who
put their trust in Him.

PSALM 2:12

A man once asked Dwight L. Moody, "How can you accept the Bible with all its mysteries and contradictions, you with your fine mind?"

Moody replied, "I don't explain it. I don't understand it. I don't make anything of it. I simply believe it."

In his classic book entitled *Prayer,* Dr. O. Hallesby echoed this attitude. He wrote, "Prayer and helplessness are inseparable. Only he who is helpless can truly pray. . . . Prayer [therefore] consists simply in telling God day by day in what ways we feel helpless. We are moved to pray every time the Spirit of God, which is the spirit of prayer, emphasizes anew to us our helplessness, and we realize how impotent we are by nature to believe, to love, to hope, to serve, to sacrifice, to suffer, to read the Bible, to pray, and to struggle against our sinful desires."

God isn't looking for your perfection and strength today. He's looking for you to trust in His perfection and strength.

———✦———

Prayer requires that we stand in
God's presence . . . proclaiming
to ourselves and to others that
without God we can do nothing.

What AREAS
OF WEAKNESS
CAN I TURN
OVER TO GOD?

It's How High You Bounce

You, O Lord, are a shield for me.
PSALM 3:3

How CAN
I LET GOD
TURN MY
TROUBLES
INTO
TRIUMPHS?

Max Cleland was a typical, all-American boy, who starred in sports and was voted his high school's most outstanding senior. At age twenty-four, he volunteered for combat duty in Vietnam as a first lieutenant in the U.S. Army. One month before his return home, Cleland noticed a grenade that had been dropped accidentally. Moving to retrieve it, he was thrown backward by its explosion. He looked down in horror to find his right hand and leg missing and his left leg badly mangled. He tried to cry out, but shrapnel had ripped his throat.

No one expected Cleland to survive. But as he recovered from a triple amputation, he recalled two things: Paul the apostle had said that hope did not disappoint, and General George Patton had said, "Success is how high you bounce after you hit bottom."

Upon his return to civilian life, Cleland entered politics, learned to drive a special car, and traveled extensively, mobilizing support for veterans' causes. At age thirty-four, he became the youngest man ever to head the Veterans Administration and was later elected Georgia's secretary of state. Max says, "Life doesn't revolve around an arm and a leg. People look at you the way you look at yourself."

Effort is the supreme joy. Success is not a goal, but a means to aim still higher.

Forgiveness and Trust

*Blessed are the merciful, for
they shall obtain mercy.*

MATTHEW 5:7

Lisa was shocked when she discovered that David had run up thousands of dollars on every one of their credit cards. Not only was she furious about the mountain of debt, she was frustrated with herself for not recognizing David's compulsive spending habits.

In the days that followed, she wondered if she could ever trust her husband again and whether they would ever get out of debt.

Rather than wait for something to happen, she took two bold steps. The first was to convince David he needed help, and the second was to seek out a financial planner. She learned that if she carefully monitored the family funds, they could be out of debt in a few years. This brought hope for their financial future and for the future of their marriage.

Another turnaround in their marriage came when David asked Lisa to forgive him. She found that forgiving David freed her to turn away from the matter of money and to focus on their relationship. She decided it was possible to love someone even though they had messed up. Forgiving him made trust possible again, and once trust was reestablished, their marriage began to heal.

Forgiveness turns the heart away from what was and is to what can be. Is it time for you to take some bold steps? If love is your motive, be encouraged! When you replace frustration and fear with forgiveness and trust, situations and circumstances are subject to change.

What DO I
NEED TO GIVE
UP IN ORDER
TO FORGIVE?

*Forgiveness is giving love when
there is no reason to.*

Right Words

*Let your "Yes" be "Yes," and your
"No," "No." For whatever is more
than these is from the evil one.*
MATTHEW 5:37

Who IN MY
LIFE NEEDS
TO HEAR ME
SPEAK
POSITIVE
AND
AFFIRMING
WORDS?

While in training, surgeons are encouraged to weigh the importance and potential impact of each word spoken during an operation. As the anesthetic is administered, fear may strike a patient upon hearing someone say, "I'm going to shoot her now." Even a phrase such as "hook up the monitor" may be interpreted by a drugged patient as "shake up the monster." Can you imagine the impact on a half-dazed patient if a doctor were to say, "This just isn't my day!"

The same directions given by two different physicians could encourage or discourage a patient, simply by their tone of voice. One doctor's voice might suggest a prescription will work, while another's might convey reservations. Sometimes these subtle differences can drastically affect the morale of a patient.

Theodore Roosevelt popularized an expression about the need for clear, precise communication. He called words with several possible meanings "weasel words." By using them, a speaker might weasel out of any commitment, claiming a different interpretation of a word.

The Bible also tells us to always speak words of encouragement, hope, and faith to those around us. Even if we aren't performing surgery, we should carefully choose our words and how we communicate. Our words have an impact on those who hear them. Let's make it a positive one!

*The sweetest music isn't in
oratorios, but in kind words.*

Broken Silence

If you forgive men their trespasses,
your heavenly Father will
also forgive you.

MATTHEW 6:14

Meredith was surprised to find a letter in the mailbox from her brother, Tim. It had been three years since she had spoken to him, even though they lived in the same town. In the letter, Tim told her he and his wife were expecting twins and he hoped she would come to visit the babies after they were born. He expressed his sorrow that they had not communicated more and apologized for whatever it was he had done to cause them to become estranged.

Meredith's initial reaction was one of anger. *Whatever it was? Didn't he know?* She immediately sat down and wrote a five-page letter, detailing all the things Tim had done to hurt her. Before she could put the letter into an envelope, the phone rang, and it was several hours before she returned to her writing desk. Upon rereading her letter, she was horrified by what she found. She had thought she was being matter-of-fact, but her words were full of anger and pain. Tears of forgiveness filled her eyes. Perhaps it wasn't all Tim's fault. She called him the next day to say, "I can hardly wait to be the aunt of twins!"

You may not even realize you're harboring past hurts until something comes along to expose your pain. But when you forgive and release your hurts into God's hands, He can cleanse your heart and mind with His love and forgiveness and give you the power to forgive.

—⊙⊙⊙—

To forgive is to set a prisoner free
and discover the prisoner was YOU.

TO KEEP MY RELATIONSHIPS STRONG, WHERE DO I NEED TO LET GO OF PRIDE?

Pleasing One

No one can serve two masters; for either he will hate the one and love the other, or else he will be loyal to the one and despise the other. You cannot serve God and mammon.

MATTHEW 6:24

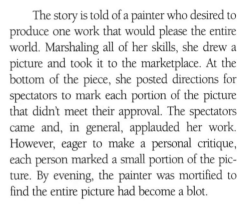

Whose
OPINION AM
I BUILDING
MY LIFE
AROUND?

The story is told of a painter who desired to produce one work that would please the entire world. Marshaling all of her skills, she drew a picture and took it to the marketplace. At the bottom of the piece, she posted directions for spectators to mark each portion of the picture that didn't meet their approval. The spectators came and, in general, applauded her work. However, eager to make a personal critique, each person marked a small portion of the picture. By evening, the painter was mortified to find the entire picture had become a blot.

The next day, the painter returned with a copy of the original picture. This time she asked the spectators to mark the portions of the work they admired. The spectators again complied. When the artist returned several hours later, she found that every stroke that had been panned the day before had received praise by this day's critics.

The artist concluded, "I now believe the best way to please one-half of the world is not to mind what the other half says."

People will always have an opinion about what we say or do. That's why we need to live our lives according to the words of the Bible— God's opinion. When we do, we will not fret over the opinions of others, because God's opinion is the only one that merits our efforts.

The formula for failure:
try to please everybody.

Small Kindnesses

Whatever you want men to do to you, do also to them, for this is the Law and the Prophets.

MATTHEW 7:12

Millie was a mentally retarded adult who lived with her mother in a small town. She was well known for her green thumb. Lawns, hedges, and flowerbeds flourished under her loving attention. Millie also volunteered by cutting grass and weeds, raking leaves, and planting flowers in vacant lots throughout the town.

As Millie went from place to place, working in gardens and yards, she always carried an oilcan with her. She would apply a dose of oil to any squeaky door, hinge, or gate she encountered.

On Sundays, Millie went to church with her mother. When teased, she always responded with good humor and unflappable cheer.

When Millie died, everyone in town showed up for her funeral. There were scores who traveled from distant places to attend, including many of those who had once teased her.

Without consciously doing so, Millie exemplified good citizenship. She worked hard, was an optimist, eased tensions, and was a faithful church member.

The Bible's admonition to "Do to others what you would have them do to you" (Matthew 7:12 NIV) calls us to live our lives as Millie did. It doesn't mean that those you "do to" will ever do to you the way you've done to them, but every small kindness you perform is noticed—by people, and most importantly, by God.

What CAN I DO FOR OTHERS THAT ONLY GOD WILL SEE?

Forget yourself for others and others will not forget you!

The Law of Christ

My son, do not forget my law, but
let your heart keep my commands.

PROVERBS 3:1

Whose
BURDEN WILL
I SHARE
TODAY?

Andrew Davison had a rare and life-impacting opportunity to visit Dr. Albert Schweitzer at his jungle hospital on the banks of the Ogooué River. For three days, he engaged in leisurely conversation with the great humanitarian, theologian, musician, and physician. He reported later that his three-day visit had a deep and profound effect on him. In writing of his visit, however, Davison didn't relay the content of their conversations, only this incident:

"It was about eleven in the morning. The equatorial sun was beating down mercilessly, and we were walking up a hill with Dr. Schweitzer. Suddenly he left us and strode across the slope of the hill to a place where an African woman was struggling upward with a huge armload of wood for the cookfires. I watched with both admiration and concern as the eighty-five-year-old man took the entire load of wood and carried it on up the hill for the relieved woman. When we all reached the top of the hill, one of the members of our group asked Dr. Schweitzer why he did things like that, implying that in that heat and at his age he should not. Albert Schweitzer, looking right at all of us and pointing to the woman, said simply, 'No one should ever have to carry a burden like that alone.'"

God has not called us to carry our burdens alone, but rather to bear one another's burdens. When we do so, we are fulfilling the law of Christ, which is the law of love.

Rank does not confer privilege or give power.
It imposes responsibility.

Misdirected?

Trust in the Lord with all your heart, and lean not on your own understanding; in all your ways acknowledge Him, and He shall direct your paths.

PROVERBS 3:5-6

A church once sent a man to spend two months as a volunteer at Mother Teresa's mission in Calcutta, caring for India's poor, sick, and dying. He left on his mission with great joy; the trip was a dream come true.

Standing by a luggage carousel in Bangkok forty hours later, he felt anything but elation. Somewhere between South Korea and Thailand, his luggage had been misdirected. With nerves worn raw by sleeplessness, he collapsed into a nearby chair and wondered, *Was this trip a mistake?* He felt as lost as his bags.

As his eyes wandered around the walls of the lobby, which was mostly empty because of the late hour, he noticed a row of clocks on one wall. They displayed the time in London, New York, Sydney, and Bangkok. He quickly noted that it was noon at his home church, and it was Sunday.

His church had promised to pray for him at noon services that day. *They're praying for me right now,* he thought. A tremendous peace came with that realization. *I'm not alone now. And I won't be alone in the months ahead!*

Luggage may often be misdirected, but not our prayers. God knows your needs, and He knows right where you are.

———⊗⊗⊗———

Prayer is a direct link to peace of mind and perspective. It reminds us of who we are.

How CAN I SHOW MY GRATITUDE TO GOD FOR HIS CONSTANT AWARENESS OF MY NEEDS?

Nothin' Outside Can Lick Us

Do not be wise in your own eyes;
fear the LORD and depart from evil.
PROVERBS 3:7

HOW CAN
I REMEMBER
TO TURN
FIRST TO
GOD FOR MY
STRENGTH?

In *Gone With the Wind*, at the funeral of Gerald O'Hara (a heavy drinker who dies in an alcohol-related accident), his prospective son-in-law gives this eulogy:

"There warn't nothin' that come to him from the outside that could lick him. He warn't scared of the English government when they wanted to hang him. He just lit out and left home. And when he come to this country . . . he warn't scared to tackle this section when it was part wild and the Injuns had just been run out of it. He made a big plantation out of a wilderness. And when the war come on and his money begun to go, he warn't scared to be poor again. And when the Yankees came through Tara and might of burnt him out or killed him, he warn't fazed a bit and he warn't licked neither. . . .That's why I say he had our good points. . . .

"All you all and me, too, are like him. We got the same weakness and failin'. There ain't nothin' that walks can lick us, any more than it could lick him, not Yankees nor Carpetbaggers nor hard times nor high taxes nor even downright starvation. But that weakness that's in our hearts can lick us in the time it takes to bat your eye."

The world of self is truly the toughest frontier, but with humility and patience, we can conquer it!

Character is not made in a crisis,
it is only exhibited.

Honor the Lord

Honor the LORD with your possessions, and with the firstfruits of all your increase.

PROVERBS 3:9

A businessman was once concerned about selling a warehouse property he owned. Since he had last surveyed the building, vandals had damaged the doors, smashed the windows, and strewn trash inside it. The building had been empty for several months and needed additional repairs due to weather and a general lack of maintenance. As the man showed a prospective buyer the building, he took great pains to assure him that he would replace the broken windows, correct any structural damage, mend the roof, and clean out the garbage. He felt as if he was apologizing for the condition of the building at every turn, but he wanted to present the building in the best possible light.

To his surprise, the buyer finally said to him, "Forget about the repairs. I'm going to build something completely different on this land. I don't want the building. I want the site."

So often, we attempt to present to our Creator what we think is good, justifying our actions, promising to do better, and trying to put the best spin on the state of our souls. In the end, what God wants is us. When we honor Him with our whole selves, He gives us the best He has.

Today I WILL HONOR GOD BY . . .

God can make you anything you want to be, but you have to put everything in His hands.

21

Praying God's Prayer

We know that all things work together for good to them that love God, to them who are the called according to his purpose.

ROMANS 8:28 KJV

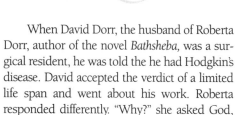

What DO
I NEED TO
PUT ASIDE IN
ORDER FOR
GOD'S WILL
TO BE DONE
IN MY LIFE?

When David Dorr, the husband of Roberta Dorr, author of the novel *Bathsheba*, was a surgical resident, he was told the he had Hodgkin's disease. David accepted the verdict of a limited life span and went about his work. Roberta responded differently. "Why?" she asked God, but no answer came.

Finally, in total relinquishment, she asked God, "How do you want me to pray for my husband?" She soon felt this strong impression: "Pray that your husband will be able to use for the good of others the medical training he has been given." As soon as she prayed this prayer, the heavy burden lifted from her heart. She felt she was praying *God's* prayer, sharing His concern for all humanity.

A year later, during a periodic test, the doctors at Johns Hopkins were astonished to find no trace of the disease in David. Three years later, they dismissed him entirely, unable to explain what had happened. David completed his residency and went to the Gaza Strip where he was desperately needed as a surgeon.

To pray God's will, we first must discover what His will is. All we need to do is ask. He *will* answer us.

Prayer is the chief agency and activity whereby men align themselves with God's purpose.

Today

Happy is the man who finds wisdom.

PROVERBS 3:13

Psychologist William Marston once asked three thousand people, "What have you to live for?" He was shocked to discover that 94 percent of the people he polled were simply enduring the present while they waited for the future. Some indicated they were waiting for something to happen—waiting for children to grow up and leave home, waiting for next year, waiting to take a trip, waiting for someone to die, or waiting for tomorrow. They had hope, but no ongoing purpose for their lives.

Only 6 percent of the people identified relationships and activities in the present tense of their lives as valuable reasons for living!

The 94 percent would be wise to recall the words of this poem by an unknown author:

During all the years since time began,
Today has been the friend of man;
But in his blindness and his sorrow,
He looks to yesterday and tomorrow.
Forget past trials and your sorrow.
There was, but is, no yesterday,
And there may be no tomorrow.

Instead of dwelling on your past mistakes, make a new start today by thanking God for all the good in your life.

⸺❧⸺

Guilt is concerned with the past.
Worry is concerned about the future.
Contentment enjoys the present.

What KEEPS ME FROM BEING CONTENT WHERE GOD HAS PLACED ME TODAY?

O God, Help!

You will find rest for your souls.
MATTHEW 11:29

How CAN
I BE MORE
HONEST WITH
GOD WHEN
I PRAY?

"Dad," a little boy once asked, "does the Lord know everything?"

"Yes, Son," the father replied. The boy nodded, but didn't look convinced, prompting the father to ask a question of his own, "Why do you ask?"

"Because," the boy replied, "when the preacher prays, he prays so long telling God everything that I thought maybe God wasn't clued in on what's happening to folks around here."

God is much more concerned about our motives than the type, amount, or form of the words we use in prayer. He looks on the heart. Sometimes a simple SOS is all that's required.

One Sunday morning as the great preacher Charles H. Spurgeon passed through the door on his way to the pulpit, the great crowd of people who had already gathered for the service overwhelmed him. As strong in faith and as profound and experienced a preacher as he was, an assistant overheard him pray, "O God, help!" Spurgeon's prayer needed no elaboration. And often, ours don't either.

The fewer words the better prayer.

Opportunity

The LORD will be your confidence, and
will keep your foot from being caught.

PROVERBS 3:26

Are you waiting for the perfect conditions before you set out to pursue your dreams? This poem by Edward Rowland Sill challenges that mindset.

What GIFT
DO I ALREADY
POSSESS
THAT GOD
COULD USE?

Opportunity

This I beheld, or dreamed it in a dream:
There spread a cloud of dust along a plain;
And underneath the cloud, or in it, raged
A furious battle, and men yelled, and swords
Shocked upon swords and shields.
  A prince's banner
Wavered, then staggered backward,
  hemmed by foes.
A craven hung along the battle's edge
And thought, "Had I a sword of keener steel—
That blue blade that the king's son bears—
  but this
Blunt thing—!" He snapt and flung it from
  his hand,
And lowering, crept away and left the field.
Then came the king's son, wounded,
  sore bestead,
And weaponless, and saw the broken sword,
Hilt-buried in the dry and trodden sand,
And ran and snatched it, and with
  battle-shout
Lifted afresh, he hewed his enemy down,
And saved a great cause that heroic day.

Don't overlook the potential of what you already hold in your hand. Use your God-given gifts and talents to change the world in which you live.

I couldn't wait for success . . .
so I went ahead without it.

The Charity of Happiness

Do not withhold good from those to
whom it is due, when it is in the
power of your hand to do so.

PROVERBS 3:27

What
ARE THE
BLESSINGS
IN MY LIFE?

His mother, Eliza, was an intelligent woman with strong common sense and strait-laced conduct. A disciplinarian, she was devoutly religious and a believer in hard work and thrift. Her strong will and deep piety gave her a remarkable serenity, which she transmitted to her son, John. A diligent and serious student, John was trained by his mother in matters of piety, neatness, and industry. Attendance at church and Sunday school was weekly.

His father was full of the joy of life and loved song, talk, and sociability. He taught John to develop his innate gift for business. William was as anxious as Eliza that all their children grow up self-reliant, honest, keen-witted, and dependable. John recalled later that both of his parents were examples of courtesy and patience. He said, "I cannot remember to have heard the voices of either Father or Mother raised in anger or complaint in speaking to any of us."

William and Eliza also instilled in their son a rich heritage of giving to church and charities, the gifts being made from their childhood earnings. In all, William and Eliza gave their son, John D. Rockefeller, a happy childhood—a gift he valued throughout his life far more than the millions of dollars he made.

—◦◦◦—

A happy childhood is one of the
best gifts that parents have it
in their power to bestow.

Heavenly Home

*The curse of the LORD is on the
house of the wicked, but He
blesses the home of the just.*

PROVERBS 3:33

Home has been called "Heaven's fallen sister." Our homes can't help but bear at least a partial imprint of our fallen world. And yet, home holds the greatest potential for being like Heaven of any place on earth. A godly home, built upon Heaven's principles, can be the sweetest, happiest, and most perfect place to dwell!

When we think of our earthly homes as being reflections of our heavenly home, we must ask ourselves, "What must God's home be like?"

Surely it is a place where there are no harsh or unkind words and no prolonged silence born of anger. It must be a place where each person is made to feel special, important, and valued beyond measure. It is a place of laughter and gladness, a place each person would desire to return to at the end of a difficult day. It must be a place of nourishment and growth, a place of total acceptance and unconditional love. Every person in God's home would surely be vulnerable enough to share his or her innermost secrets, dreams, and hopes. Communication flows freely, as do hugs and kisses.

The good news is that we have the privilege of creating our homes to mirror Heaven. It is within our power—with God's help—to do so!

❦

*A good thing to remember, a better thing
to do—work with the construction
gang, not the wrecking crew.*

I WILL MAKE
MY HOME A
PLACE OF
SANCTUARY
BY . . .

Hop for It

Do not throw away your confidence;
it will be richly rewarded.

HEBREWS 10:35 NIV

What

ACTIONS CAN
I TAKE TO
OVERCOME
THE
CHALLENGES
IN MY LIFE?

An author once sought to escape city life by moving to a little house in the country. His house was located across the street from a farm, and he often looked up from his writing to watch from his library window as his neighbor engaged in a wide variety of farm chores. He was intrigued to the point of distraction.

He watched as the man mended the fence after his cattle had broken through it. He marveled as the man replanted a field after a heavy deluge washed out a new planting. He observed as the farmer made repairs to his tractor and removed several large stones from his field after a tractor blade broke. The farmer seemed to work from sunup to sundown, battling against the elements and facing one problem after another with unlimited energy and enthusiasm. The author began to wonder about the man's optimism.

One day the author strolled from his cottage to talk to the farmer. "You amaze me," he said after greeting his neighbor. "You never seem to lose heart. Do you always hope for the best?"

The farmer thought for a moment and then, eyes flashing, he replied, "No, I don't hope for it—I hop for it!"

It takes more to plow a field than
merely turning it over in your mind.

Christmas in December

*Through wisdom a house is built, and
by understanding it is established.*

PROVERBS 24:3

Two lifelong friends in their early fifties began to argue over the forthcoming marriage of one of them to a man who was only in his thirties.

"I just don't believe in May-December marriages," the friend said. "After all, December is going to find in May the strength and virility of springtime, but whatever is May going to find in December?"

The bride-to-be thought for a moment and then replied with a twinkle in her eye, "Christmas."

Many couples who claim they "fell in love at first sight" look back after years of marriage and adjust their opinions, saying, "I was infatuated," or "We felt an immediate attraction," or "There was electricity between us when we first met." "Love," however, is a word they have come to cherish. It is something they now share that is far richer and more meaningful than the emotions they felt "at first sight."

One of the great qualities about genuine love is that it grows and deepens over time. Time is life's nursery for love. Tend to it as you would your most cherished plant, and love's fragrance will continually remain.

———— ✆ ————

*Nothing beats love at first sight
except love with insight.*

How CAN
I ENCOURAGE
THE LOVE
IN MY LIFE
TO GROW?

Try and Try Again

In the LORD *I put my trust.*
PSALM 11:1

What
HOLDS ME
BACK FROM
TRYING NEW
EXPERIENCES?

Franklin D. Roosevelt said, "It is common sense to take a method and try it. If it fails, admit it frankly and try another. But above all, try something."

In *The Pursuit of Excellence,* Ted W. Engstrom gives this advice about the importance of trying: "Starting today, you can begin to enjoy using and developing your gifts. For a start, you may want to risk something small—like a toe rather than a neck.

"For example, if you've always wanted to write, then write something, a short article, a poem, an account of your vacation. Write it as if it were going to be published; then submit it somewhere. If you're a photographer, gather your best pictures together and submit them as entries in a contest. If you think you're a fair tennis player or golfer, enter some tournaments and see how you do. You may not win the top prize, but think how much you'll learn and experience just by trying."

The first step in trying may be taking a course at a local college, getting some private lessons, or conducting your own simple experiments. Trying is perfected by practice.

The only true failure is the failure to try.

⤞⤝

*Consider the turtle. He makes progress
only when he sticks his neck out.*

Hope for the Homeless

*"For the oppression of the poor, for the sighing
of the needy, now I will arise," says the LORD;
"I will set him in the safety for which he yearns."*

PSALM 12:5

Some thought Les Goldberg was crazy when he cashed in his personal investments to buy a home to lease to the homeless. Goldberg, a retired engineer, felt it was the only right decision he could make.

Since his retirement, Goldberg has been a busy volunteer, serving on six service boards and leading a crew of homeless people at odd jobs and charity work. He spends at least an hour a day with his homeless friends and has helped renovate several properties on their behalf. In all his efforts, Goldberg never regarded the homeless as irresponsible or unreliable. He only saw them as people. He figured the house he purchased could be used as both a temporary shelter and a drop-in center, a place where homeless people might pick up mail, make phone calls, follow up job leads, and receive donated commodities. Four homeless men live at the house, paying minimal rent to offset expenses. House rules are strict—no alcohol, no drugs, no loitering.

Goldberg has never been rich. For twenty years he ran his own business, making about twenty-five thousand dollars a year, designing and installing fire sprinklers. He simply saw a need and found a way to help meet it. What can you do today to help meet the needs of those around you?

—◊◊◊—

*God never asks about our ability or
our inability—just our availability.*

I CAN
ACTIVELY
SEEK OUT
OPPORTUNITIES
TO HELP
OTHERS BY . . .

From a Dump to a Meadow

He answered her not a word.
MATTHEW 15:23

How CAN
I HELP
TURN MY
NEIGHBOR-
HOOD INTO
A TRUE
COMMUNITY?

A bus driver became annoyed with what he saw. At the end of his run lay an open field which local litterbugs had turned into an unofficial dump. The driver had at least a seven-minute layover there several times a day. One day he decided to get out of his bus and spend his few minutes of waiting time picking up a few of the bottles and cans.

The next day he took along a little bigger sack and some gloves, and during each layover, he gathered up a little more of the trash. After a week of doing this, he was so encouraged by the change he had made in the field that he decided to spend all his free moments cleaning up the site. He worked all through the winter months, and when spring came, he decided to sow some flower seeds on the land.

By the end of the summer, some of his regular riders actually began riding with him to the end of the line just to see what the driver had accomplished. He had turned a dump into a meadow, just a few minutes at a time, and the entire community benefited.

Our neighborhoods are only as good as those who live in them. One step, one minute, one day at a time, you can make yours an even better place for you and your neighbors to call home.

---

*It's not how many hours you put in but
how much you put into the hours.*

An Up-stretched Hand

The LORD looks down from heaven upon the children of men, to see if there are any who understand, who seek God.

PSALM 14:2

Matthew Huffman, the son of missionaries in Salvador, Brazil, awoke one morning complaining of a fever. As his temperature soared, he began to lose his eyesight. His mother and father put him in the car and raced to the nearest hospital. As they drove, the boy lay in his mother's lap, listless. Then suddenly, he put one hand into the air. His mother took it gently and pulled it down to his body, but he extended it again. Again, she pulled it down. He reached into the air a third time. Confused at this unusual behavior, the mother asked her son, "What are you reaching for?" "I'm reaching for Jesus' hand," he answered.

With those words, Matthew closed his eyes and slid into a coma from which he never awakened. He died two days later, a victim of bacterial meningitis.

Matthew did not have a long life, but he learned the most important lesson a person can learn before he or she dies: He learned for whom to reach in the hour of death.

Matthew's up-stretched hand was more eloquent than any prayer he might have spoken. It said in action what words could never fully convey.

Reaching for God is not only for the dying, it is for the living. While reaching for God's hand, we find the strength to live every day.

Are you looking to God with an up-stretched hand today? He is always reaching down to you.

What KEEPS ME FROM REACHING OUT TO GOD?

Prayer is not eloquence, but earnestness.

Weep with the Weeping

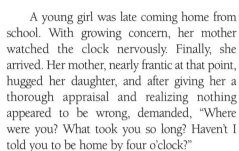

When she opened it, she saw the child, and behold, the baby wept. So she had compassion on him, and said, "This is one of the Hebrews' children."

EXODUS 2:6

What AM I WILLING TO RISK IN CARING FOR OTHERS?

A young girl was late coming home from school. With growing concern, her mother watched the clock nervously. Finally, she arrived. Her mother, nearly frantic at that point, hugged her daughter, and after giving her a thorough appraisal and realizing nothing appeared to be wrong, demanded, "Where were you? What took you so long? Haven't I told you to be home by four o'clock?"

The girl answered her mother's first question: "I was at Mary's house."

"And what was so important that you couldn't get home on time?" her mother scolded.

The daughter replied, "Her favorite doll got broken."

"Did you break it?" the mother asked. When her daughter shook her head no, she then asked, "Could the doll be fixed?" Again, the girl replied with a "no." Both bewildered and frustrated, the mother asked a third time, "So what was the point of staying so long?"

Tears began to well up in the little girl's eyes and stream down her face under her mother's inquisition. "I helped her cry," she said softly.

The Scriptures tell us to "Rejoice with those who rejoice, and weep with those who weep" (Romans 12:15). Mothers may not be able to do everything for their children, but we can all do that for them!

Who ran to me when I fell, and would some pretty story tell, or kiss the place to make it well? My mother.

The Power of Teamwork

Where two or three are gathered together in My name, I am there in the midst of them.

MATTHEW 18:20

Debora Dempsey, captain of the transport ship *Lyra*, was glad to be home. The storm that raged off Cape Fear on January 26, 1993, was a sailor's nightmare. She thought she had seen her 634-ton ship for the last time the day it left the Chesapeake Bay on its way to a buyer in New Orleans. Then Dempsey received a call. Northeast of Cape Fear, the *Lyra* had broken loose from its towline. The crewless ship—with 387,000 gallons of oil on board to run its engines—was being pushed toward land by the strong winds. An ecological disaster was in the making, not to mention the loss of the twenty-two-million-dollar vessel. Dempsey and four volunteer crew members were called upon to save the ship and avert disaster.

Lowered from a helicopter onto the pitching deck, they immediately began to let down the two, five-and-a-half-ton anchors. After they got the first anchor safely down, the generator failed. Without the aid of a power winch and only flashlights by which to see, they finally got the second anchor down, stopping the ship's deadly drift. It was a dangerous mission, accomplished only by a strong team effort. Dempsey received the Admiralty of the Ocean Sea award, a high honor, for her leadership and courage.

Effort may be self-rewarding, and the accomplishment of a goal can bring recognition. However, teamwork usually yields the best results. Focus on helping others today.

With GOD'S HELP, I CAN HELP . . .

Obstacles are those frightful things you see when you take your eyes off the goal.

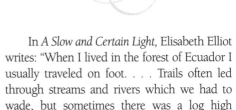

The Guide

You will show me the path of life; in Your presence is fullness of joy; at Your right hand are pleasures forevermore.

PSALM 16:11

IS THERE ANYTHING THAT KEEPS ME FROM SEEING GOD?

In *A Slow and Certain Light,* Elisabeth Elliot writes: "When I lived in the forest of Ecuador I usually traveled on foot. . . . Trails often led through streams and rivers which we had to wade, but sometimes there was a log high above the water which we had to cross.

"I dreaded those logs and was always tempted to take the steep, hard way down into the ravine and up the other side. But the Indians would say, 'Just walk across, señorita,' and over they would go, light-footed and confident. I was barefoot as they were, but it was not enough. On the log, I couldn't keep from looking down at the river below. I knew I would slip. I had never been any good at balancing myself . . . so my guide would stretch out a hand, and the touch of it was all I needed. I stopped worrying about slipping. I stopped looking down at the river or even at the log and looked at the guide, who held my hand with only the lightest touch. When I reached the other side, I realized that if I had slipped he could not have held me. But his being there and his touch were all I needed."

A major source of comfort in prayer is simply realizing that God is present, gently guiding us along our way. Any fear of falling vanishes if we but keep our eyes on Him.

Prayer is not only "the practice of the presence of God," it is the realization of His presence.

Complaining Against God

Uphold my steps in Your paths,
That my footsteps may not slip.

PSALM 17:5

In *The Pursuit of Holiness,* Jerry Bridges has written: "I still vividly recall how God first dealt with me over twenty-five years ago about complaining against Him. In response to His will, I had settled in San Diego, California, and had begun to look for a job. When several weeks went by without success, I mentally began to accuse God. 'After all, I gave up my plans to do His will and now He has let me down.' God graciously directed my attention to Job 34:18-19: 'Is it fitting to say to a king, "You are worthless," and to nobles, "You are wicked"? Yet He is not partial to princes, nor does He regard the rich more than the poor; for they are all the work of His hands.'

"As soon as I read that passage I immediately fell to my knees, confessing to Him my terrible sin of complaining and questioning His holiness. God mercifully forgave and the next day I received two job offers."

God graciously directs our paths. The One who placed you on the path is the One who steadies your steps upon it.

If your life is not turning out the way you had planned . . .

If your day seems to be haphazard and out of control . . .

If your hour isn't as productive as you had desired . . .

If you can't seem to find peace . . .

It's time to pray.

God MOVED IN MY LIFE AS THE ALMIGHTY PROVIDER WHEN HE . . .

You will not stumble while on your knees.

37

Making Our Best Better

The last will be first, and the first last.
MATTHEW 20:16

How CAN I MAKE MY LIFE MORE OTHER-CENTERED THAN SELF-CENTERED?

Johann Olav Koss was a star at the 1994 Winter Olympic Games at Lillehammer, Norway. A hometown favorite, he skated his way to three gold medals and three world records in the 1,500-, 5,000-, and 10,000-meter races. Perhaps no one was as surprised as Koss when he won his first medal. He said, "There was so much joy over this gold medal that it made me think a little bit before the next race. . . . I decided, if this will happen to me again, I want to give the bonus that I get to Olympic Aid. . . . It made me strong, I think, to be skating for someone else."

At a press conference after winning the second gold medal, Koss made his announcement: He would donate all his bonus money from equipment sponsors and the Norwegian Olympic Committee to Olympic Aid—a gift of more than $175,000. Koss challenged his countrymen to donate 10 kroner (U.S. $1.37) for every Norwegian gold medal. The response was tremendous; more than $200,000 was raised during the Games, and up to a million dollars came in afterward.

Koss, who entered medical school after the Olympics, was surprised by all the fuss he had caused. Helping children and the less fortunate was not only his future career, it was his nature.

Our best efforts become even better when we perform for the benefit of others, rather than for our own gain.

Kindness gives birth to kindness.

"Heave!"

Whoever desires to be first among you,
let him be your slave.

MATTHEW 20:27

Many years ago, a rider on horseback came across a squad of soldiers who were trying to move a heavy piece of timber. The rider noticed that a well-dressed corporal was standing by, commanding the men to "heave." The piece of timber was just a little too heavy for the group of men to move, however.

"Why don't you help them?" the rider quietly asked the corporal.

"Me?" the corporal responded with shock in his voice. "Why, I'm a corporal, sir!"

The rider then dismounted and took his place with the soldiers. Smiling at them, he said encouragingly, "Now, all together boys—heave!" The big piece of timber moved easily with the help of one more man. The stranger then mounted his horse. As he prepared to ride on, he said to the corporal, "The next time you have a piece of timber for your men to handle corporal, send for the commander-in-chief." It was only then that the corporal and his men realized that the helpful stranger was none other than George Washington.

No person is too great to help others. In truth, only a little person fails to do so.

———∞∞∞———

Give me the ready hand
rather than the ready tongue.

How CAN I BE ON THE LOOKOUT FOR WAYS TO HELP OTHERS?

No Shortcuts

*A little sleep, a little slumber, a little
folding of the hands to sleep—so shall
your poverty come on you like a prowler,
and your need like an armed man.*

PROVERBS 6:10-11

In WHAT
AREA OF MY
LIFE HAVE I
BEEN TAKING
SHORTCUTS?

Award-winning figure skater Erin Sutton, thirteen, and world-class figure skater Brian Boitano have something in common: a love for ice-skating and an intense dedication to their sport. They both know a great deal about getting up before dawn in order to put in hours of practice on the ice.

Erin has been skating since she was four years old. As an eighth-grader, her workday on the ice began at 5:30 A.M. Even on Saturday mornings, she was usually at the rink by 6:30. Boitano also knew that schedule as a young skater. For years, he skated from 5 to 10 A.M. before going to school. His dedication paid off. In 1988, he won Olympic gold, and in 1995, he was the professional world champion.

Being a champion hasn't changed Boitano's schedule a great deal. He is still at the ice rink before sunrise each day to practice for the competitive figure-skating season. Whether a skater is a veteran or a novice, it takes months of work to produce the three to five-minute routines of leaps, spins, and intricate footwork that keep fans on the edge of their seats and judges awarding high scores.

If you want to be a champion, there are no shortcuts.

*There is a close correlation between
getting up in the morning
and getting up in the world.*

God Is Always Near

The LORD is my strength and song, and He has become my salvation; He is my God, and I will praise Him; my father's God, and I will exalt Him.

EXODUS 15:2

In *Love and Duty,* Anne Purcell writes about seeing Major Jim Statler standing with her pastor outside his study after a Sunday service. She knew instantly that he was there with news about her husband, Ben, who was on active duty in Vietnam. As she had feared, Jim had chilling news: "He was on a helicopter that was shot down . . . he's missing in action."

Anne recalls, "Somewhere in the back of my mind, a little candle flame flickered. This tiny flame was the vestige of my faith." Days passed without word. To her, being the wife of an MIA was like being caught in limbo. She found herself able to pray only one thing: "Help me, dear Father." She says, "I hung onto this important truth—that He would help me—and the flickering flame of my candle of faith began to grow." Then one day, she noticed a white dove sitting in her yard. It was particularly beautiful—still and quiet—and a highly uncommon sight in her neighborhood. She took it as a sign from God that He was, indeed, always near.

For five years, Anne Purcell clung to the fact that God was close by. Little did she know that during those years before she was reunited with her husband, he was whispering to her from a POW cell, "Anne, find solace and strength in the Lord."

Remember: God is always near—in the good times and bad. Rest in His strength, and your faith in Him will grow into a blazing fire.

What WOULD IT TAKE FOR ME TO TOTALLY DEPEND ON THE LORD'S HAND?

Sorrow looks back. Worry looks around. Faith looks up.

A Gentle Answer

You have also given me the shield of Your salvation; Your right hand has held me up, Your gentleness has made me great.

PSALM 18:35

IS THERE ANYTHING THAT KEEPS ME FROM RESPONDING TO OTHERS WITH PATIENCE AND A SMILE?

Mentor Graham was so absorbed in evaluating assignments that he failed to notice the youthful giant who slouched into his Illinois classroom one day after school. The brightness of the late-afternoon sun silhouetted the young man before him. When his eyes adjusted, he recognized the youth as a newcomer to the community. The lad already had a reputation for "whipping the daylights" out of all the local tough guys.

Graham would have been justified in thinking, *What does he want? Am I in danger?* But instead, he looked up and down the six foot, four inches of muscle and ignorance before him and offered to help the lad with his reading. When the young man left the schoolroom an hour later, he had several books under his arm—a loan from Mentor Graham, with a promise of more in the future.

Few people remember Graham. He was a quiet man, simply willing to do his best for any student who came his way. His pupil, however, is well remembered. His name was Abraham Lincoln.

A kind, helpful response to others is often perceived as strength. It is this gentle strength to which we are drawn. When you find yourself in a sensitive situation, try a gentle touch!

*Nothing is so strong as gentleness.
Nothing is so gentle as real strength.*

Bargaining with God

Jesus said to him, "'You shall love the LORD your God with all your heart, with all your soul, and with all your mind.'"

MATTHEW 22:37

Janette Oke, a best-selling novelist with more than forty books to her credit, is considered the modern-day pioneer author for Christian fiction. Since her first novel was published in 1979, her books have sold millions of copies.

When she first decided to write, she said to God, "Lord, I'm going to write this book. If it works, and if I discover I have talent, I'll give it all to You."

Janette sensed God was not pleased with the bargain she was trying to strike with Him. She felt in her heart as if He was responding, "If you're serious about this, then I want everything before you start." Thus she gave Him her ambitions and dreams and trusted Him with the outcome of her efforts. She left it up to Him to teach her, whether she was successful or not.

Out of that resolve came a secondary resolve. She refused to compromise her principles. Although she would write realistically, her stories would be "wholesome and good and encouraging." Many thought that approach was doomed to failure at the outset, but a shelf of novels later, Janette Oke has proven "God can teach spiritual truths through fictional characters."

The greatest step of faith is to trust God before we see the results of our efforts. Whether we fail or succeed, God will still be with us. When we give Him everything, He can take our best and make it better!

How CAN I TRUST GOD MORE COMPLETELY?

The world wants your best but God wants your all.

True Rewards

He who is greatest among you
shall be your servant.
MATTHEW 23:11

Today I
WILL MAKE
A SPECIAL
EFFORT TO
BE OF
SERVICE
TO...

A recent plot of the soap opera *All My Children* called for high-society philanthropist Brooke English to move into a shelter in order to better understand the plight of the homeless. Julia Barr, who plays Brooke, felt prompted to take some real-life action of her own. She became a participant in First Step, a New York City job-readiness program for homeless and formerly homeless women. The eight-week session included one-on-one mentoring, résumé advice, access to job internships, interview clothing, and pep talks from people such as herself.

"I know how it feels to lack motivation and self-esteem," Julia says. "I tend to procrastinate, I'm rarely on time, I'm rather bossy, I'm very stubborn—we all have things that hold us back and so I share mine."

Julia is not only giving her time, but her money as well. When her maternal grandmother, Myrtle, died at the age of 104, she left Julia "a nice amount of money." It was all donated to First Step.

Julia Barr has received an Emmy award and six nominations, but those in First Step will remember her, not for the accolades she's received as an actress, but for the care she showed to them.

You have something to give others today—a word of encouragement, a gentle hug, a bit of advice. Those are the eternal things that will not pass away. Awards will eventually crumble, and accolades will be forgotten, but those little things you do in service to others will remain.

The greatest achievements are
those that benefit others.

A Time for Rest

Six days you shall do your work, and on the seventh day you shall rest, that your ox and your donkey may rest, and the son of your female servant and the stranger may be refreshed.

EXODUS 23:12

Our grandparents may have worked hard, with less sophisticated technology, but most analysts today agree that at the day's end, our grandparents gave themselves a chance to unwind. In today's world, there seems to be no downtime. The home has become a branch office, with cell phones in cars, beepers in pockets, and e-mail, fax machines, and answering machines waiting to be attended to. Some have estimated that more than 80 percent of all white-collar employees are in the habit of taking work home on a daily basis.

A report in *Newsweek* magazine quoted Dr. Mark Moskowitz of Boston University Medical Center as saying, "A lot of people are working 24 hours a day, seven days a week, even when they're not technically at work." Moskowitz sees this as a classic formula for first-class exhaustion. Stewart Noyce would probably agree. He is reported in the same magazine to have slept on his couch for an entire week in a fit of exhaustion after graduating from business school. Noyce concluded, "It's really important to have some balance. Otherwise, it won't be fun anymore."

The writer of Ecclesiastes would no doubt say today, "There's a time for work . . . and for rest!"

What CHANGES CAN I MAKE IN MY DAILY ROUTINE TO GET THE REST I NEED?

For peace of mind, resign as general manager of the universe.

Praying through the Window

This gospel of the kingdom will be preached
in all the world as a witness to all the nations,
and then the end will come.

MATTHEW 24:14

How CAN I
PRAY MORE
EFFECTIVELY?

Back in 1993, a group called AD 2000 United Prayer Track came up with an innovative idea. In order to help realize their goal of "a church for every people and the Gospel for every person by AD 2000," they established a program called "Praying through the Window."

The "window" refers to an area on the globe from ten degrees to forty degrees north of the equator, from North Africa and southern Spain eastward to Japan and the northern Philippines. More than 2.5 billion people live in this area, where the most prominent religions are Buddhism, Islam, and Hinduism. For the entire month of October 1993, and again in 1995, millions of Christians from around the world prayed for the people in the 10/40 window.

The goal was that new churches might be established and new missionaries sent to these areas. In 1993 alone, the number of churches in Albania grew from fifty to more than three hundred, and the number of Christian fellowship groups formed daily in India rose from an average of three to seventeen.

In praying for people around the world, we are called to remember not only those who already are believers, that they might grow in their faith and be equipped to endure persecution and hardships, but we are called to pray for new believers to enter the kingdom of God.

———

The best way to remember
people is in prayer.

Fulfilling Your Purpose

*May He grant you according
to your heart's desire, and
fulfill all your purpose.*

PSALM 20:4

At forty-three, Lenny felt the time had come to give something back to his community, so he volunteered at a feeding program for homeless people. Soon he was counseling the families who came for food, directing them to places that provided shelter, and helping several of the men find jobs. The director of the program told him he had a talent for working with people and encouraged him to develop it.

Lenny had been working in a semi-clerical position as an administrative aide to a corporate executive. There wasn't any higher place he could go in his field or within the company. His biggest regret was that he had never gone to college. Armed with the encouraging words of his fellow volunteers, he and his wife sold their home and went back to school. They both eventually earned doctoral degrees and became full-time family therapists. They opened a clinic together and rebuilt their lives, this time enjoying a much greater sense of personal fulfillment.

It's never too late to start a new career. And it's never too late to make a new start in your spiritual life. Genuine success is found in establishing a relationship with God, discovering who He created you to be, and then developing talents and gifts He has given you!

*To know the will of God is the greatest
knowledge, to find the will of God is
the greatest discovery, and to do the
will of God is the greatest achievement.*

Am I USING
THE GIFTS
AND TALENTS
THAT GOD HAS
GIVEN TO ME?

He Is Risen

*Some trust in chariots, and some
in horses; but we will remember
the name of the LORD our God.*

PSALM 20:7

In SPITE
OF MY
DIFFICULTIES,
I CAN
STILL BLESS
OTHERS BY . . .

_____
_____
_____
_____
_____
_____
_____
_____
_____
_____
_____
_____
_____
_____
_____
_____

When British minister W. E. Sangster first noticed an uneasiness in his throat and a dragging in his leg, he went to his physician. It was found that he had an incurable muscle disease that would result in gradual muscular atrophy until he died. Rather than retreat in dismay, Sangster threw himself into his work in British home missions. He figured he could still write and that he would have even more time for prayer. He prayed, "Lord, let me stay in the struggle. . . . I don't mind if I can no longer be a general." He wrote articles and books and helped organize prayer cells throughout England. When people came to him with words of pity, he insisted, "I'm only in the kindergarten of suffering."

Over time, Sangster's legs became useless. He completely lost his voice. However, at that point, he could still hold a pen and write, although shakily. On Easter morning just a few weeks before he died, he wrote a letter to his daughter, saying, "It is terrible to wake up on Easter morning and have no voice to shout, 'He is risen!'—but it would be still more terrible to have a voice and not want to shout."

Are you using all of your capabilities to serve God today? In spite of your circumstances, there is something you can do. Go on in God's grace, shouting, "He is risen!"

———————

*It is impossible for that man to
despair who remembers that
his Helper is omnipotent.*

Honoring the Sabbath

You shall keep the Sabbath, therefore, for it is holy to you. Everyone who profanes it shall surely be put to death; for whoever does any work on it, that person shall be cut off from among his people.

EXODUS 31:14

For months, Eric Liddell trained with his heart set on winning the 100-meter race at the Olympics of 1924. Many sportswriters predicted that he would win. When he arrived at the Games, however, Liddell learned that the 100-meter race was scheduled to be run on a Sunday. This posed a major problem for him, because Liddell did not believe he could honor God by running on the Sabbath. He bowed out of the race, and fans were stunned. Some who had praised him in the past now called him a fool. He came under intense pressure to change his mind, but Liddell stood firm.

Then a runner dropped out of the 400-meter race that was scheduled on a weekday, and Liddell offered to fill the slot. This was not really his race—the distance was four times as long as the race for which he had diligently trained. Even so, Liddell crossed the tape as victor and set a record of 47.6 seconds in the process. He had earned an Olympic gold medal and made an uncompromising stand for his faith.

Liddell went on to become a missionary in China, where he died in a war camp in 1945. He lives in history as a man known more for his inner mettle than for his gold medal.

When we stand firm in our convictions, God will always reward us. It may not always be as quickly as in this case, or maybe not even in our lifetime on earth, but the reward is inevitable. God always desires to bless us!

Have I COMPROMISED IN GOD'S VALUE SYSTEM?

The smile of God is victory.

Teaching Responsibility

*O you simple ones, understand
prudence, and you fools, be of
an understanding heart.*

PROVERBS 8:5

Am I
BLAMING
OTHERS FOR
MY MISTAKES
OR TAKING
RESPONSI-
BILITY FOR
MY ACTIONS?

Some have theorized that it is a fear of taking responsibility that led to the development of "errorless" machines—ones that allow for work to be done in a repetitive way so that it is "perfect" every time. Columbia University psychologist Herbert Terrace argues this approach. He contends that errorless machines fail to help people deal with the real world, where "you have to cope when you make a mistake."

In support of his view, he cites a study in which pigeons were taught to distinguish green from red. If they pecked a green light, they received no food. If they pecked a red light—half of the birds got food every time, but the rest of them received food on an erratic basis. When the pigeons that received a reward every time they pecked the right light were switched over to the group that received rewards irregularly, they hit their heads against the wall, flapped their wings, and pecked at everything in sight. The birds trained on the intermittent system didn't go wild when a correct peck failed to produce food. Instead, they remained calm and just continued pecking only at the red light until they were rewarded with a snack.

Responsibility is built as we take life in stride and acknowledge failures, disappointments, and faults. That's a valuable lesson we can teach our children. When we let them take responsibility for their own mistakes, rather than always trying to fix things for them, they become responsible people who won't end up directionless, hitting their heads against the wall.

*Character is much easier
kept than recovered.*

The Vigil

He went a little farther and fell on His face, and prayed, saying, "O My Father, if it is possible, let this cup pass from Me; nevertheless, not as I will, but as You will."

MATTHEW 26:39

In the Middle Ages, an elaborate ceremony surrounded the conferring of knighthood. After certain rites had been performed, the candidate was conducted into his lord's chapel, where he was told to keep a vigil until sunrise. He was to pass the night by "bestowing himself in visions and prayer."

This ritual was vividly captured by artist John Pettie in a painting he entitled *The Vigil*. In it, a young armor-clad knight is seen kneeling before an altar. The light of dawn illuminates the dim aisles of the chapel behind him, but the knight doesn't seem to notice that his vigil is over. His noble, but weary young face is still turned to the altar. His eyes have the look of one who has meditated at length on divine and holy things. His helmet and armor are laid on the steps leading to the altar, but he holds his sword in front of him. Its silhouette is the shape of a cross.

It is the cross that speaks to us of complete surrender to God's will and compels us to follow Christ wherever He leads. It is the cross that unites us to God.

What is it that compels you to keep a prayer vigil? Are you holding the cross before you as you pray?

❦

Prayer unites the soul to God.

Have I SURRENDERED TO GOD'S WILL FOR MY LIFE?

O Rugged Land of Gold

I, wisdom, dwell with prudence, and
find out knowledge and discretion.
PROVERBS 8:12

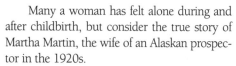

The
SCRIPTURE
THAT HAS
SUSTAINED
ME THE MOST
IN HARD
TIMES IS . . .

Many a woman has felt alone during and after childbirth, but consider the true story of Martha Martin, the wife of an Alaskan prospector in the 1920s.

While she was pregnant, her husband left her at their camp and went to a neighboring island to run an errand. A series of disasters struck almost immediately. First, an avalanche pinned her under a rock on the mountainside, where she lay unconscious for several days. She finally managed to crawl back to their cabin and reset the broken bones she had suffered, making a splint for her leg and a cast for her arm. Then a storm prevented her husband's return. Injured, alone, and with supplies almost gone, she quickly learned how to be self-sufficient, killing animals for food and using their fur to make coverings for the coming baby. Bit by bit, she began burning pieces of the cabin for heat.

Martha had never seen a child born before, but when she went into two days of hard labor, she kept her head and helped herself after her daughter finally arrived. She later baptized the infant, Dannas. Several weeks later, some Indians appeared, and she finally had help until her husband, who had been stranded on the other island, arrived. Her published diary was appropriately entitled, *O Rugged Land of Gold.*

When you feel alone, the Bible and the wisdom you gain from reading it will sustain you through any trial.

Wisdom is the wealth of the wise.

Coming Clean

Thus Moses did; according
to all that the LORD had
commanded him, so he did.
EXODUS 40:16

As a professional stock-car racer, Darrell Waltrip was once proud of his image as "the guy folks loved to hate." When the crowds booed, he'd just kick the dirt and smile. Then things began to change. After miraculously surviving a crash in the Daytona 500, he began going to church with his wife, Stevie. They tried to have a family, but Stevie suffered four miscarriages.

One day their pastor came to visit. "Your car is sponsored by a beer company," he said. "Is that the image you want?" Darrell had never thought about it. He had always loved watching kids admire his car, but the more he thought about it, he discovered that he did care about his image. He thought, *If our prayers were answered for a child, what kind of dad would I be?* He remembered his pastor's admonition to "walk the walk, not just talk the talk."

He didn't know what to do to convince his car's owner to change sponsors, but amazingly, an opportunity opened for him to sign with a new racing team sponsored by a laundry detergent company. After much thought and more prayer, he switched teams. Two years later, daughter Jessica was born, and a few years later, daughter Sarah. In 1989, he won Daytona.

Obedience to God and His Word opens up the doors for God to rain down blessings on our lives.

Am I WILLING TO RISK RIDICULE TO ADHERE TO GOD'S TRUTH?

In order to receive the direction from God, you must be able to receive the correction from God.

Talk to God

Blessed is the man who listens to me, watching daily at my gates, waiting at the posts of my doors. For whoever finds me finds life, and obtains favor from the LORD.

PROVERBS 8:34-35

What
PROBLEMS
HAVE I NOT
BEEN
TRUSTING
THE LORD
WITH?

In the midst of her intense grief, Betty found it difficult to pray. She was drowning in a sea of turbulent emotions and hardly knew her own name, much less what to request from God.

One afternoon a friend of Betty's came by, and soon, Betty was pouring out all of her hurts, fears, and struggles. She admitted she was angry with God and disappointed that her prayers for her husband's healing weren't answered. She admitted she was having difficulty believing God would do anything for her—in the present or the future. Finally, as the well of her emotions began to run dry, Betty's friend said quietly, "I have only one piece of advice to give you. Let's talk to God."

Betty's friend put her arms around her and prayed a simple, heartfelt prayer, claiming Christ's promise to heal her broken heart and restore her soul. After she had finished, she said, "Christ is with you. He is in you. And where He is, because of who He is, He heals."

No matter what you may be going through today, your best recourse is to invite Jesus Christ to manifest Himself in you and through you. He knows the answer. He is the answer. He gives you Himself, and in Him is all the power, strength, encouragement, love, and comfort you need.

Prayer is the breath of the soul, the organ by which we receive Christ into our parched and withered hearts.

Worry Is Worthless

Yea, though I walk through the valley of the shadow
of death, I will fear no evil; for You are with me;
Your rod and Your staff, they comfort me.

PSALM 23:4

Opera star Marguerite Piazza was at the height of her career, married to a devoted husband, and the mother of six healthy children. Then her world seemed to turn upside down. Her husband died suddenly, and soon after, a spot on her cheek was diagnosed as a melanoma, a deadly type of cancer. She was told that a disfiguring surgery to remove her cheek was her only hope for survival. The same day she received that news, she was scheduled to sing to a sold-out audience.

"What do you do at a time like that?" she said. "You do what you are paid to do, and I was paid to lift people with my talent. So, as I stood in the wings of the opera house, I prayed. Then I hung my troubles on a hanger and left them in the closet." She performed her heart out, and even after her surgery, she kept her beauty, raised her family, and continued to sing.

Rather than hang his worries in a closet, one man took another approach. He put them in a box. Each time he had a worry, he'd write it down and deposit it. Then on "Worry Wednesday," he read the contents of his box. To his amazement, most of the things he had worried about had already been resolved. He soon discarded the box!

Worry doesn't produce anything; it only slows you down. When you give your worries to God, you have the freedom to accomplish more in life.

Today I
AM GOING
TO GIVE UP
WORRYING
ABOUT . . .

Sometimes the Lord calms the storm;
sometimes He lets the storm
rage and calms His child.

Just Visiting

The earth is the LORD's, and all its fullness, the world and those who dwell therein.

PSALM 24:1

Is SOMETHING PREVENTING ME FROM PURSUING A DEEPER RELATIONSHIP WITH GOD?

In the last century, an American tourist heard that a renowned Polish rabbi, Hofetz Chaim, lived in the area where he was traveling. A great admirer of Rabbi Chaim, he asked if he might be able to visit him at his home. Word came back from the rabbi that he was welcome to stop by at any time.

The excited young tourist arrived at the rabbi's home and was invited to take off his knapsack and come inside. He entered the doorway and found a simple one-room lodging filled with books. The furnishings were limited to a table, a lamp, and a cot.

The tourist asked in amazement, "Rabbi, where is the rest of your furniture?" Hofetz Chaim replied, "Where is yours?"

The puzzled American replied, glancing out the door at his knapsack. "My furniture? But I'm only a visitor here." The rabbi responded, "So am I."

Often it is when we empty ourselves not only of our pride, but also of the possessions in which we pride ourselves, that we truly can find those things that will last for eternity. It is impossible to grasp hold of Heaven and earth with the same outstretched hand.

It is right to be contented with what we have, never with what we are.

Alone with the Eternal

The fear of the LORD is the beginning
of wisdom, and the knowledge of
the Holy One is understanding.

PROVERBS 9:10

Dr. Alexander MacLaren is considered one of the clearest Bible expositors of his time. He attributed becoming such a great Bible scholar to a habit he never broke—spending one hour a day "alone with the Eternal."

The hour that Dr. MacLaren designated was from nine to ten in the morning. At times, he allowed others into his prayer closet, but they were never allowed to utter a word. MacLaren would sit in his well-worn armchair, with his big Bible lying across his knees. Sometimes he would read its pages, but most often he would just sit with his hand over his face.

During that hour, he did not allow himself to read the Bible as a student or to search for texts to use in sermons or lessons. One of his assistants noted, "He read the Bible as a child would read a letter from an absent father, as a loving heart would drink in again the message from a loved one far away."

When we pray, we open our hearts to a clearer and deeper understanding of God's Word. As we read His Word, we open our minds to a greater understanding of how and for what to pray.

How CAN I REARRANGE MY SCHEDULE TO ALLOW FOR REGULAR PRAYER TIME?

We should never pray without reading the Bible, and we should never read the Bible without praying.

A Real Role Model

Do not remember the sins of my youth,
nor my transgressions; according
to Your mercy remember me,
for Your goodness' sake, O LORD.
PSALM 25:7

Would I
BE ABLE TO
SHARE MY
SHORTCOM-
INGS TO HELP
OTHERS?

His name conjures up memories of booming home runs, tremendous speed, and enormous natural ability. Mickey Mantle was a baseball giant. And yet, just a month after receiving a liver transplant, Mantle had the graciousness to say, "You talk about your role models. This is your role model: Don't be like me." Mantle squarely faced the fact that while he was a superstar on the field, his personal life was not worthy of emulation.

Nevertheless, in the ninth inning of his life, with two outs and a full count, Mantle hit a personal home run. With humility, humor, and no self-pity, he eloquently pleaded with others to take heed of his mistakes. In return, his final days were marked by a great outpouring of love—not only in response to the great memories he had made on the baseball fields of America, but in response to his honest self-appraisal.

Because of his pleas, organ donations increased all across America virtually overnight, giving countless people what Mantle himself did not enjoy—extra innings.

———

Character is made by what you stand for;
reputation by what you fall for.

Paths of Mercy and Truth

All the paths of the LORD are mercy and truth, to such as keep His covenant and His testimonies.

PSALM 25:10

Many people have thrilled to the voice of the opera great Beverly Sills. Few know, however, that her natural daughter was born deaf and that she has a stepdaughter who is also severely handicapped. She writes in her autobiography, *Bubbles:*

"I was now only thirty-four, but a very mature thirty-four. In a strange way my children had brought me an inner peace. The first question I had when I learned of their tragedies was self-pitying 'Why me?' Then gradually it changed to a much more important 'Why them?' Despite their handicaps they were showing enormous strength in continuing to live as normal and constructive lives as possible. How could Peter and I show any less strength?"

Oscar Wilde once wrote: "In this world there are only two tragedies. One is not getting what one wants, and the other is getting it." A third tragedy may be added: the tragedy of not being able to go forward after tragedy has occurred. When a tragedy strikes, our first tendency is to ask, "Why?" We may never know why, but God promises to be with us always. When we make the decision to go on with life, He leads us in His paths of mercy and truth.

How CAN I TACKLE MY PROBLEMS WITH THE COURAGE THAT ONLY COMES FROM GOD?

Adversity is the diamond dust Heaven polishes its jewels with.

Unseen Details

He who has a slack hand becomes poor,
but the hand of the diligent makes rich.

PROVERBS 10:4

Do I PAY
ATTENTION
TO THE
SMALL
DETAILS IN
MY LIFE?

On a shelf sits a beautiful and expensive carving from the Orient. It is a statue of a woman wearing a tall headdress, and balanced atop the headdress is an intricately carved ball. Inside that seamless sphere is another slightly smaller sphere of equal intricacy—and inside that still another, and then another—until one can no longer see through the tiny carved holes to see how many more balls there actually are.

Several things make this orb truly remarkable. Each of the nested balls is seamless, completely free from the one outside it and inside it, and magnificent in its airy, lacy design. The orb was carved from a single piece of ivory more than one hundred years ago, before the days of electronic magnifying instruments.

Why did the artist carve so many layers with such precision? The smallest orbs would not be clearly seen by most people, yet each one was finished with as much skill and artistry as was applied to the larger, outer ones.

The small details of a job may not always remain unnoticed or unseen. Like this artist, your excellence in small things can bring you prosperity in this life and make you a legend for future generations to follow.

Everything requires effort. The only thing
you can achieve without it is failure.

Listen and Obey

He said to them, "He who has
ears to hear, let him hear!"

MARK 4:9

Am I PAYING
ATTENTION
TO THE STILL,
SMALL VOICE
OF GOD?

While skiing in Colorado one day, a man noticed some people on the slope wearing red vests. Moving closer, he could read these words on their vests: blind skier. He couldn't believe it. He had difficulty skiing with twenty-twenty vision! How could people without sight manage to ski?

He watched the skiers for a while and discovered their secret. Each skier had a guide who skied beside, behind, or in front, always in a position where the two could easily communicate. The guide used two basic forms of communication. First, tapping his ski poles together to assure the blind person that he was there, and second, speaking simple, specific directions: "Go right. Turn left. Slow. Stop. Skier on your right."

The skier's responsibility was to trust the guide to give good instructions, as well as to immediately and completely obey those instructions.

We can't see even five seconds into the future. We cannot see the struggles to come. Other people may run into us, or we into them, like errant skiers on a crowded slope. But God has given us the Holy Spirit to be our guide through life—to walk before and behind us and to dwell in us. Our role is to listen and obey.

May the strength of God pilot us. May the
power of God preserve us. May the wisdom
of God instruct us. May the hand of God
protect us. May the way of God direct us.
May the shield of God defend us.

Integrity, Not for Sale

*He who walks with
integrity walks securely.*

PROVERBS 10:9

Am I
WALKING IN
INTEGRITY?

When Orv Krieger, a hotel broker, received a call about a property for sale in Spokane, Washington, he decided to take the plunge and buy it himself rather than list it for sale. He knew the 140-unit Holiday Inn—minutes from the airport and located on thirteen acres of fir-covered hillside overlooking the city—was a prime property.

Krieger quickly discovered that the Inn's restaurant was the big moneymaker. The bar grossed an average of $10,000 a month. However, Krieger's Christian principles were incompatible with running a business subsidized by alcohol sales. The manager argued that if guests couldn't get a drink at the Inn, they'd be off to other hotels in a flash. He had convincing statistics for his argument, but Krieger closed the bar anyway. The manager resigned.

Krieger remodeled the hotel lobby and replaced the bar area with a cozy coffee shop filled with greenery. In the first five years of business, food sales went up 20 percent and bookings were up 30 percent. Profits might not have been what they could have been, but they were substantial enough to satisfy Krieger. He has said, "Beliefs aren't worth much if a fella's not ready to live by them."

When you walk in integrity, God will reward you and people will respect you.

───❦───

*The strength of a man consists
in finding out the way God is
going and going that way.*

Adequate Enough

When You said, "Seek My face,"
my heart said to You,
"Your face, LORD, I will seek."

PSALM 27:8

On a bitterly cold night in February of 1943, one of the great maritime losses of World War II occurred—the sinking of the SS *Dorchester* in the North Atlantic. Of the 904 men aboard, 678 lost their lives.

Clark Poling was a young chaplain assigned to the ship. Before going to sea, he asked his father, Daniel A. Poling, to pray for him. But he had one stipulation: pray not for his safety, but that he would be adequate for any situation. Poling prayed as his son had requested.

When the enemy's torpedo struck the *Dorchester* and the ship began to sink, many of the men became paralyzed with fear. Young Poling, along with three other chaplains, strapped their own life belts to the fear-stricken men. They helped load the lifeboats and then joined hands in a circle of prayer as they sank to their watery graves. Poling's prayer had been answered. Although his son had not remained in safety, he had been more than adequate for the situation.

Ultimately, our adequacy to face any challenge is found only in the Lord. He provides what we need to remain true to Him and to be His brightest light in the darkest of circumstances.

To pray does not only mean to seek help;
it also means to seek Him.

Today
I WILL ASK GOD HOW TO PRAY FOR . . .

Thy Will Be Done

The labor of the righteous leads to life,
The wages of the wicked to sin.

PROVERBS 10:16

IS THERE SOMETHING I'M HOLDING ONTO IN MY LIFE THAT IS NOT GOD'S WILL FOR ME?

An overweight man decided it was time to shed a few pounds. One morning, however, he arrived at work carrying a gigantic coffee cake. His coworkers scolded him, but he smiled and said, "This is a very special coffee cake. I drove by the bakery this morning and there in the window was a host of goodies. I felt this was no accident, so I prayed, 'Lord, if You want me to have one of these delicious coffee cakes, let me have a parking place directly in front of the bakery.' And sure enough, the eighth time around the block, there it was!"

In *A Lamp for My Feet,* Elisabeth Elliot writes about the relationship in prayer between our will and God's will: "Does prayer work? The answer to that depends on one's definition of work. It is necessary to know what a thing is for in order to judge whether it works. It would be senseless, for example, to say that if a screwdriver fails to drive nails into a board it doesn't 'work.' A screwdriver works very well for driving screws. Often we expect to arrange things according to our whims by praying about them, and when the arrangement fails to materialize, we conclude that prayer doesn't work. God wants our willing cooperation in the bringing in of His kingdom. If 'Thy kingdom come' is an honest prayer, we will seek to ask for whatever contributes to that end."

When we go to God in prayer, we should ever be mindful of surrendering our will to His. His will—His plan for our life—is far better than anything we can dream up. When we pray, "Thy will be done," we're opening the way for God's best to be poured into our lives.

True prayer brings a person's will
into accordance with God's will,
not the other way around.

Grateful Giving

Besides the Sabbaths of the LORD, besides your gifts, besides all your vows, and besides all your freewill offerings which you give to the LORD.

LEVITICUS 23:38

The story is told of a man and woman who gave a sizable contribution to their church to honor the memory of their son, who lost his life in war. When the generous donation was announced to the congregation, a woman whispered to her husband, "Let's give the same amount in honor of each of our boys."

The husband replied, "What are you talking about? Neither one of our sons was killed in the war."

"Exactly," said the woman. "Let's give it as an expression of our gratitude to God for sparing their lives!"

All of our charitable giving in life produces benefits in three ways: (1) it helps those in need, (2) it inspires others to give, and (3) it builds character in us—selflessness, temperance, generosity, and compassion.

Keep in mind that when you give, you are ultimately giving to people, even though your gift might be made to an institution or organization. Churches and other charitable organizations are comprised of people. Your giving not only brings sunshine to the lives of others, but to your life as well.

What ARE MY MOTIVES WHEN I GIVE TO OTHERS?

Those who bring sunshine to the lives of others cannot keep it from themselves.

Conserving Words

*In the multitude of words
sin is not lacking, but he
who restrains his lips is wise.*

PROVERBS 10:19

In WHAT
SITUATION
RIGHT NOW
SHOULD I
HOLD MY
TONGUE?

During World War I, Eleanor Roosevelt made a valiant effort to conserve food, but things didn't turn out exactly as she had planned. In July of 1917, the Food Administration picked their household as "a model for other large households." The *New York Times* sent a newswoman to interview Mrs. Roosevelt about her food-saving methods, and she later wrote: "Mrs. Roosevelt does the shopping, the cooks see that there is no food wasted, the laundress is sparing in her use of soap, each servant has a watchful eye . . . and all are encouraged to make helpful suggestions in the use of leftovers." The article ended with a quote from Mrs. Roosevelt: "Making ten servants help me do my saving has not only been possible but also highly profitable."

As might be expected, the story created a great deal of mirth in Washington. FDR joined in teasing his wife, saying, "Please have a photo taken showing the family, the ten cooperating servants, the scraps saved from the table, and the handbook." To which Mrs. Roosevelt moaned in reply, "I feel dreadfully about it because so much is not true and yet some of it I did say. I will never be caught again, that's sure, and I'd like to crawl away for shame."

The book of Proverbs tells us that even a fool is thought wise when he holds his tongue. When in doubt about what to say— don't say anything!

*I regret often that I have spoken;
never that I have been silent.*

The Headboard Diary

The memory of the righteous is blessed,
but the name of the wicked will rot.

PROVERBS 10:7

The bed was about forty-five years old when Elaine's mother offered it to her. Elaine decided to refinish it for her daughter's room. However, as she prepared to strip the wood, she noticed that the headboard was full of scratches. She realized one scratch was the date her parents were married. Above another date was a name she didn't recognize. A call to her mother revealed the details of a miscarriage that occurred before Elaine was born.

Elaine realized the headboard had been something of a diary for her parents. She wrote down all the scratches she could decipher, and over lunch with her mother, she heard stories about the time when her mother lost her purse at a department store, a rattlesnake was shot just as it was poised to strike her brother, a man saved her brother's life in Vietnam, her sister nearly died after falling from a swing, and a stranger broke up a potential mugging.

Elaine couldn't strip and sand away so many memories, so she moved the headboard into her own bedroom. She and her husband began to carve their own dates and names. "Someday," she says, "we'll tell our daughter the stories from her grandparents' lives and the stories from her parents' lives. And someday the bed will pass on to her."

Memories are a powerful tool we can use in teaching our children. They tell our children of trust in God's faithfulness, patience with His timing, and reliance on His goodness.

I THANK GOD
FOR THE
MEMORIES
OF . . .

The best things you can give children,
next to good habits, are good memories.

Holding On

*When the storm has swept by,
the wicked are gone, but the
righteous stand firm forever.*

PROVERBS 10:25 NIV

What AM
I HOLDING
ONTO IN
THE STORMS
OF LIFE?

Tracy's grandmother was a survivor of a prison camp. Tracy often spent her time after school at Gram's house but had never heard her grandmother's stories. She decided that she would write about Gram for her English assignment, a paper on "Modern-Day Heroes."

After explaining to Gram what she wanted to do, Tracy sat down with her grandmother to work on the report. Tracy's heart was almost broken as Gram told story after story of the suffering of her friends and the deaths of so many she loved. Tracy made some notes and asked some questions along the way, but finally she put down her pen and paper and asked Gram, "How did you do it? How did you live through such an awful experience?"

After thinking a moment, Gram answered honestly, "I don't think all of me did live through it. You lose part of yourself in the face of so much evil. But there was a part of me that believed this was the evil of men, not of God. Part of me never forgot there was a power greater than this evil, and only love would help me find that power to make it through."

"You ARE a hero, Gram," Tracy said.

"Maybe to you I am," Gram said with a smile, "but to me I am someone who was fortunate enough to have something to hold on to when the storm came by."

Vision is the art of seeing things invisible.

From Catching Footballs to Flipping Burgers

As vinegar to the teeth and smoke to the eyes, so is the lazy man to those who send him.

PROVERBS 10:26

In 1961, Jerry Richardson faced an important decision. As a wide receiver for the Baltimore Colts, he had a job that was considered glamorous and secure. But when the raise he had requested was turned down, he felt the time had come to take a risk and do what he had always wanted to do. He would start his own business.

Richardson and his family moved back to South Carolina, where an old college buddy invited him to buy into a hamburger stand. Richardson took the plunge and bought Hardee's first franchise. He went from catching footballs to flipping hamburgers twelve hours a day. After hours, he scrubbed stoves and mopped floors. His reward? Four hundred and seventeen dollars a month. Some would have thought, *It's time to punt.*

Tired and frustrated as he was, Richardson refused to give up. He employed the same discipline he had used on the football field to focus on making his restaurant more efficient, his employees the friendliest in town, and his prices affordable. Before long, his business boomed.

Today, Richardson heads one of the largest food-service companies in the United States with $3.7 billion a year in sales and owns an NFL team as well!

When God plants dreams and desires in your heart, He also will help you achieve them, but you must still apply discipline and diligence. When it looks like you're not getting anywhere, turn up the heat and keep going. Hard work pays off!

What
DREAMS HAVE
I ASKED GOD
TO HELP ME
ACHIEVE?

What comes with ease, goes with ease.

Forgiveness Heals

*O Lord my God, I cried out
to You, and You healed me.*

PSALM 30:2

Have I
ALLOWED
BITTERNESS
TOWARD
SOMEONE
TO KEEP
ME FROM
FORGIVENESS?

In his book, *With Justice for All*, John Perkins tells how God gave him a real compassion for white people.

The incident began when a van load of students who had participated in a civil-rights march were pulled over by a highway patrolman and taken to jail. The driver of a second van called Perkins, who went to post bail for the students. No sooner had Perkins arrived at the jailhouse than he was beaten by the sheriff and tortured by several other officers.

He later testified in court that, although he was unconscious most of the night, he had ample opportunity to see the faces of those who had beaten him. They were faces "twisted with hate," the "victims of their own racism." Rather than hate them back, though, Perkins felt pity for them. He prayed, "God . . . I really want to preach a Gospel that will heal these people, too."

In the months that followed, God brought the faces of numerous white people to Perkins' mind, and one by one, he forgave them. Forgiveness healed the wounds that had long kept him from loving whites. He wrote, "How sweet God's forgiveness and healing was!"

Are you at odds with someone today? Pray for that person, so that you both might be healed.

*Prayer can change what
arguments can't settle.*

Scientific Selflessness

When pride comes, then comes shame;
But with the humble is wisdom.

PROVERBS 11:2

Everybody knows of Isaac Newton's famed encounter with a falling apple and how he introduced the law of gravity and revolutionized the study of astronomy. But few know that if it weren't for Edmund Halley, the world may never have heard of Isaac Newton.

Halley challenged Newton to think through his original theories. He corrected Newton's mathematical errors and prepared geometrical figures to support his discoveries. It was Halley who coaxed the hesitant Newton to write his great work, *Mathematical Principles of Natural Philosophy.* And it was Halley who edited and supervised its publication. He even financed its printing, although Newton was wealthier and could better afford the cost.

Historians have called Halley's relationship with Newton one of the most selfless in science. Newton began almost immediately to reap the rewards of prominence; Halley received little credit. He did use the principles Newton developed to predict the orbit of a comet that would later bear his name, but since Halley's Comet only returns every seventy-six years, few hear his name. Still, Halley didn't care who received the credit as long as the cause of science was advanced. He was content to live without fame.

Sometimes the reward of what we are doing far outweighs any recognition we may or may not receive. Though no one else may see or hear of our efforts, the God who sees what is done in secret will reward us openly. And His rewards are always far better than any accolades of man.

IS MY DESIRE FOR REWARD GREATER THAN MY DESIRE TO SERVE GOD?

Authority makes some people grow—
and others just swell.

Good Advice

Immediately the father of the
child cried out and said with tears,
"Lord, I believe; help my unbelief!"

MARK 9:24

Today, I
AM PRAYING
THAT GOD
WILL . . .

A woman once accepted a job in a field for which she had a college degree and past experience. She had community contacts, she enjoyed this type of work, and her family could use the extra income. In fact, the job seemed to be a perfect fit. Almost immediately, however, problems emerged. As the weeks wore on, she wore out. Being a diehard, she held on, trying to force the job to work for her and to be successful in it. "God, please show me what I should do!" she prayed.

One cold winter day, her phone rang, and a young woman said, "You probably don't remember me, but I was in a seminar group you taught about a year ago. Could I come talk to you today?" Although her schedule was full, she made an appointment with the young woman. She discovered that the young woman was in despair about her job and was yearning to enter a field where she could express her strengths and gifts. The woman urged her to recognize that her gifts were from God and to choose a career of excellence.

It was only after the young woman left that the woman realized, "That advice I gave was for my benefit!"

Don't be surprised at how God may answer your prayers today. It may even come through something you say to help someone else.

⸺∘∞∘⸺

How deeply rooted must unbelief be
in our hearts when we are surprised
to find our prayer answered.

Are You a Slave or a Servant?

He sat down, called the twelve, and said to them, "If anyone desires to be first, he shall be last of all and servant of all."

MARK 9:35

For more than a quarter of a century, Arnold Billie was a rural mail carrier in southern New Jersey. His daily route took him sixty-three miles through two counties and five municipalities. Mr. Billie, as he was affectionately known, did more than deliver the mail. He provided personal service. Anything a person might need to purchase from the post office, Mr. Billie provided—stamps, money orders, pickup service. All customers needed to do to let Mr. Billie know they needed something was to leave the flag up on their mailbox.

One elderly woman had trouble starting her lawn mower, so whenever she desired to use it, she would simply leave it by her mailbox, raise the flag, and when Mr. Billie came by, he would start it for her. Mr. Billie added a new dimension to the label of public servant.

True Christian servants rarely think of themselves as doing anything out of the ordinary, when what they do is actually quite extraordinary. The apostle Paul called himself a slave to Christ, yet he was too concerned about being a good servant to ever worry about being a real slave. Why? True servants are motivated by love. It is love they know they have received from Christ, and it is love they give.

As women and mothers, we are called upon to serve in many areas of life—sometimes all at once. Always remember that the difference between a slave and a servant is love.

Today I WILL TAKE THE OPPORTUNITY TO SERVE...

The fellow who does things that count doesn't usually stop to count them.

From Local to Long Distance

*Jesus looked at them and said, "With men
it is impossible, but not with God;
for with God all things are possible."*
MARK 10:27

Are MY EYES
OPEN TO THE
OPPORTUNI-
TIES GOD HAS
PROVIDED
FOR ME TO
SUCCEED?

In order to communicate among themselves, Serbian shepherd boys developed an ingenious system. They would stick the blades of their long knives into the ground of a pasture, and when one of the boys sensed an approaching cattle thief, he would strike the handle of his knife. The vibration created a signal that could be picked up by other shepherd boys, their ears pressed tightly against the ground. It was by using this unique system that they outwitted thieves who tried to creep up on their flocks and herds under the cover of darkness and tall corn.

Most of the shepherd boys grew up and forgot about their ground signals, but one boy remembered. Twenty-five years after he left the pastures, he developed one of the greatest inventions of the modern era. Michael Pupin expanded the use of the telephone from speaking only across a city to a long-distance instrument that could be heard across an entire continent.

Something you take for granted today, something others may consider insignificant or ordinary, might actually become your key to greatness. Look around you. What has God placed at your disposal?

*God has a history of using the insignificant
to accomplish the impossible.*

Speak Out and Stand Up

*Be of good courage, and He
shall strengthen your heart,
all you who hope in the LORD.*

PSALM 31:24

While he was a pastor in Indianapolis, Henry Ward Beecher preached a series of sermons about gambling and drunkenness. He soundly denounced the men of the community who profited by these sins.

The next week, a would-be assailant accosted Beecher on the street. Brandishing a pistol, the man demanded that Beecher make some kind of retraction about what he had said the previous Sunday.

"Take it back, right here!" the man demanded with an oath, "Or I will shoot you on the spot!"

Beecher calmly replied, "Shoot away!" The man was taken back by the response. Beecher just walked away, saying over his shoulder as he left the scene, "I don't believe you can hit the mark as well as I did!"

Courage is more than just having convictions. It requires being willing to speak and act in order to bring about change, whether in individual lives, families, neighborhoods, cities, or nations. It's not enough to just believe in something. In order to be a truly courageous person, you must be willing to speak out and stand up. Your voice can make a difference.

Courage is fear that has said its prayers.

If I KNEW GOD WOULD GIVE ME COURAGE, I WOULD SPEAK OUT FOR . . .

Don't Cut Corners

The wicked man does deceptive work,
but he who sows righteousness
will have a sure reward.

PROVERBS 11:18

Have I
EVER CUT
CORNERS?

Joe Smith was a loyal carpenter who worked nearly two decades for a successful contractor. One day the contractor called him into his office and said, "Joe, I'm putting you in charge of the next house we build. I want you to order all the materials and oversee the job from the ground up." Joe accepted the assignment with great enthusiasm. He studied the blueprints and checked every measurement and specification. Suddenly, he had a thought, *If I am really in charge, why couldn't I cut a few corners, use less expensive materials, and put the extra money in my pocket? Who will know? Once the house is painted, it will look great.*

So Joe went about his scheme. He ordered second-grade lumber and inexpensive concrete, put in cheap wiring, and cut every corner he could. When the home was finished, the contractor came to see it.

"What a fine job you have done!" he said. "You have been such a faithful carpenter to me all these years that I have decided to show you my gratitude by giving to you this very house which you have built."

Build well today. You may have to live with the reputation you create.

———————

Character is like the foundation
of a house—it is below the surface.

Small Beginnings

I will instruct you and teach
you in the way you should go;
I will guide you with My eye.

PSALM 32:8

Near the top of one of the highest peaks in the Rocky Mountain range—more than 10,000 feet above sea level—are two natural springs. They are so close together and level in height that it would not take a great deal of effort to divert one streamlet toward the other. Yet if you follow the course of one of these streams, you will find that it travels easterly, and after traversing plateaus and valleys and receiving water from countless tributaries, it becomes part of the great Mississippi River and empties into the Gulf of Mexico.

If you follow the water from the other fountain, you will find that it gradually descends in a westerly direction, also combining with other tributaries, until it becomes part of the Columbia River, which empties into the Pacific Ocean.

The terminal points of the two streams are more than five thousand miles apart, separated by one of the highest mountain ranges in the world. Yet at their onset, the two streams are close neighbors. Little effort would be required to make the easterly stream run west or the westerly stream run east.

The direction of any person, project, or plan is determined at the beginning. Our greatest opportunity to impact the lives of our children for the long haul is to teach them while they're young. It's never too early to start!

❧❧❧

Train your child in the way in which
you know you should have gone yourself.

As A CHILD,
I REMEMBER
LEARNING
THAT . . .

The Worry Table

Casting all your care upon
Him, for He cares for you.
1 PETER 5:7

What AM
I ANXIOUS
ABOUT?

I've suffered a great many catastrophes
in my life. Most of them never happened.

A military chaplain once drew up a worry table based upon the problems men and women had brought to him through his years of service. He found their worries fit into the following categories:

- Worries about things that never happened—40 percent.

- Worries about past, unchangeable decisions—30 percent.

- Worries about illness that never happened—12 percent.

- Worries about adult children and friends (who were able to take care of themselves)—10 percent.

- Worries about real problems— 8 percent.

According to his chart, 92 percent of all our worries are about things we can't control—things that are better left to God. The truth is, anxiety is rooted in a failure to trust God.

We simply don't believe He is big enough, or cares enough, to help with our problems, give us the desires of our hearts, and keep us and our loved ones from harm.

Once we know God's character, we can easily see how we worry for nothing most of the time. God is more than big enough and cares more than enough to help us, bless us, and protect us. Give your worries to Him, and He will replace them with His peace.

Kindness Returns

*The generous soul will be made
rich, and he who waters will
also be watered himself.*

PROVERBS 11:25

Many years ago, an elderly man and his wife entered the lobby of a small Philadelphia hotel. "All the big places are filled," the man said. "Can you give us a room?" The clerk replied that with three conventions in town, no accommodations were available anywhere. "Every guest room is taken," he said, but then added, "I can't send a nice couple like you out into the rain at one o'clock in the morning, though. Would you be willing to sleep in my room?"

The next morning, as he paid his bill, the elderly man said to the clerk, "You are the kind of manager who should be the boss of the best hotel in the United States. Maybe someday I'll build one for you." The clerk laughed and forgot about the incident. About two years later, however, he received a letter containing a round-trip ticket to New York and a request that he be the guest of the elderly couple he had befriended.

Once in New York, the old man led the clerk to the corner of Fifth Avenue and Thirty-fourth Street, where he pointed to an incredible new building and declared, "That is the hotel I have just built for you to manage." The young man, George C. Boldt, accepted the offer of William Waldorf Astor to become the manager of the original Waldorf-Astoria, considered the finest hotel in the world in its time.

When you go out of your way to help someone, they often return the favor. Even if they don't, someone else will, and most importantly—God will.

Who IN MY LIFE HAS GONE OUT OF THEIR WAY TO HELP ME?

_____

Kindness will always attract kindness.

A Warm Heart and Willing Hands

He who earnestly seeks good
finds favor, but trouble will
come to him who seeks evil.
PROVERBS 11:27

What OPPORTUNI-
TIES ARE
PRESENT
IN MY LIFE
TO TOUCH
SOMEONE
ELSE'S?

Bob Richie, a former truck driver and Marine "no longer on active duty," found that the idleness of early retirement got on his nerves. So he created an unusual, full-time volunteer job for himself at Saint Christopher's Hospital for Children in Philadelphia. He makes beds, picks up toys, and changes diapers—whatever needs to be done. But the activities he enjoys most are sitting for hours rocking irritable babies and walking toddlers up and down the hall all afternoon.

Richie came to his volunteer work after his own experience in a hospital. A three-packs-a-day smoker for thirty years, he'd lost a lung to cancer. He said, "My wife stayed with me the whole time. That's when I realized how important it was to have somebody there." A ward full of children fighting devastating diseases might seem like the last place that a man battling cancer would want to be. Richie sees it differently. "Being here keeps my mind off it. One reason I've done so well with the cancer is seeing how the children fight. These kids—they're the real heroes."

It doesn't take great talent, exhaustive energy, or huge chunks of time to do good deeds. All it takes is a warm heart and willing hands. If you have those, you'll find all the time, energy, and ability that you need.

Kindness has converted more people
than zeal, science, or eloquence.

Watch and Pray

*Take heed, watch and pray; for you
do not know when the time is.*

MARK 13:33

Lawrence Cunningham sometimes visits a nearby Trappist monastery. For him, the best part of the monastic day comes in the two hours between 3:15 and 5:15 A.M., a time set aside for vigilance.

"O Watchman, what of the night?" he writes (Isaiah 21:11). "I think of those who lie awake staring at the ceiling, worrying about money or children or the nagging pain in the belly that keeps them from sleep. I think of those who work in all-night diners or convenience stores. . . . Have the bars closed? . . . Have the street hustlers and the young-but-so-old hookers quit the streets yet? Have the dopers found some rest? Are the street people now snoring in wine-drenched quiet? Is it easy for the cops in their patrol cars and the firemen in their stations and the nurses in the ER? Have the sirens silenced a bit? Do the people on death row sleep easily amid the coughs and groans of the prison population? . . . Is it now too late for the rapist and housebreaker? . . . Are the milkers and produce buyers and long-haul truckers at work? . . . Are my kids and wife and friends and students safe?"

Each question becomes a prayer to Cunningham, who agrees with what Thomas Merton wrote: "The more we are alone with God, the more we are with one another in darkness." It is always a good time to watch and pray!

*"Christian! Seek not yet repose,"
hear thy guardian angel say; Thou art
in the midst of foes, "Watch and pray."*

The LAST TIME I "WATCHED AND PRAYED" WAS . . .

Encouraging Words

No eye has seen, no ear has heard,
no mind has conceived what God
has prepared for those who love him.
1 CORINTHIANS 2:9 NIV

How CAN
I ENCOURAGE
OTHERS TO
BE WHO
GOD CREATED
THEM TO BE?

Abraham Lincoln is often held up to children as a model of achievement, the embodiment of "The Great American Dream." He is regarded by many as the greatest president the United States has ever seen. His second Inaugural Address is one of the noblest political speeches ever given, and his Gettysburg Address is still studied and memorized by many a student. Amazingly, Lincoln had only four months of formal education and that in a one-room country schoolhouse where the students ranged from age five to twenty-five.

One day a father was reciting all of Lincoln's achievements to his son. "Where else but in America could this happen?" he mused. And then, hoping to motivate his son to study, he asked, "Do you know what Abe Lincoln was doing when he was your age?"

The boy answered, "No, but I do know what he was doing when he was your age."

We nearly always err when we suggest to someone, especially our children, that they become like anybody other than their own best selves. While we can urge our children to follow good examples, we should always encourage them to be just who God created them to be.

It is better to fail in originality
than to succeed in imitation.

Staying Together

*Watch and pray, lest you enter
into temptation. The spirit indeed
is willing, but the flesh is weak.*

MARK 14:38

Mike and Teri had one major goal in common: They both wanted to make their first million dollars by the age of thirty. Teri wasn't a Christian when they met, but Mike was, and after attending church with Mike and reading Christian books he gave to her, she accepted the Lord. They were married a short while later and for the next two years lived what both called an ideal life.

Their focus on financial success, however, caused their dreams to unravel. They began to drift apart and drift away from Jesus Christ. Eventually, they separated and divorced. A year after the divorce, Teri attended a conference and came away believing that God could restore their marriage. She began to pray earnestly for Mike.

Not long after, Mike began to recognize that God was not finished with him. He set his heart toward God, walked away from the life he had been leading, and made contact with Teri. They remarried and reordered the focus of their lives.

Can prayer keep a marriage together? Mike and Teri believe it can, and so did Rev. and Mrs. Robert Newton. They met twice a day to pray with and for each other, every day of their more than fifty years of marriage. At their jubilee wedding anniversary, Rev. Newton said, "I know not that an unkind look or an unkind word has ever passed between us."

The old saying is still true: "The family that prays together, stays together."

What CAN
I SURRENDER
TO GOD THAT
IS KEEPING
ME FROM
MAKING
PRAYER
AN ACTIVE
PART OF MY
FAMILY LIFE?

*Prayer is a virtue that prevaileth
against all temptations.*

Five More Minutes

See then that you walk circumspectly, not as fools but as wise, redeeming the time, because the days are evil.

EPHESIANS 5:15-16

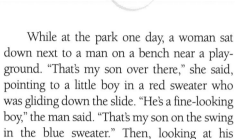

Are THERE PRECIOUS MOMENTS WITH MY FAMILY I AM LETTING PASS ME BY?

While at the park one day, a woman sat down next to a man on a bench near a playground. "That's my son over there," she said, pointing to a little boy in a red sweater who was gliding down the slide. "He's a fine-looking boy," the man said. "That's my son on the swing in the blue sweater." Then, looking at his watch, he called to his son, "What do you say we go, Sam?"

Sam pleaded, "Just five more minutes, Dad. Please? Just five more minutes." The man nodded, and Sam continued to swing to his heart's content.

Minutes passed, and the father stood and called again to his son, "Time to go now." Again Sam pleaded, "Five more minutes, Dad. Just five more minutes." The man smiled and said, "Okay."

"My, you certainly are a patient father," the woman responded.

The man smiled and then said, "My older son, Tommy, was killed by a drunk driver last year while he was riding his bike near here. I never spent much time with Tommy and now I'd give anything for just five more minutes with him. I've vowed not to make the same mistake with Sam. He thinks he has five more minutes to swing. The truth is, I get five more minutes to watch him play."

Too much love never spoils children.

Deep in the Earth

A good man obtains favor from the LORD, but a man of wicked intentions He will condemn.

PROVERBS 12:2

When England needed to increase its coal production during World War II, Winston Churchill called labor leaders together to enlist their support. He asked them to picture in their minds a parade in Piccadilly Circus after the war. First, he said, would come the sailors who had kept the critical sea-lanes open. Then would come the soldiers who had returned from Dunkirk after defeating Rommel in Africa. Then would come the pilots who had wiped the *Luftwaffe* from the skies.

Next would come a long line of sweat-stained, soot-streaked men in miner's caps. As Churchill painted the scene for the labor leaders, he depicted someone crying out from the crowd, "'And where were you during the critical days of our struggle?' And from ten thousand throats would come the answer, 'We were deep in the earth with our faces to the coal.'"

Whatever your profession, not every person can be number one. Not everyone can be the star. But anyone can be a hero. Nothing worthwhile is ever accomplished by one person alone. No matter what the role, every person can make a significant contribution. Whether it's behind the scenes or on the front lines, each person plays an important part in the success of the whole.

Success for the striver washes away the effort of striving.

What KEEPS ME FROM WORKING WITH ALL MY MIGHT IN THE POSITION GOD HAS PLACED ME IN?

85

De Forest's Worthless Glass Bulb

Those who passed by blasphemed Him,
wagging their heads and saying, "Aha!
You who destroy the temple and build
it in three days, save Yourself, and
come down from the cross!"

MARK 15:29-30

Am I
PURSUING
THE DREAM
GOD HAS
GIVEN
TO ME?

Years ago in a federal courtroom in New York, a sarcastic district attorney presented to a jury a glass gadget which looked something like a small electric light bulb. With great scorn and ridicule, the attorney accused the defendant of claiming that this "worthless device" might be used to transmit the human voice across the Atlantic! He alleged that gullible investors had been persuaded by preposterous claims to buy stock in the company—an obvious act of fraud. He urged the jury to give the defendant and his two partners stiff prison terms. Ultimately, the two associates were convicted, but the defendant was given his freedom after he received a severe scolding from the judge.

The defendant was inventor Lee De Forest. The "worthless glass bulb" that was also on trial was the audion tube he had developed—perhaps the single greatest invention of the twentieth century. It was the foundation for what has become a multibillion-dollar electronics industry.

No matter how harsh the criticism or how stinging the sarcasm aimed at your original ideas, pursue them further. Take them to their logical end, either convincing yourself that you were wrong, or creating something new and beneficial!

What lies behind us and what lies
before us are tiny matters
compared to what lies within us.

An Audience with the King

Do not fear or be discouraged.
DEUTERONOMY 1:21

Long ago, a band of minstrels traveled from town to town performing music to make a living. However, they were not financially successful. Times were hard, and there was little money for common folk to spend on entertainment. Attendance at their performances was sparse.

One night the troupe met to discuss their plight. One said, "I see no reason for singing tonight. It's starting to snow. Who will venture out on a night like this?" Another said, "I agree. Last night we performed for only a handful. Fewer will come tonight. Why not give back the price of their tickets and cancel." A third added, "It's hard to do one's best for so few."

Then an older man rose, and looking straight at the group as a whole, he said, "I know you are discouraged. I am, too. It's not the fault of those who come that others do not. They should not be punished with less than the best we can give. We will go on and we will do our best."

Heartened by his words, the minstrels went on with their show. Even though the audience was small, they had never performed better. After the concert, the old man called the troupe together. "Listen to this," he said, as he began to read a note he held in his hand: "'Thank you for a beautiful performance.'" The note was signed simply, "Your king."

There are always at least two people who see what you do and how well you do it—you and God.

Do I do my best every time regardless of my audience?

Many people have the ambition to succeed; they may even have a special aptitude for their job. And yet they do not move ahead. Why? Perhaps they think that since they can master the job, there is no need to master themselves.

"You're Special!"

*Command Joshua, and encourage
him and strengthen him; for he
shall go over before this people.*
DEUTERONOMY 3:28

I WILL MAKE
MY FAMILY
FEEL SPECIAL
TODAY BY . . .

*Happiness is a perfume you cannot
pour on others without getting
a few drops on yourself.*

While on vacation in New England the year after they were married, Sue and Kevin purchased two red "You're Special" plates at an outlet mall. They liked them so much they decided to use them as everyday dishes. Then one day, one of the plates broke. That night, Kevin said, "You should get the special plate tonight." "Why?" Sue asked. "Because you finished that big project that you were working on."

The next night, Sue insisted that Kevin dine from the "You're Special" plate, in honor of the help he had given to a neighbor in need. Thereafter, Sue and Kevin vied nightly for the "You're Special" plate honors—not to receive the plate, but for the privilege of awarding it to the other!

When the plate finally broke, Sue said sadly, "I had never been affirmed as much in my entire life as I was those eight months that Kevin and I bestowed upon each other the 'You're Special' honors. What seemed like courtesy the first night Kevin gave me the plate actually set a precedent for our encouraging each other on a daily basis. We're looking for another set of plates now, including one for the baby who is on the way!"

There are many little things you can do every day to make your family feel special. Encouraging them on a daily basis sets a tone of warmth, peace, and comfort in your home. Think of ways to make each member of your family feel special today.

Courage Under Fire

With God nothing will be impossible.

LUKE 1:37

Many years ago a huge oil refinery caught fire. Flames shot hundreds of feet into the air and filled the sky with grimy smoke. The heat was so intense that firefighters parked a block away, hoping for the heat to die down. Instead, the fire raged ever closer to a nearby row of oil tanks.

Suddenly, a fire truck came careening down the street. Brakes screeching, it hit the curb directly in front of the blaze. The firefighters jumped out to battle the blaze. Inspired by this courageous act, the other firefighters drove closer and joined in the fight. As a result of their cooperative effort, the fire was brought under control in the nick of time.

Those who witnessed these events decided to honor the man who had driven the lead fire truck to the brink of the blaze. In preparing for the awards ceremony, the mayor said, "Captain, we want to honor you for your fantastic act. You prevented the loss of property, perhaps even the loss of life. Is there something we can give you as a token of our appreciation?" The captain replied without hesitation, "Your Honor, a new set of brakes would be dandy!"

Acts of heroism all begin the same way: One person is willing to try when others are not.

The right angle to approach a difficult problem is the "try-angle."

With GOD'S HELP I CAN TACKLE...

A Gardener's Prayer

Commit your way to the LORD,
trust also in Him, and He
shall bring it to pass.

PSALM 37:5

Today
I WILL
COMMIT TO
THE LORD . . .

This prayer from *The Gardener's Year* reminds us that when we tell God what to do in prayer, we are speaking from our limited, finite point of view. We are much better off when we simply state our requests and then trust Him to respond from His eternal storehouse with His great generosity and unquestionable wisdom.

"O Lord, grant that in some way it may rain every day, say from about midnight until three o'clock in the morning, but you see, it must be gentle and warm so that it can soak in; grant that at the same time it would not rain on campion, alyssum, helianthemum, lavender, and the others which You . . . know are drought-loving plants—I will write their names on a bit of paper if You like—and grant that the sun may shine the whole day long, but not everywhere (not, for instance, on spiraea or on gentian, plantain lily and rhododendron) and not too much; that there may be plenty of dew and little wind, enough worms, no plant-lice and snails, no mildew, and that once a week thin liquid manure and guano may fall from Heaven. Amen."

Our business in prayer is not to prescribe
but to subscribe to the wisdom and
will of God; to refer our case to
Him and then leave it with Him.

Somebody's Mother

Love the stranger.

DEUTERONOMY 10:19

She stood at the crossing and waited long,
Alone, uncared for, amid the throng.
Past the woman so old and gray
Hastened the children on their way.
No one offered a helping hand to her—
So meek, so timid, afraid to stir
Lest the carriage wheels or the horses' feet
Should crowd her down in the slippery street.
He paused beside her and whispered low,
"I'll help you cross, if you wish to go."
Her aged hand on his strong young arm
She placed, and so, without hurt or harm,
He guided the trembling feet along,
Proud that his own were firm and strong.
Then back again to his friends he went,
His young heart happy and well content.
"She's somebody's mother, boys, you know.
For all she's aged and poor and slow.
And I hope some fellow will lend a hand
To help my mother, you understand,
If ever she's poor and old and gray,
When her own dear boy is far away."

—Anonymous

Every DAY, AM I LOOKING FOR SOMEONE WHO NEEDS A HELPING HAND?

If it is desirable that children be
kind, appreciative, and pleasant, those
qualities should be taught—not hoped for.

The Teacher

You shall lay up these words of mine in your heart and in your soul, and bind them as a sign on your hand, and they shall be as frontlets between your eyes. You shall teach them to your children, speaking of them when you sit in your house, when you walk by the way, when you lie down, and when you rise up.

DEUTERONOMY 11:18-19

I WILL
SAY "THANK
YOU" FOR
TEACHING ME
VIRTUE TO...

A king once decided to honor the greatest of his subjects. Word spread throughout the kingdom, and various nominations were immediately forthcoming. A man of wealth and property was singled out. One person was lauded for her healing skills, another for his fair practice of the law. Still another was praised for his honesty in business and yet another for his bravery as a soldier. Each candidate was brought to the palace and presented to the king. He admitted to his counselors that this choice was going to be difficult.

As the last day before the ceremony arrived, the last candidate was finally brought before the king—a white-haired woman whose eyes sparkled with the light of knowledge, love, and understanding.

"Who is this?" the king asked. "What has she accomplished of note?" An aide replied, "You have seen and heard all the other candidates. This woman is their teacher." The king's court erupted into applause, and the king immediately stepped from his throne to honor her.

Virtues do not happen by accident or as a natural part of growth. As with any skill or means of success, they must be taught.

Life affords no greater responsibility, no greater privilege, than the raising of the next generation.

Caution: Watch for Falling Eggs!

Do you see a man hasty in his words?
There is more hope for
a fool than for him.

PROVERBS 29:20

In his autobiography, Lee Iacocca gives us an opportunity to learn from a mistake he once made. In 1956, the Ford Motor Company emphasized auto safety, rather than performance and horsepower. The company introduced crash padding for dashboards and sent out a film to dealers explaining how much safer the new dashboards were. The narrator on the film claimed the padding was so thick a person could drop an egg on it from a two-story building and it would bounce right off without breaking. As a district assistant sales manager for Ford, Iacocca decided he'd demonstrate!

With eleven hundred salesmen watching him, he climbed a high ladder and proceeded to drop an egg on a strip of the dash padding he had placed on the floor of the stage. The egg missed the padding and splattered on the floor. A second egg bounced off his assistant's shoulder. Eggs three and four landed on target, but broke on impact. Finally, with the fifth egg, he got the desired result. Iacocca writes, "I learned two lessons that day. First, never use eggs at a sales rally. And second, never go before your customers without rehearsing what you want to say—as well as what you're going to do—to help sell your product."

In other words, think before you speak.

—⚬⚬⚬—

Learn from others' mistakes
rather than making them all yourself.

DO I ALWAYS KEEP A CLOSE WATCH ON MY TONGUE?

Turning the Other Cheek

*You shall be blameless
before the LORD your God.*
DEUTERONOMY 18:13

THE BATTLE
I WILL TRUST
TO THE LORD
TODAY IS...

Ruth Bell Graham tells a humorous story about her daughters, Anne and Bunny. One day Ruth was in another room in the house when she heard some loud cries coming from the kitchen. When she ran to the kitchen to investigate, she found three-year-old Bunny holding her hand to her cheek, looking disapprovingly at her sister. "Mommy," explained five-year-old Anne, "I'm teaching Bunny the Bible. I'm slapping her on one cheek and teaching her to turn the other one so I can slap it, too."

When we are wronged, our first response is more likely to fight back than to turn the other cheek. But many have found that fighting back is usually counterproductive.

Missionary E. Stanley Jones found himself being publicly slandered by someone he had once helped. Jones' first response was to write his accuser a letter he says was "the kind of reply you are proud of the first five minutes, the second five minutes you're not so certain, and the third five minutes you know you're wrong."

Jones knew his comments would win the argument, but lose the person. "The Christian," he said, "is not in the business of winning arguments, but of winning people," and he tore up the letter. A few weeks later, without having said a word, Jones received a letter of apology from the one who had turned on him.

When we turn the other cheek and let God fight the battle, He can bring about a greater victory than we can imagine.

*Silence is one of the hardest
arguments to refute.*

A Basic Survival Skill

Anxiety in the heart of
man causes depression.
PROVERBS 12:25

Business consultant C. W. Metcalf tells how he once signed up for a hospice-training program to work with terminally ill patients. He was assigned to Roy, an elderly man with colon cancer. Offering to assist Roy one day, Metcalf said, "Maybe you want me to help you out of those Mickey Mouse pajamas and into something more respectable." Despite his great pain, Roy whispered back, "I like these PJs. Mickey reminds me that I can still laugh a little, which is more than the doctor has ever done. Maybe you should get some Goofy PJs." Roy laughed, but Metcalf didn't. "Young man," Roy continued, "you're one of the most depressing people I've ever met. I'm sure you're a nice person, but if you're here to help, it ain't working." Such blunt truth made Metcalf angry.

On the last day of his training, Metcalf learned that Roy had died. His instructor handed him a paper bag that Roy had left for him. Inside, he found a T-shirt with the grinning face of Goofy and a note that read: "Put on this shirt at the first sign you're taking yourself too seriously. In other words, wear it all the time." Metcalf finally laughed. Roy had taught him one of the best lessons he ever learned: Humor is a basic survival skill for living life to its fullest!

A good laugh is sunshine in a house.

I HAVE RECENTLY SEEN THE FUNNY SIDE OF LIFE IN . . .

Pedal Faster!

The lazy man does not roast what
he took in hunting, but diligence
is man's precious possession.
PROVERBS 12:27

Have I
QUIT TRYING
IN ANY AREA
OF MY LIFE?

Success in business is often closely associated with a person's courage and ability to recover from a recent failure.

In 1928, a thirty-three-year-old man by the name of Paul Galvin found himself staring at failure—again. He had failed in business twice at this point, his competitors having forced him to fold his latest venture in the storage-battery business. Convinced, however, that he still had a marketable idea, Galvin attended the auction of his own business. With $750 he had managed to raise, he bought back the battery eliminator portion of the inventory. With it, he built a new company—one in which he succeeded. He eventually retired from his company, but not before it became a household name: Motorola. Upon his retirement, Galvin advised others: "Do not fear mistakes. You will know failure—continue to reach out."

A failure isn't truly a failure until you quit trying. If a venture begins to slow down, try speeding up your efforts. Consider the child who quits pedaling his bike. Eventually, the bicycle wobbles to the point where the child falls off. The key to avoiding the crash? Faster pedaling! The same holds true for many an enterprise. Don't give up; just pedal faster!

The train of failure usually
runs on the track of laziness.

Encouraging Your Children

He who guards his mouth preserves
his life, but he who opens wide
his lips shall have destruction.

PROVERBS 13:3

Glenn Van Ekeren tells about an experience he had with his son on one summer vacation. For the first couple of days, his son Matt seemed to misbehave constantly. And Glenn seemed to be continually rebuking and correcting his son. Thinking, *No son of mine is going to act this way,* he made it clear to Matt in no uncertain terms that he expected him to start behaving.

Matt tried hard to live up to his father's standards. In fact, later in the week, a day went by in which he hadn't done a single thing that called for correction. That night, after Matt had said his prayers and jumped into bed, Glenn noticed that his bottom lip began to quiver. "What's the matter, buddy?" he asked his son. Barely able to speak, Matt looked up at his father with tear-puddled eyes and asked, "Daddy, haven't I been a good boy today?"

Glenn said, "Those words cut through my parental arrogance like a knife. I had been quick to criticize and correct his misbehavior, but failed to mention my pleasure with his attempt to be a good boy. My son taught me never to put my children to bed without a word of appreciation and encouragement."

Statistics show that most parents make ten negative statements to their children for every positive one. Furthermore, studies have concluded that it takes four positive statements to overcome one negative statement. Take a moment and check yourself. Do you need to play catch-up with your children today?

Whom CAN
I ENCOURAGE
WITH A
POSITIVE
STATEMENT
TODAY?

❧

A critical spirit is like poison ivy—it only
takes a little contact to spread its poison.

Blessed in All Your Works

*You shall surely give to him, and your heart
should not be grieved when you give to him,
because for this thing the LORD your
God will bless you in all your works
and in all to which you put your hand.*

DEUTERONOMY 15:10

When
HAS GOD
REWARDED
ME FOR
DOING
SOMETHING
GOOD?

In *The Seven Habits of Highly Successful People,* Stephen Covey tells about a small computer software company that had developed a new program, which it sold on a five-year contract to a bank. The bank president was excited about the product, and his people were highly supportive. A month later, though, the bank changed presidents. The new president said he wanted to back out of the deal.

The computer company was in financial trouble. The president knew he had every legal right to enforce the contract, but he also knew the right thing to do. He told the bank president, "We have a contract. Your bank has secured our products and services to convert you to this new software program. But we understand that you're not happy about it. So what we'd like to do is give you back the contract, give you back your deposit, and if you are ever looking for a software solution in the future, come back and see us."

Just like that, he walked away from an $84,000 contract. It was nearly financial suicide for his company. However, three months later, the new bank president called to say, "I'm now going to make changes in my data processing, and I want to do business with you." They signed a contract worth $240,000.

Who says nice guys always finish last?

———

Success that is easy is cheap.

Transplanting

Blessed are you when men hate you, and when they exclude you, and revile you, and cast out your name as evil, for the Son of Man's sake. Rejoice in that day and leap for joy! For indeed your reward is great in heaven, for in like manner their fathers did to the prophets.

LUKE 6:22-23

Japanese bonsai trees are tiny, perfectly formed miniatures. They remain small no matter how old they get. Most are only fifteen to eighteen inches tall. To make a bonsai tree, a young sapling is pulled from the soil. Then, its taproot and some of the feeder roots are tied off. Thus, the growth of the bonsai is deliberately stunted.

In sharp contrast, California sequoia trees grow extremely large. The General Sherman stands 272 feet and measures 79 feet in circumference. If felled, this giant tree would provide enough lumber to build thirty-five, five-room homes! The sequoia begins life as a small seed, no larger than the seed of the bonsai. However, its sapling is allowed to be nourished in the rich California soil and sunshine.

Neither the bonsai nor the giant sequoia has a choice in determining how large it will become. But we human beings do! We cannot blame others, including our parents, for what they have done or are doing to us. We have the opportunity to transplant ourselves into a nurturing, positive environment.

If others are trying to prune you back today, move away from their shears. Rejoice in who you are and who you can be. Find a new place to put down roots.

Whom HAS GOD CREATED ME TO BE?

People who try to whittle you down are only trying to reduce you to their size.

Give, and It Shall Be Given

Give, and it will be given to you: good
measure, pressed down, shaken together,
and running over will be put into your bosom.
For with the same measure that you use,
it will be measured back to you.

LUKE 6:38

IS THERE
SOMETHING
I NEED THAT
I COULD
PROVIDE FOR
SOMEONE
ELSE?

_____

The best way to cheer yourself up
is to cheer up somebody else.

The grief-stricken mother sat in a hospital room in stunned silence, tears slipping down her cheeks. She had just lost her only child. As she gazed into space, the head nurse asked her, "Did you notice the little boy sitting in the hall just outside?" The woman shook her head no.

"His mother was brought here by ambulance from their poor one-room apartment," the nurse continued. "The two of them came to this country only three months ago, because all of their family members had been killed in war. They don't know anyone here. That little boy has been sitting outside his mother's room every day for a week in hopes his mother would come out of her coma and speak to him."

By now the woman was listening intently. The nurse continued, "Fifteen minutes ago his mother died. It's my job to tell him that at age seven, he is all alone in the world—no one even knows his name." The nurse paused and then asked, "I don't suppose you would tell him for me?" The woman stood, dried her tears, and went out to the boy.

She put her arms around the homeless child and invited him to come to her childless home. In the darkest hour of both their lives, they became lights to one another.

God's law of sowing and reaping works in every area of life—not just finances. When you need a friend, be a friend. When you need comfort, be a comforter. When you need light, be a light. Even in your darkest hour, you have something to give. In return, you'll receive from God exactly what you need.

God's Work—God's Pay

He also brought me up out of a horrible pit,
out of the miry clay, and set my feet
upon a rock, and established my steps.

PSALM 40:2

As a young man, J. C. Penney ran a butcher shop. He was told that if he gave a fifth of Scotch to the head chef in a popular hotel, the business of that hotel would be his. Penney did this for some time. Then he felt convicted that what he was doing was wrong. He discontinued the gifts of liquor and sure enough, lost the hotel's business, causing him to go broke. God, however, had better things planned for him. In time, he began a merchandise business that grew into a nationwide enterprise.

Unsuccessful years alone don't create success. Remaining true to principles and doing the right thing—even when you seem to be failing—produce success in time. A poem by an unknown writer says it well:

Who does God's work will get God's pay,
However long may seem the day,
However weary be the way;
Though powers and princes thunder "Nay,"
Who does God's work will get God's pay.
He does not pay as others pay,
In gold or land or raiment gay;
In goods that vanish and decay;
But God in wisdom knows a way,
And that is sure, let come what may,
Who does God's work will get God's pay.

I WILL DO
GOD'S WORK
TODAY IN . . .

Behind every successful man
there's a lot of unsuccessful years.

A Sweet Song of Prayer

*Praise the LORD! Oh, give thanks
to the LORD, for He is good!
For His mercy endures forever.*

PSALM 106:1

What
BLOCKS THE
SONG OF GOD
IN MY LIFE?

Although they may not have known the title of the painting, or the name of its painter, almost everyone has seen a copy of *The Song of the Lark,* a famous painting by the French artist, Jules Breton.

The painting depicts a peasant girl on her way to the field for a hard day's work. Breton captures her upturned face, alive with hope and joy, thrilled to hear the lilting beauty of the lark's sweet song. From her dress, she obviously is just another peasant girl with a difficult work life. But Breton captures something of her inner soul—a human being glorying in one of nature's loveliest voices, a person enriched by the beauty of God's creation.

The painting has no image of a bird in it. The lark that gives rise to such pleasure is unseen.

So it is in our relationship with God. We cannot see with our physical eyes the One with whom we walk and to whom we pray. Even so, He is the One who gives our lives meaning. His words of comfort, admonition, encouragement, and direction prompt us to look upward with thanksgiving and praise.

Have you heard the song He is singing to you today?

*A single grateful thought raised
to Heaven is the most perfect prayer.*

Where to Go

The eternal God is your refuge, and underneath
are the everlasting arms; He will thrust out the
enemy from before you, and will say, "Destroy!"

DEUTERONOMY 33:27

Mary George, known to her friends as "the girl of prayer," tells of a time when she, her six sisters, and her brother were facing eviction. Mary's parents had died, and the owners of the house in which she and her siblings were living wanted to convert the home into an apartment house. The house itself was in dire need of repair. The roof leaked, the water heater was broken, and the ceilings were about to cave in. Mary wasn't at all sorry at the prospect of leaving the old house, but finding a house large enough for a family of eight, and more importantly, one they could afford, wasn't easy. They prayed and prayed, both individually and as a family.

Soon Mary felt led to ask about a house just a block away. She was told that a buyer was closing on the sale the next day. But later that same week, the owner phoned her to tell her that the buyer had backed out. The house was theirs. Unfortunately, it was in an equal state of disrepair to the house they were vacating. "The next day we signed the lease," Mary recalled, "and word got around the neighborhood how God took care of the Georges. Immediately, neighbors and friends volunteered to help us clean and do repairs, and make the house livable."

When you think you have nowhere to turn, the best place to go is the throne room of Heaven.

❧

I have been driven many times to
my knees by the overwhelming conviction
that I had nowhere else to go.

What PROBLEM IN MY LIFE HAVEN'T I TURNED OVER TO GOD'S CONTROL?

Then What?

This Book of the Law shall not depart from your mouth, but you shall meditate in it day and night, that you may observe to do according to all that is written in it. For then you will make your way prosperous, and then you will have good success.

JOSHUA 1:8

What ARE
MY GOALS
IN LIFE?

Early one morning Charles G. Finney, a young apprentice lawyer, was sitting in a small-town law office in the state of New York. He was alone when he sensed the Lord speaking to him.

"Finney, what are you going to do when you finish your course?" Finney answered, "Put out a shingle and practice law."

"Then what?" "Get rich," he replied.

"Then what?" "Retire," he said.

"Then what?" "Die."

"Then what?" And as he spoke his next words, his voice trembled, "The judgment."

Finney immediately left the office and ran for the woods a half-mile away. He prayed there all day and vowed that he would not leave until he had made peace with God. He had studied law for four years, but he emerged from the woods that evening with the high purpose of living to the glory of God and enjoying Him forever. God began to use him in a mighty way, not as a lawyer, but as a preacher. He led thousands of people to a personal relationship with Jesus Christ over the next fifty years of his life.

Any career can bring glory to God, as long as you know you are working to further His kingdom, and not simply to build one of your own.

Three qualities vital to success:
toil, solitude, prayer.

Perfect Timing

Why are you cast down, O my soul? And why are
you disquieted within me? Hope in God, for I shall
yet praise Him for the help of His countenance.

PSALM 42:5

Carolyn, a preacher's wife, had just found evidence that her daughter was involved in activities that Carolyn knew were not only wrong, but potentially deadly. Because of her position, however, Carolyn felt that to tell anyone this family secret might expose her husband and his ministry to ridicule or shame. To keep the secret was painful; she needed a friend. In near desperation, she cried out to God, "I've got to talk to someone! Can't You send me somebody I can trust?"

Almost before she had finished praying, the doorbell rang. When she opened the door, there stood another preacher's wife. She was new to the city and had come to make her acquaintance. Almost immediately, the women developed a rapport as they discussed their lives, their many moves, and the difficulties of raising children.

Carolyn discovered her newfound friend also had gone through the struggle of raising a rebellious teenager. She poured out her problem to her new friend, who offered, "Would you mind if I prayed for you before I go?" Within minutes, Carolyn felt a profound peace fill her heart. She realized God had sent her help the minute she needed it. Because of it, she felt confident she could trust Him to begin a healing in her daughter's heart, and in her own heart, just as quickly!

Hope in God is never misplaced. He always comes through. The moment we pray, He sends the answer, and sometimes it arrives before we even finish.

When I HAVE PRAYED FOR GOD'S HELP, I HAVE RECEIVED IT...

Prayer is a cry of hope.

The Loudest Message

He said to them all, "If anyone desires to come after Me, let him deny himself, and take up his cross daily, and follow Me."

LUKE 9:23

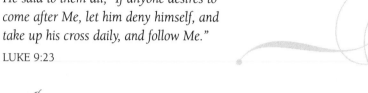

Are MY ACTIONS SPEAKING TO OTHERS ABOUT GOD'S LOVE?

Dorothy Canfield Fisher has written a poignant story about a physically powerful, but dim-witted farmhand named Lem who lived in a Vermont valley. His mother resented him from the day he was born. She often ridiculed her son with harsh and demeaning words. Even so, the boy served her faithfully until she died.

Lem was the brunt of many village jokes. But then, he came upon a huge dog killing some farmer's sheep one night. Using his bare hands as his only weapon, he strangled the dog to death. When morning came, the villagers discovered the dog was really a giant timber wolf. Lem quickly earned the villagers' silent admiration.

Later, an unwed village girl falsely accused Lem of being the father of her baby. Even though he was innocent, he married the girl so the baby would have a father. Unfortunately, the mother died within a year, so Lem raised the little girl by himself. After she was grown and married, her own baby became desperately ill, and Lem sold all his sheep to pay for the baby's medical care.

Confronted with meanness, misunderstanding, and loneliness all his life, Lem had no recourse in professing the true nature of his own life except to live it out in serving others. And that he did!

The way you live your life is the loudest message you will ever speak.

God can do tremendous things through people who don't care who gets the credit.

A Good Name

A good man leaves an inheritance to his children's children, but the wealth of the sinner is stored up for the righteous.

PROVERBS 13:22

The first major movie star to wear a uniform in World War II was Jimmy Stewart. Unlike so many other prominent people who sought excuses not to serve, Jimmy willingly accepted the draft and tried to get into the Army Air Corps, since he already had a pilot's license. The corps, however, had a strict weight requirement—for Jimmy's height, a minimum of 153 pounds. He weighed 143. When he suggested that they forget to weigh him, the officer responded, "That would be highly irregular." Jimmy replied, "Wars are highly irregular, too." Without weighing in, Jimmy won his new role, one in which he often prayed, not for himself, but that he "wouldn't make a mistake."

Over the course of the war, Stewart worked his way up from buck private to full-fledged pilot and completed twenty-five missions over enemy territory, many of them as command pilot of a B-24 bomber wing. By the time he returned to Hollywood, he was a full colonel with the Air Medal, Croix de Guerre, Distinguished Flying Cross, and seven battle stars. He remained in the Air Force Reserve and was promoted to brigadier general in 1959. He once said, "There's a tremendous difference between a warmonger and a patriot."

Although he was a general, Jimmy Stewart was better known as "the nice guy." When we are more concerned with our character than our reputation, we will leave a good name for our children and our children's children.

What ASPECTS OF MY CHARACTER NEED CLOSER EXAMINATION?

Take care of your character and your reputation will take care of itself.

In the Very Hour

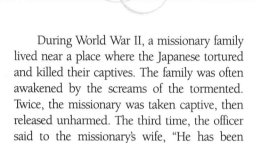

Joshua spoke to the Lord in the day when the Lord delivered up the Amorites before the children of Israel, and he said in the sight of Israel: "Sun, stand still over Gibeon; and Moon, in the Valley of Aijalon." So the sun stood still, and the moon stopped, till the people had revenge upon their enemies. Is this not written in the Book of Jasher? So the sun stood still in the midst of heaven, and did not hasten to go down for about a whole day.

JOSHUA 10:12-13

Is my communication with God based on the expectation of results?

During World War II, a missionary family lived near a place where the Japanese tortured and killed their captives. The family was often awakened by the screams of the tormented. Twice, the missionary was taken captive, then released unharmed. The third time, the officer said to the missionary's wife, "He has been returned to you two times—don't think he will be spared a third time. This time he dies."

After she had put her five children to bed, the wife began a prayer vigil. At four o'clock, she awoke her family to join her, saying, "The burden has become so heavy I cannot bear it alone." A short while later, they heard footsteps approaching—ones she recognized as those of her husband!

Safely inside their home, he told her what had happened. He had been the last in a row of ten men. A Japanese soldier had gone down the row, slashing off the head of each man with a sword. Just as he raised his sword to kill the missionary, the officer shouted, "Stop!" Then he roared to the missionary, "Go home. Quick, get out of here!" He pushed the missionary past the guard and toward the gate. "I looked at my watch," the missionary said. "It was 4 A.M."

Nothing impacts the impossible like prayer.

Prayer is invading the impossible.

Jesus Loves Me

He answered and said, "'You shall love the
LORD your God with all your heart, with all
your soul, with all your strength, and with all
your mind,' and 'your neighbor as yourself.'"

LUKE 10:27

I BELIEVE IN
GOD'S LOVE
FOR ME
BECAUSE...

A woman minister received a call from a friend that she had not seen in two years. The friend said, "My husband is leaving me for another woman. I need for you to pray with me." The minister said, "Come quickly."

When her friend arrived, the minister could not help but notice that her friend was carelessly dressed, had gained weight, and had not combed her hair or put on makeup. As they began to converse, the friend admitted to being an uninteresting, nagging wife and a sloppy housekeeper. The minister quickly concluded to herself, *My friend has grown to hate herself!*

When her friend paused to ask for her advice, the minister said only, "Will you join me in a song?" Surprised, her friend agreed. The minister began to sing, "Jesus loves me, this I know." Her friend joined in, tears flooding her eyes. "If Jesus loves me, I must love myself, too," she concluded.

Amazing changes followed. Because she felt loved and lovable, this woman was transformed into the confident woman she once had been. In the process, she recaptured her husband's heart.

We can never accept God's love beyond the degree to which we are willing to love ourselves. We rarely receive more than we are willing to believe God has for us. Our part is to believe, to receive, and to give.

Unanswered yet! Nay do not say
UNGRANTED; perhaps your
part is not yet fully done.

Teach Us How to Pray

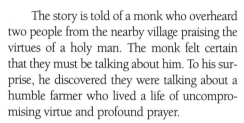

Now it came to pass, as He was praying in a certain place, when He ceased, that one of His disciples said to Him, "Lord, teach us to pray, as John also taught his disciples."

LUKE 11:1

Are MY PRAYERS MORE SELF-CENTERED THAN GOD-CENTERED?

The story is told of a monk who overheard two people from the nearby village praising the virtues of a holy man. The monk felt certain that they must be talking about him. To his surprise, he discovered they were talking about a humble farmer who lived a life of uncompromising virtue and profound prayer.

The monk was determined to meet this man and discover what it was that had motivated such great admiration. He found the farmer selling vegetables and asked him for overnight shelter. The farmer, overjoyed to be of service, welcomed the monk into his home.

After supper, the monk suggested to his host that they pray. Almost immediately, the monk heard the sound of vulgar songs coming from a group of drunks as they passed along the road outside the farmer's home. With great annoyance, the monk exclaimed, "Tell me, what kind of prayer can be made with such noise and vulgarity!" The farmer replied, "A prayer that they travel safely on their way to the kingdom of God."

The old monk marveled. He returned to his monastery, aware that he had never prayed a prayer as noble as that of the humble farmer.

The key to profound prayer is to first let go of the prideful notion that you know how to pray. Like the disciples, we should ask Jesus, "Teach us how to pray," and never cease listening or asking.

There are few men who dare to publish to the world the prayers they make to Almighty God.

A Small Piece of Butter

A faithful witness does not lie,
But a false witness will utter lies.

PROVERBS 14:5

Do MY WORDS ALWAYS FOLLOW THE PRECEPTS OF GOD?

When the elderly head of the trust department at a bank retired, four competent young men competed to fill the vacancy. After considering the merits of each applicant, the board of directors made its decision. They decided to notify the young man of his promotion, which included a substantial raise in salary, at a meeting scheduled for after lunch.

During the noon hour, the young man they had selected went to the cafeteria for lunch. One of the directors was a few spots behind him in the line. The director saw the young man select his food, including a small piece of butter. As soon as he flipped the butter onto his plate, he shuffled some food on top of it to hide it from the cashier. Thus, he avoided paying for it.

That afternoon the directors met to notify the young man of his promotion, but prior to bringing him into the room, the entire board was told of the incident. Rather than giving the young man the promotion, they called him in to discharge him from the bank. They had concluded that if he were willing to lie to a cashier about what was on his plate, he would be just as willing to lie about what was in the bank's accounts.

Lying isn't a matter of degrees. A lie is a lie. And truth is the truth. You can bank on it!

Character is what you are in the dark.

Procrastination

*How long will you neglect to go and
possess the land which the LORD
God of your fathers has given you?*

JOSHUA 18:3

What AM I
PUTTING OFF
THAT COULD
EASILY BE
DONE TODAY?

When Beth's boss asked her to take on an extra project, Beth saw the opportunity to prove she could handle greater responsibility. She immediately began to think how she might approach the task, and her enthusiasm ran high. But when the time came to start the project, Beth found herself telling her boss she was too busy to do it justice. The project was given to someone else, who earned a promotion for completing it successfully. Beth didn't receive any new opportunities and eventually took a position with another firm.

What had kept Beth from doing the project? Simple procrastination. She put off getting started on the job until she was paralyzed with fear—fear that she might not be able to do the job or that her performance would not meet her boss' expectations. In the end, Beth didn't move ahead and thus reinforced her fears with a bigger sense of insecurity about her own ability.

If you find yourself procrastinating, ask God to show you how to overcome your fear, then do what He says. He wants you to succeed and live a fulfilled life, but you must step out in faith. He's waiting to bless you!

———∞———

*If you want to make an easy job seem
mighty hard, just keep putting off doing it.*

One Percent

*Do not fear, little flock, for it is
your Father's good pleasure
to give you the kingdom.*

LUKE 12:32

A philosophical clock—one capable of deep pondering and meditation—once spent a great deal of time thinking about its own future. It noticed that it had to tick twice each second. *How much ticking might that be?* the clock questioned.

The clock calculated that it ticked 120 times each minute, which was 7,200 times every hour. In the twenty-four hours of a day, it would tick 172,800 times. This meant 63,072,000 ticks every year. At that point in his calculations, the clock had begun to perspire profusely at the very thought.

Finally, the clock calculated that in a ten-year period, it would have to tick 630,720,000 times! At that point, the clock collapsed from nervous exhaustion.

An equally scientific and philosophical person has concluded that 95 percent of everything that we worry about doesn't happen. Of the 5 percent that does happen, 4 out of 5 times, things turn out much better than anticipated. In the end, only about 1 percent of all the bad that we think might happen actually does, and of this, it's rarely as bad as we imagine. Therefore, what profit is there in worry? Enjoy life!

I WILL TRUST
IN MY
FATHER'S
GOOD
PLEASURE
BY . . .

*Worry is like a rocking chair:
It gives you something to do,
but doesn't get you anywhere.*

Something Better

There is a way that seems right to a man, but its end is the way of death.
PROVERBS 14:12

I HAVE SEEN
THAT GOD
KNOWS BEST
IN . . .

A little girl desperately wanted a new bicycle. She had been playing with a neighbor girl who had a new bicycle, and more than anything, she wanted to trade in her "baby bike" for a real "big girl" model like the one her friend rode. When she asked her parents for a new one, they both said, "Wait until your birthday."

Two weeks later, the little girl saw a picture of a bicycle in the newspaper. She stared at it in awe. The ad read, "Three speeds. Gear shifts. Light and easy to handle. Hand brakes. In many colors. The works!" She asked her parents if they might visit the store where the bike was sold, and they agreed. To her delight, she found the bicycle came in hot pink! "But don't you want a bike just like your friend has?" Mom asked with a smile. "No way," the little girl replied. "I've got something better in mind!"

Often, we can look back with thanksgiving that God did not answer our prayers the way we thought they should be answered. His answer reflected something better that we hadn't known about or thought to request!

Praying "Thy kingdom come, Thy will be done" is not a prayer of passivity. It is a powerful prayer of submission and faith. We want God's best, but at the same time, we recognize only He knows what His best may be!

Nothing lies beyond the reach of prayer except that which lies beyond the will of God.

The Importance of Agreement

Choose for yourselves this day whom you will serve. . . . As for me and my house, we will serve the LORD.

JOSHUA 24:15

As *Train 8017* made its way through Salerno, Italy, on March 2, 1944, it gave no sign that disaster was in the making. The chugging train didn't collide with anything on that rain-soaked evening. It didn't derail or burn. But shortly after 1:00 A.M., the train loaded with six hundred passengers lumbered into the Galleria delle Armi.

When the two locomotives pulling the train reached mid-tunnel, the drive wheels began to slip. Sand was sprayed on the tracks but to no avail. The wheels lost traction, and the train stopped. Any other details are pure speculation since both engineers died. Carbon monoxide snuffed out the lives of nearly five hundred people.

As analysts surveyed the wreckage, they found that the leading locomotive was unbraked, its controls set in reverse. The second locomotive was also unbraked, but its throttle was positioned "full ahead." The two locomotives had pulled and pushed against each other, their engineers obviously having fatally different ideas about what to do! Some have speculated that no lives would have been lost if the engineers had only been in agreement about which direction to go.

Today, make a decision with your spouse that you will both move your thought life in the direction of God—then stay ready by the controls of your minds.

What IN MY LIFE HAVE I NOT COMMITTED TOWARDS SERVING THE LORD?

Any plant growing in the wrong place is a "weed."

Silence Beyond Words

Whoever exalts himself will be humbled, and he who humbles himself will be exalted.

LUKE 14:11

What
WORDS HAVE
I SPOKEN
THAT ARE
UNPLEASING
TO GOD?

Marie Louise de la Ramée says in *Ouida*, "There are many moments in friendship, as in love, when silence is beyond words. The faults of our friend may be clear to us, but it is well to seem to shut our eyes to them. Friendship is usually treated by the majority of mankind as a tough and everlasting thing which will survive all manner of bad treatment. But this is an exceedingly great and foolish error; it may die in an hour of a single unwise word."

If the words "I love you" are the most important three words in a marriage, the words "I'm sorry" are probably the most important two! The more a spouse is willing to admit fault, the greater the likelihood the other spouse also will grow to be vulnerable enough to admit error. However, that doesn't mean a person should apologize for an error that has not been made; to do so would be to become a doormat or to exhibit false humility.

When you are right, although the other cannot see it, the better approach is silence—not saying, "I'm not speaking to you until you apologize." Remember: Silence is golden.

Silence is a great peacemaker.

Allowed to Serve

*Whoever of you does not forsake all
that he has cannot be My disciple.*

LUKE 14:33

When British Prime Minister William E. Gladstone was facing one of the greatest crises of his political life, he sat down at two o'clock one morning to write a speech he hoped would help him win a great political victory in Parliament the following day.

At that hour, the mother of a poor, dying cripple saw the light on in his home and knocked at the door. She asked him to come and bring a message of hope to her son.

Without hesitation, Gladstone left the half-finished speech on his desk and spent the remainder of the night with the child, leading him to Christ before he died. As morning light was breaking, he went back to his study and faced his own day with a smile of confidence and peace. Later that morning he said to a friend, "I am the happiest man in the world today." When asked why, he replied that the previous night he had been allowed to serve a child in the name of the Master.

Later in the day, Gladstone made the greatest speech of his life in the House of Commons and carried his cause to a triumphant success. Were the two events related? Gladstone could never be convinced that they weren't.

What OPPORTUNI-TIES HAS GOD LAID AT MY DOORSTEP TO SERVE OTHERS?

*The world is full of two kinds of people:
the givers and the takers. The takers
eat well—but the givers sleep well.*

Reaching Out

*He who has mercy on
the poor, happy is he.*
PROVERBS 14:21

What ONE
SMALL
ACTION
WILL I TAKE
TO HELP
ANOTHER
TODAY?

When thirteen-year-old Bobby Hill, the son of a U.S. Army sergeant stationed in Italy, read a book about the work of Nobel Prize winner Albert Schweitzer, he decided to do something to help the medical missionary. He sent a bottle of aspirin to Lieutenant General Richard C. Lindsay, Commander of the Allied air forces in Southern Europe, asking if any of his airplanes could parachute the bottle of aspirin to Dr. Schweitzer's jungle hospital in Africa.

Upon hearing of the letter, an Italian radio station issued an appeal that resulted in more than $400,000 worth of donated medical supplies. The French and Italian governments each supplied a plane to fly the medicines and the boy to Dr. Schweitzer. The grateful doctor responded, "I never thought a child could do so much for my hospital."

Not one of us can solve all the problems in the world, but we can feed a hungry family in a nearby neighborhood, clothe the homeless person who has just arrived at a local shelter, or give a blanket to a street person who sleeps near our office building. It's amazing what can happen when just one of us reaches out to help those in need. Inevitably, we are joined by many others who want to help as well.

*If you can't feed a hundred
people, then just feed one.*

The Examen

In all labor there is profit, but idle chatter leads only to poverty.

PROVERBS 14:23

Dennis Hamm has noted the "examen," or examination of conscience, is an ancient practice among Christians. In the early days of the Church, the examen was a time for confession. Specifically, it was a process of examining one's daily behavior against the criteria of the Ten Commandments.

Hamm proposes five practices that can help a person examine his or her day in prayer:

1. *Pray for light.* Ask God to give you illumination to help you see His plan in the buzzing confusion of your day.

2. *Review the day in thanksgiving.* Walk through your day, hour by hour, thanking God for each task He gave you and each person He allowed you to encounter.

3. *Review the feelings that surface as you replay your day.* Both positive and negative feelings are signals to you about your own spiritual state.

4. *Take one of the feelings that surfaces (positive or negative) and use it as a guide for your prayers.* You may be led to praise, petition, repent, or cry for help or healing.

5. *Finally, look toward tomorrow.* What feelings do you have about the tasks and appointments that lie ahead? Whatever you are feeling, ask for God's help.

Any one of the five prayer practices listed above will enhance your prayer time; all five can revolutionize it. You can implement them gradually, one at a time, or all at once. Either way, you'll find your prayers becoming more effective and meaningful in your life.

I WILL INVEST TIME TO REVOLUTIONIZE MY PRAYER LIFE BY . . .

Prayer should be the key of the morning and the bolt of the night.

More Than All Right

Only deliver us this day, we pray.
JUDGES 10:15

I TRUST
IN GOD'S
KNOWLEDGE
OF WHAT'S
BEST BY...

A mother was awakened one night to hear the news that her son, who was away at college, had fallen and was seriously injured. As she and her husband raced to the hospital, she prayed over and over again, "Dear God, please let our son be all right." The doctor greeted them with grim news. Their son had injured his spinal cord in the fall and would be permanently paralyzed from the neck down.

The mother thought it would be impossible for her son to finish college, but he remained determined to do so. Within three months after his hospitalization and rehabilitation at a spinal center, he enrolled at a college near home.

His mother was concerned about how he would get around campus in a wheelchair or take notes wearing the special brace he was just beginning to learn how to use. But four years later, her son graduated with his bachelor's degree. He then went on to law school, and within three years, received his law degree. He passed the bar exam and began to work for a law firm.

She has said about her experience, "No, God didn't answer my prayers in the way I had thought He would . . . [my son] had to struggle, but . . . he has done more than all right!"

*She who does not pray when
the sun shines will not know
how to pray when the clouds roll in.*

Shattered

*Take heed to yourselves. If your
brother sins against you, rebuke
him; and if he repents, forgive him.*

LUKE 17:3

One Sunday afternoon, Doris Louise Seger opened the door of her office at the church to practice a violin solo she was to play that night, only to find her violin in pieces, scattered across the floor. Doris was crushed. She had received the violin as a high school graduation present from her parents fifty years before. She thought, *Who? Why? How can I forgive the person who did this?*

A week later, police found the vandal, and Doris went to his home. When she saw the skinny, blond eleven-year-old sitting next to his father, she understood that the real tragedy was not her shattered violin, but a young life that seemed headed for a shattered future. She explained to the family what the violin had meant to her life, and then she found herself saying, "I forgive you, and God will, too, if you ask Him."

A few days later, the boy came to the pastor's office, asking hesitantly, "Is there any work that I can do at the church to pay for the violin?" At the sign of his repentant heart, the pastor shared the Gospel with him, and the boy received Jesus as his Savior that day.

Doris purchased a new violin, but she later wrote, "It would never compare with this 'new creature' in Christ Jesus. I learned anew that God's grace is sufficient enough to give me a forgiving heart."

His grace is sufficient enough for you, too.

Whom DO
I NEED TO
FORGIVE?

*He who cannot forgive breaks the
bridge over which he himself must pass.*

Following Orders

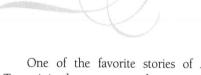

He who is slow to wrath has great understanding, but he who is impulsive exalts folly.

PROVERBS 14:29

How WILL
I HELP
SOMEONE
TO FOLLOW
GOD'S
LEADING FOR
THEIR LIVES
TODAY?

One of the favorite stories of Arturo Toscanini, the great symphony conductor, was this:

An orchestra was playing Beethoven's *Leonore Overture,* which has two great musical climaxes. Each of these musical high points is followed by a trumpet passage, which the composer intended to be played offstage.

The first climax arrived, but no sound came from the trumpet offstage. The conductor, annoyed, went on to the second musical high point. But again, no trumpet was heard.

This time, the conductor rushed, fuming, into the wings, with every intention of demanding a full explanation. There he found the trumpet player struggling with the house security guard who was insisting as he held on to the man's trumpet for dear life, "I tell you, you can't play that trumpet back here! You'll disturb the rehearsal!"

Like the security guard, we often jump to conclusions when we try to judge the actions of others. The trumpet player knew what the conductor had directed him to do; the security guard did not. We are not called to be God's security men, we are called to obey the conductor, and allow—even help—others to do so as well.

* * *

Ignorance is always swift to speak.

Mother's Anchor

*Assuredly, I say to you, whoever does
not receive the kingdom of God as a
little child will by no means enter it.*

LUKE 18:17

Henry Ward Beecher, considered by many to be one of the most effective and powerful pulpit orators in the history of the United States, not only had a reputation for having an extremely sensitive heart, but also for having a great love of the sea. Many of his sermons were laced with loving anecdotes with a seafaring flavor.

Beecher once said, "Children are the hands by which we take hold of Heaven." And he had this to say about a mother's relationship with her child:

"A babe is a mother's anchor. She cannot swing far from her moorings. And yet a true mother never lives so little in the present as when by the side of the cradle. Her thoughts follow the imagined future of her child. That babe is the boldest of pilots, and guides her fearless thoughts down through scenes of coming years. The old ark never made such voyages as the cradle daily makes."

What a wonderful image to think of a child as being on a voyage from Heaven, through life, to return to Heaven's port one day. What a challenge to think that our children have not come along to join us in our sail through life, but we are to join in their voyage!

*The most valuable gift you can
give another is a good example.*

I WILL HELP THE CHILDREN IN MY LIFE SUCCESSFULLY SAIL IN THEIR VOYAGE BY . . .

World-changing Prayer

*He said, "The things which are
impossible with men are
possible with God."*

LUKE 18:27

I HAVE SEEN
THE WORLD-
CHANGING
POWER OF
PRAYER
THROUGH...

Billy Graham had planned a meeting in Germany in 1992, but when the Berlin Wall came down in 1989, his plans were changed. On March 10, 1990, Graham spoke at the Platz der Republik, the great open area in front of the Reichstag, the historic site where Nazis once paraded by torchlight, preaching their doctrine of ethnic bitterness and hatred. In sharp contrast, Graham spoke of the Good News of God's forgiveness and love. Just a few yards away, workers with saws and torches continued to rip out the bars that had supported the wall.

Graham told the large congregation, "God has answered our prayers." Members of the press corps asked if he truly believed the dismantling of the Iron Curtain was an answer to prayer. He told them yes. Christians in the East and the West had been praying for decades for the day the wall would be demolished. He told them the prospect of liberation, reunification, and the freedom to worship God made this the happiest hour for Germany.

Often, we mistakenly assume that major world events just happen. In nearly all cases, however, you will find that those headlines that mark major changes for good have been birthed in prayer. God commands us to pray for all those in authority. Your prayers do make a difference in the world!

*Prayer moves the hand
that moves the world.*

Word Echoes

A soft answer turns away wrath,
But a harsh word stirs up anger.

PROVERBS 15:1

I shouted aloud and louder
While out on the plain one day;
The sound grew faint and fainter
Until it had died away.
My words had gone forever,
They left no trace or track,
But the hills nearby caught up the cry
And sent an echo back.
I spoke a word in anger
To one who was my friend,
Like a knife it cut him deeply,
A wound that was hard to mend.
That word, so thoughtlessly uttered,
I would we could both forget,
But its echo lives and memory gives
The recollection yet.
How many hearts are broken,
How many friends are lost
By some unkind word spoken
Before we count the cost!
But a word or deed of kindness
Will repay a hundred-fold,
For it echoes again in the hearts of men
And carries a joy untold.

—C. A. Lufburrow

Whom IN
MY LIFE CAN
I TOUCH
TODAY WITH
A WORD OF
AFFIRMATION?

We should seize every opportunity
to give encouragement.
Encouragement is oxygen to the soul.

125

The Stepladder

Ruth said: "Entreat me not to leave you, or to turn back from following after you; for wherever you go, I will go; and wherever you lodge, I will lodge; your people shall be my people, and your God, my God."

RUTH 1:16

What CAN I DO TO MAKE CHRIST THE ULTIMATE HEAD OF MY HOUSEHOLD?

A child once asked his father to draw a picture of a stepladder for him. The father did as he was asked. Then his son said, "No, Dad, you left out something." The father looked again at the double upside-down V he had drawn on the page and the lines he had drawn as the ladder's steps. "What did I leave out?" he asked. The little boy replied, "The part where you put the paint can."

The little boy may have been more interested in paint cans than a properly engineered ladder, but what the father later realized was that the crosspiece that extends to provide a resting place for paint cans is the one part of a stepladder that is truly indispensable! Without it, the inverted V shape of a ladder would collapse. The crosspiece is what makes a stepladder useful by allowing it to support weight.

Similarly, when Christ is the crosspiece that holds a couple together in a sturdy triangle, the marriage can withstand the pressures of life. Let Christ support your marriage.

───── ✺ ─────

A personal relationship with Jesus Christ is the cornerstone of marriage.

A Lonely Tree

Blessed are you of the LORD, my daughter!
For you have shown more kindness
at the end than at the beginning.

RUTH 3:10

When American poet and writer Edgar Guest was a young man, his first child died. He wrote about the experience: "There came a tragic night when our first baby was taken from us. I was lonely and defeated. There didn't seem to be anything in life ahead of me that mattered very much.

"I had to go to my neighbor's drugstore the next morning for something, and he motioned for me to step behind the counter with him. I followed him into his little office at the back of the store. He put both hands on my shoulders and said, 'Eddie, I can't really express what I want to say, the sympathy I have in my heart for you. All I can say is that I'm sorry, and I want you to know that if you need anything at all, come to me. What is mine is yours.'"

Guest recalls that this man was "just a neighbor across the way—a passing acquaintance." He says of the druggist that he "may long since have forgotten that moment when he gave me his hand and his sympathy, but I shall never forget it—never in all my life. To me it stands out like the silhouette of a lonely tree against a crimson sunset."

Is there someone who needs a kind word from you today?

⟶⟵

Kind words can be short and easy to
speak, but their echoes are truly endless.

I HAVE
RECEIVED
KIND WORDS
WHEN I
NEEDED IT
FROM . . .

Without Ransom

*For this child I prayed, and
the LORD has granted me my
petition which I asked of Him.*
1 SAMUEL 1:27

I WILL
PLACE MY
ENTIRE FAITH
IN GOD'S
ABILITY TO
ANSWER
PRAYER BY...

One night while Kao Er was attending a prayer meeting, his eight-year-old son and baby daughter were kidnapped. The kidnappers demanded 1,000 yuan in ransom. Mr. Er painted a large sign and posted it in front of his place of employment. It said, "I am not a wealthy man. I cannot pay 1,000 yuan ransom. I cannot pay 500 yuan. I cannot even pay 50 yuan. But I believe God. He is able to bring my children back without ransom."

The sign brought a great deal of ridicule from those who saw it. No sane man could expect a kidnapped child to be returned alive without ransom! Weeks passed. Finally, soldiers clashed with bandits in the Chinese countryside, and the bandits were routed. In hot pursuit of the bandits, some soldiers heard a sound coming from a ditch beside the road. They found a skeleton-like child lying there, abandoned by the bandits. It was Mr. Er's son!

After a second battle between the bandits and soldiers, the wife of the bandit chief was captured. She was nursing two babies—one of whom was Mr. Er's daughter. Both children were returned home safely. God had done the impossible—returned kidnapped children without ransom.

God's answers to prayer are not dependent upon our ability to pray, but on His ability to answer.

*God answers prayers because
His children ask.*

Bravery Under Fire

Having confidence in your obedience,
I write to you, knowing that you
will do even more than I say.

PHILEMON 1:21

In 1769, Mary Ludwig, daughter of a Dutch dairyman, was sent to Carlisle, Pennsylvania, to become a domestic servant in the home of a doctor. A few months later, not yet sixteen, she married a barber named John Hays. When Hays enlisted in the Pennsylvania artillery, Mary followed her husband's outfit, washing and cooking for the soldiers.

In the summer of 1778, the American army was pursuing British troops, and they met at the Battle of Monmouth. It was a blistering hot day, and fifty soldiers died of thirst during the battle. Not content to stay back in the camp, Mary braved the gunshots and cannon fire to carry water from a stream to the parched American troops. This brave act earned Mary her legendary nickname, "Molly Pitcher."

As the battle wore on, Mary saw her husband fall wounded next to his cannon. His commanding officer ordered the cannon to be pulled back from the front lines, but Mary, who had watched her husband in training, stepped into his place and kept firing for the rest of the battle. In the end, the battle ended as a draw, but Mary won the admiration of the other soldiers, who called her "Sergeant Molly." Legend has it that General Washington himself gave her a noncommissioned title and made up songs about her.

Extra effort above and beyond the expected never goes unnoticed or unrewarded by God.

I WILL
EXPEND EXTRA
EFFORT TODAY
IN . . .

It is the amount and excellence of what is
over and above the required that determines
the greatness of ultimate distinction.

Clear Away the Brambles

Do you see a man who excels in his work? He will stand before kings; he will not stand before unknown men.

PROVERBS 22:29

Is THERE
A TASK I
DESPAIR OF
THAT COULD
BE MADE
MANAGEABLE
THROUGH
PLANNING
SMALL STEPS?

A man who owned a plot of land was about to leave the area on a journey that would take several years. Before he left, he leased his land to others. When he returned, he discovered his renters had been careless, and brambles had sprung up, turning his plot of land into a wilderness of thorns. Desiring to cultivate the land, he said to his son, "Your job is to go and clear that ground."

The son visited the acreage and quickly concluded that it would take forever to get the land cleared! Overwhelmed by the task, he lay down on the ground and went to sleep. He did the same day after day. When his father came to see what had been done, he found his son asleep and the land untouched.

When his father woke him, the son complained that the job had looked so monumental, he could never make himself begin to tackle the project. His father replied, "Son, if you had only cleared the area on which you lay down for a nap each day, your work would have advanced and you would not have lost heart." After the father left, the son began to do what his father had advised. In a short time, the plot of land was cleared and cultivated.

Daily prayer clears away the brambles in our hearts. Don't give up! God is working something good in you—prayer by prayer!

By far the most important thing about praying is to keep at it.

The Best Medicine

All the days of the afflicted are evil,
but he who is of a merry heart
has a continual feast.

PROVERBS 15:15

Stand-up comedian and author David Brenner was signing books in a San Francisco bookstore when a young man handed him a newly purchased copy to be signed and said softly, "I want to thank you for saving my life." Brenner replied flippantly, "That's okay." The young man stood his ground and said, "No, I really mean it."

Brenner stopped signing the book and looked at him. The man said, "My father died. He was my best friend. I loved him and couldn't stop crying for weeks. I decided to take my own life. The night I was going to do it, I happened to have the TV on. You were hosting *The Tonight Show* and doing your monologue. Next thing I knew, I was watching you and laughing. Then I started laughing hysterically. I realized then that if I was able to laugh, I was able to live. So I want to thank you for saving my life." Humbled and grateful, Brenner shook his hand and said, "No, I thank you."

Laughter does more than help us escape our problems. It sometimes gives us the courage to face them. As humorist Barbara Johnson has said: "Laughter is like changing a baby's diaper. It doesn't permanently solve any problems, but it makes things more acceptable for a while."

Humor is to life what shock
absorbers are to automobiles.

How CAN I IMPROVE SOMEONE'S LIFE THROUGH LAUGHTER TODAY?

131

Praying on Your Fingers

Evening and morning and at noon
I will pray, and cry aloud, and
He shall hear my voice.

PSALM 55:17

Whom CAN
I PRAY FOR
BY NAME
TODAY?

Many children learn to count on their fingers, but a nurse once taught a child to pray on his fingers.

This was her method:

Your thumb is the digit nearest to your heart, so pray first for those who are closest to you. Your own needs, of course, should be included, as well as those of your beloved family and friends.

The second finger is the one used for pointing. Pray for those who point you toward the truth, whether at church or school. Pray for your teachers, mentors, pastors, and those who inspire your faith.

The third finger is the tallest. Let it stand for the leaders in every sphere of life. Pray for those in authority—both within the body of Christ and those who hold office in various areas of government.

The fourth finger is the weakest, as every pianist knows. Let it stand for those who are in trouble and pain—the sick, injured, abused, wounded, or hurt.

The little finger is the smallest. Let it stand for those who often go unnoticed, including those who suffer abuse and deprivation.

What a great tool to use in teaching children how to pray for themselves and others! What a simple and wonderful reminder to use as we pray ourselves!

Daily prayers will diminish your cares.

Fixing Your Spouse

A man has joy by the answer of his mouth, and a word spoken in due season, how good it is!

PROVERBS 15:23

A demanding wife continually nagged her husband to conform to her high standards: "This is how you should act, this is how you should dress, this is what you should say, this is where you should be seen, and this is how you should plan your career!" She insisted every aspect of his life be honed to perfection. Feeling thoroughly whipped, the man finally said, "Why don't you just write it all down? Then you won't have to tell me these things all the time." She gladly complied.

A short time later, the wife died. Within the course of a year, the man met another woman and married. His new life seemed to be a perpetual honeymoon. He could hardly believe the great joy and relief he was experiencing with his new bride.

One day he came across the list of "do's and don'ts" his first wife had written. He read them and realized, to his amazement, he was following all of the instructions—even though his second wife had never mentioned them.

He thought about what might have happened and finally said to a friend, "My former wife began her statements, 'I hate it when. . . ,' but my new wife says, 'I just love it when. . . .'"

The most important way we can help our husbands become the men God created them to be is to pray for them and always speak encouraging words to and about them. When we trust in God to fix what we think is wrong with our spouses, we often find it is we who need fixing.

Whom CAN I ENCOURAGE WITH AN "I JUST LOVE IT WHEN . . . ?"

———

Ninety percent of the friction of daily life is caused by the wrong tone of voice.

Divert the Ice Cream Man

Whenever I am afraid,
I will trust in You.

PSALM 56:3

Have
I BEEN
PLACING
MY TRUST
IN GOD
TO PROVIDE
THE POWER
TO AVOID
TEMPTATIONS?

Sally was trying desperately to save all the pennies she could for the doll carriage she wanted to buy. She was turning in aluminum cans, offering to do extra chores—anything to make a few more cents each week.

One night as she was saying her bedtime prayers, Sally's mother overheard her say in great earnest, "O Lord, please help me to save my money for the doll carriage in Mr. Brown's store window. It's so beautiful and I want it so much. It's just right for my doll. And I'd be sure to let my friends play with it, too."

Pleased at her daughter's prayer, Sally's mother was startled to hear the final line of the prayer: "And please, God, don't let the ice cream man come down our street this week!"

Just as we are each unique in our talents, abilities, and experiences, we are also unique in our temptations. What is tempting to one person may not be at all tempting to another.

Although the enemy of our souls knows our weaknesses, we know where to find our strength—in Jesus. As we stick close to Him, when temptation comes, we can draw on His strength to turn from it.

When you say yes to Jesus, saying no to temptation becomes easier!

When you flee temptations
don't leave a forwarding address.

Doing the Right Thing

My heart is steadfast, O God, my heart
is steadfast; I will sing and give praise.

PSALM 57:7

During the Great Depression, Debbie and her family lived with her grandparents because her father couldn't find work. She slept in a bed with four other relatives, and they survived by eating jackrabbits caught on the Texas plains. When she was seven, her family moved to California, and at age sixteen, she won the Miss Burbank contest, which led to a part in a movie.

As an adult, her first marriage ended in a bitter divorce, so she raised her two children alone. Her second marriage to a millionaire shoe manufacturer ended when his financial gambles brought an end to his business. He left her with millions of dollars of debt. Everything she owned was repossessed, including her home. Determined to pay back the debts and properly care for her family, she went on the road doing live theater. It took her more than ten years, working forty weeks a year, to pay back the debts of her ex-husband. But she did it.

Now out of debt and living in a home that is paid for, Debbie Reynolds has a satisfaction that only doing the right thing can produce.

Successful people accept responsibility for their mistakes and learn from their experiences. And most importantly, they never give up.

———————

No man will succeed unless he is ready
to face and overcome difficulties and
prepared to assume responsibilities.

Have I
GIVEN UP ON
SOMETHING
IN MY LIFE?

A Reason to Laugh

The light of the eyes rejoices the heart, and a good report makes the bones healthy.

PROVERBS 15:30

How CAN I
MAKE THE
JOY OF GOD
A REGULAR
PART OF
MY LIFE?

Peggy was nervous about the upcoming dinner party she and her husband were hosting. It was their first time to have guests for dinner since the birth of their son, Pete. To top off Peggy's tension, one of the guests was her husband Bill's new supervisor.

Sensing the tension in his parents, the baby became irritable and fussy, which only added to Peggy's frustration. In an attempt to comfort little Pete, Peggy picked him up, raised him high over her head, and kissed his bare tummy. To her surprise, he smiled and giggled—the first genuine laughter she had heard from her young son.

In an instant, the evening took on an entirely new tenor. Peggy became more relaxed, and the baby relaxed as well. The dinner party was a great success.

Can the laughter of a small child change a day? Yes! So can laughter shared between adults or a chuckle prompted by the memory of a funny event.

When you're feeling stressed out, don't allow yourself to explode in anger. Get alone if you have to, but find a reason to laugh, and watch the stress melt away!

―――∞∞∞―――

Humor is the sunshine of the mind.

You Are What You Think You Are

The ear that hears the rebukes
of life will abide among the wise.

PROVERBS 15:31

The story is told of a man who found an eagle's egg and put it into the nest of a barnyard chicken. The eaglet hatched with the brood of chicks and grew up with them. All his life, the eagle did what the chickens did. It scratched the dirt for seeds and insects to eat. It clucked and cackled. And it flew no more than a few feet off the ground in a chicken-like thrashing of wings and flurry of feathers.

One day the eagle saw a magnificent bird far above him in the cloudless sky. He watched as the bird soared gracefully on the wind, gliding through the air with scarcely a beat of its powerful wings.

"What a beautiful bird," the young eagle said. "What is it called?"

The chicken next to him said, "Why, that's an eagle—the king of all birds. But don't give him any mind. You could never be like him."

So the young eagle returned to pecking the dirt for seeds, and it died thinking it was a chicken.

What you think of your own potential defines who you are today and what you will become tomorrow.

Try not to become a man of success but rather try to become a man of value.

*I*S MY IMAGE OF MYSELF BASED ON WHAT GOD CREATED ME TO BE?

Six-Step Problem Solving

Teach me Your way, O LORD;
I will walk in Your truth.

PSALM 86:11

Am I
BASING MY
LIFE ON
RECEIVING
ANSWERS
FROM GOD
ABOUT
EVERYTHING?

A man once recognized Norman Vincent Peale on an airplane and told him that he had read his books and benefited from them. He then told Peale that he was a training supervisor and had spent a great deal of time listening to the problems of employees. He said, "I worked out six practical points for handling a problem. Would you like to hear them?" Peale replied, "I sure would!" These are the six points he shared, which Peale in turn shared with millions of his readers:

1. When faced with a problem, pray about it, asking that God's will, rather than your own, be done.

2. Having prayed, believe that God will bring the matter out right.

3. Write the problem out in detail.

4. Always ask yourself what is the right thing to do. Nothing that is wrong ever works out right.

5. Keep thinking and keep working at the problem. First try one thing, then another, until you find a solution.

6. When your problem is solved, thank God. Give one-tenth of your income to God's work. When you give, God's blessings will be released to flow into your life.

God has an answer for every problem you may face today or will face in the future. He is ready to give you the solution, and He is waiting to fill your life with blessings. Take it to God. He has an answer!

Everybody finds out, sooner or later,
that all success worth having is
founded on Christian rules of conduct.

Hull House

Commit your works to the LORD, and
your thoughts will be established.

PROVERBS 16:3

Jane was only seven years old when she visited a shabby street in a nearby town. Seeing ragged children there, she announced that she wanted to build a big house so poor children would have a place to play. As a young adult, Jane and a friend, Ellen Starr, visited Toynbee Hall in London, where they saw educated people helping the poor by living among them.

She and Ellen returned to the slums of Chicago, restored the old Hull mansion, and moved in. There they cared for children of working mothers and held sewing and cooking classes. Older boys and girls had clubs at the mansion. An art gallery, playground, and public music, reading, and craft rooms were created in the mansion. Her childhood dream came true.

Jane fought against child labor laws and campaigned for adult education, day nurseries, better housing, and women's suffrage. She was eventually awarded an honorary degree from Yale. President Theodore Roosevelt dubbed her, "America's most useful citizen," and she was awarded the Nobel Prize for peace.

No matter how famous she became, however, Jane Adams remained a resident of Hull House. She died there, in the heart of the slum she had come to call home.

Commit your dreams and plans to the Lord, and He will see to it that they come to pass.

❦

The secret of achievement is to not let what you're doing get to you before you get to it.

Have I BEEN TRUSTING THAT GOD WILL GIVE ME THE DESIRES OF MY HEART?

I Want It!

The LORD has made all for Himself.
PROVERBS 16:4

What IN MY
LIFE WILL I
ENTRUST TO
GOD FOR HIM
TO CHANGE?

A man once went into a pastor's office and said, "I want what my wife has found." The pastor asked, "What do you think it is that she found?" "I'm not sure," the man replied, "but whatever it is, it sure has changed her disposition."

The man's wife had been a difficult, demanding person. She had found it excruciating to give without receiving twice as much in return. Her needs kept the family in constant turmoil. She could be extremely unpleasant when things didn't go as she had planned.

What had changed her? She started attending an Enabler's Group in her neighborhood. The women, all members of the same church, opened their hearts to this woman. One day at the end of a meeting, she stayed to talk with one of the women about her life. Facing the fact of her rotten disposition, she prayed, almost as an experiment, "Jesus, if You are alive as these people say You are, help me to change." The result of that prayer came slowly but surely. She repeated the prayer each morning, and within just a few months, her husband had not only noticed the difference, but he wanted the same Jesus in his own life!

The only way to effect real and lasting change in our lives is to invite Jesus to help us. He won't force us to change or do all the work, but He will be with us every step of the way, pointing us toward the path of peace.

Prayer is God's way of doing God's will.

The Legend of David's Temple

*God so loved the world that He gave His only
begotten Son, that whoever believes in Him
should not perish but have everlasting life.*

JOHN 3:16

Most authorities believe King David's temple was built on Mount Moriah, the mount where Abraham was told to sacrifice Isaac. But there's another Hebrew legend that presents a different story.

The legend says that two brothers lived on adjoining farms that were divided from the peak to the base of the mountain. The younger brother lived alone, unmarried. The older brother had a large family.

One night during the grain harvest, the older brother awoke and thought, *My brother is alone. To cheer his heart, I will take some of my sheaves and lay them on his side of the field.*

At the same hour, the younger brother awoke and thought, *My brother has a large family and greater needs than I do. As he sleeps, I'll put some of my sheaves on his side of the field.* Each brother went out carrying sheaves to the other's field, and they met halfway. When they declared their intentions to one another, they dropped their sheaves and embraced. It is at that place, the legend claims, the temple was built.

Whether this story is true or not, it exemplifies the highest expression of love—giving. Giving is one of life's best relationship builders.

*We make a living by what we get—
we make a life by what we give.*

What RELATIONSHIP IN MY LIFE COULD BENEFIT FROM A GIVING ATTITUDE?

Start with a Step

A man's heart plans his way,
but the LORD directs his steps.
PROVERBS 16:9

What FIRST
STEP IN
FAITH CAN I
TAKE TODAY?

A comic strip created by the late Charles Schulz addresses the need for each of us to make the most of the present moment in our lives:

Charlie Brown is at bat. Strike three. He has struck out again. He slumps down on the players' bench. "Rats!" he exclaims. "I'll never be a big-league player. I just don't have it! All my life I've dreamed of playing in the big leagues, but I know I'll never make it."

Lucy turns to console him. "Charlie Brown," she says, "you're thinking too far ahead. What you need to do is set yourself more immediate goals."

Charlie Brown looks up and asks, "Immediate goals?"

Lucy responds, "Yes. Start with this next inning when you go out to pitch. See if you can walk out to the mound without falling down."

The first step toward walking into any future you can picture is the step that you take today. Make it a forward, positive, energetic, purposeful step. The steps you take today become the well-worn paths of tomorrow.

* * *

The only preparation for
tomorrow is the right use of today.

Always Useful to God

Truly my soul silently waits for God;
From Him comes my salvation.

PSALM 62:1

In *Glorious Intruder,* Joni Eareckson Tada writes about Diane, who suffers from multiple sclerosis: "In her quiet sanctuary, Diane turns her head slightly on the pillow toward the corkboard on the wall. Her eyes scan each thumbtacked card and list. Each photo. Every torn piece of paper carefully pinned in a row. The stillness is broken as Diane begins to murmur. She is praying.

"Some would look at Diane—stiff and motionless—and shake their heads . . . 'What a shame. Her life has no meaning. She can't really do anything.' But Diane is confident, convinced her life is significant. Her labor of prayer counts. She moves mountains that block the paths of missionaries. She helps open the eyes of the spiritually blind in Southeast Asia. She pushes back the kingdom of darkness that blackens the alleys and streets of the gangs in east LA. She aids homeless mothers, single parents, abused children, despondent teenagers, handicapped boys, and the dying and forgotten old people in the nursing home down the street from where she lives. Diane is on the front lines, advancing the gospel of Christ, holding up weak saints, inspiring doubting believers, energizing other prayer warriors, and delighting her Lord and Savior."

What a difference we can make, regardless of our situation in life, if we have the right attitude! God is willing and able to use us regardless of our ability or inability. He always has a plan!

IS THERE AN ATTITUDE IN MY LIFE THAT HAS GOTTEN IN THE WAY OF GOD USING ME?

There are moments when, whatever be the attitude of the body, the soul is on its knees.

Simplicity

*Do not trust in oppression, nor vainly
hope in robbery; if riches increase,
do not set your heart on them.*

PSALM 62:10

Is THERE AN
AREA OF MY
LIFE I CAN
UNCLUTTER
TODAY?

The necessary ingredients for
enjoying success: 1. Simple tastes
2. A certain degree of courage
3. Self-denial to a point
4. Love of work
5. A clear conscience.

One of the most influential and prominent people in the world is Pope John Paul II. Those who have known him through the years regard him as a man of simplicity and honor.

As a quarry worker in Poland in 1940, he endured bitterly cold temperatures dressed only in a sweat-soaked cap and a blue cloth jacket and trousers. One day he arrived at work without his jacket—he had given it to someone he met on the road.

As a village cleric, he had a reputation as a "skinny priest in a threadbare cassock." He walked on an unpaved road to his first parish, carrying all of his belongings in a battered brief-case. As a teacher of ethics at the Catholic University of Lublin, he often wore a black cassock frayed at the knees from the time he spent in prayer. As a cardinal at the Vatican, he owned practically nothing except his books, ecclesiastical robes, a few family mementos, skis, and hiking clothes.

Those who know him well have conjectured that it is because Pope John Paul has ties to so little in the way of family (most of whom died early in his life) or personal goods that he is able to reach out so warmly to millions around the world who have little to offer other than their faith.

The Bible says that whatever occupies your thoughts and time is what you truly value. Stop yourself today. What do you spend most of your time thinking about? You may find you need to simplify your life and cut back on some superfluous commitments so that you can focus your attentions on those to whom God has called you to minister.

Time to Pray

O God, You are my God; early will I seek You;
my soul thirsts for You; my flesh longs for You
in a dry and thirsty land where there is no water.

PSALM 63:1

How hollow our excuse sounds when we say, "I just didn't have time to spend with You today, Lord." Perhaps our not seeking Him is the reason so many of us have difficulty finding His answers.

I got up early one morning
And rushed right into the day;
I had so much to accomplish
I didn't have time to pray.

Troubles just tumbled about me
And heavier came each task.
Why doesn't God help me, I wondered.
He answered, "You didn't ask."

I tried to come into God's presence,
I used all my keys at the lock.
God gently and lovingly chided,
"Why child, you didn't knock."

I wanted to see joy and beauty,
But the day toiled on grey and bleak,
I called on the Lord for the reason—
He said, "You didn't seek."

I woke up early this morning
And paused before entering the day.
I had so much to accomplish
That I had to take time to pray.

—Anonymous

Does ANYTHING KEEP ME FROM SEEING PRAYER WITH GOD AS THE ONLY WAY TO BEGIN MY DAY?

Do not face a day until
you have faced God.

Handiwork

*Pride goes before destruction,
and a haughty spirit before a fall.*

PROVERBS 16:18

What

KEEPS ME
FROM DOING
MY BEST IN
THE WORK
GOD HAS
GIVEN ME?

A carpenter had a brother who was a famous musician. When his brother came to visit the construction company where he worked, the foreman said, "You must be very proud to have a brother who is known around the world for his music." Then, feeling that he may have slighted his worker, he clumsily added, "Of course, not everyone in the same family can enjoy an equal amount of talent."

The carpenter responded, "You're right. My brother doesn't know the first thing about building a home. It's fortunate he could afford to hire others to build a house." The musician nodded in agreement and added, "My brother and I both work with our hands. I hold a musical instrument in mine, and he holds a hammer in his."

Not everybody is called to walk the same path through life. If we were, we'd find our walk through life crowded indeed! Booker T. Washington wrote in *Up From Slavery:* "There is as much dignity in tilling a field as in writing a poem." Dignity resides in a person's heart and attitude, not in their job description.

---

*Show me a man who cannot bother to
do little things and I'll show you a man
who cannot be trusted to do big things.*

A Trail of Kindness

*Pleasant words are like a
honeycomb, sweetness to the
soul and health to the bones.*

PROVERBS 16:24

The words of this poem are a good reminder that everything we say and do makes a difference—especially to those whom we love:

Is anybody happier
Because you passed his way?
Does anyone remember
That you spoke to him today?
This day is almost over,
And its toiling time is through;
Is there anyone to utter now
A friendly word for you?
Can you say tonight in passing
With the days that slipped so fast,
That you helped a single person,
Of the many that you passed?
Is a single heart rejoicing
Over what you did or said?
Does one whose hopes were fading
Now with courage look ahead?
Did you waste the day, or lose it?
Was it well or poorly spent?
Did you leave a trail of kindness
Or a scar of discontent?

—Anonymous

*One kind act will teach more love of God
than a thousand sermons.*

IS MY LIFE STRUCTURED AROUND PROVIDING KINDNESS TO THOSE AROUND ME?

The Big Picture

He rules by His power forever;
His eyes observe the nations; do not
let the rebellious exalt themselves.

PSALM 66:7

What
LIVING
INSTRUC-
TIONS HAVE
I RECEIVED
FROM GOD?

Earl Weaver, former manager of the Baltimore Orioles, had a rule that no one could steal a base unless he gave the steal sign. This upset Reggie Jackson, who felt he knew the pitchers and catchers well enough to judge when he could steal. One day, he decided to steal without the sign. He got a good jump off the pitcher and easily beat the throw to second base. As he shook the dirt from his uniform, he smiled with delight, feeling he had vindicated himself.

Later, Weaver took Jackson aside and explained why he hadn't given the steal sign. The next batter was Lee May, a major power hitter. Because first base was open, the opposing team intentionally walked May. The batter after May hadn't been strong against this pitcher, so Weaver had to send in a designated hitter. That left their team without the bench strength they might need later in the game.

Jackson had seen a stolen base as involving only the relationship between pitcher and catcher. Weaver was calling signals with the entire game in mind.

Don't put your trust in what you see immediately around you. Trust the One who sees the big picture that spans all of time and eternity.

Don't bother to give God
instructions; just report for duty.

No Excuses

*Who keeps our soul among the living, and does not
allow our feet to be moved. For You, O God, have
tested us; You have refined us as silver is refined.*

PSALM 66:9-10

Some of the world's greatest achievers have been saddled with disabilities and adversities:

Sir Walter Scott, author and English poet—crippled.

John Bunyan, author of *The Pilgrim's Progress*—imprisoned.

George Washington—snowbound and freezing in Valley Forge.

Abraham Lincoln—raised in abject poverty.

Benjamin Disraeli, British prime minister, who was born Jewish and converted to Christianity—subject to bitter religious prejudice.

Franklin D. Roosevelt—struck with infantile paralysis.

Ludwig van Beethoven—deaf.

Glenn Cunningham, a world-record-holding sprinter—legs badly burned in a school fire.

Booker T. Washington, Harriet Tubman, Marian Anderson, and George Washington Carver—all outstanding African-Americans born into a society filled with racial discrimination.

Enrico Caruso, a famous dramatic tenor—the first child to survive in a poor Italian family of eighteen children.

Itzhak Perlman, concert violinist—paralyzed from the waist down at age four.

There really are no good excuses for giving up!

Do I LOOK
FOR REASONS
TO SUCCEED?

*Success is never final and failure
never fatal. It's courage that counts.*

Pray High

If I regard iniquity in my heart,
the Lord will not hear.

PSALM 66:18

*I*S THERE
SOMETHING
IN MY LIFE
BREAKING
UP THE
COMMUNI-
CATION
BETWEEN ME
AND GOD?

Buddy's busy day was over. He was actually ready to kneel by his bed and join his father in bedtime prayers. He prayed about the many activities of his day, thanking God for the ability to catch a lizard and pass a spelling test. Then he listened as his father prayed for his health, safety, and protection from evil. The customary amen was said, and Buddy was tucked into bed. Before his father left the room, however, he sat up to ask, "Daddy, how high did we pray tonight? Did our prayers get all the way to Heaven?"

His father, accustomed to fielding such difficult questions, assured Buddy that God had heard their every word, since He always hears anything we pray. Buddy fell back onto his pillow and was asleep almost before his father left the room.

Daddy, however, pondered his son's question for some time. He was reminded that the Scriptures tell us we are not forgiven unless we first forgive others and that Jesus once told a man to leave his offering at an altar and first go make amends with a person he had offended.

The daddy realized there are some things that can hinder our prayers. His son's question was not really that far off.

How high did you pray today?

—— ⌘ ——

A good man's prayers will from the
deepest dungeon climb Heaven's height,
and bring a blessing down.

A Picture-Perfect Christmas

Better is a dry morsel with quietness,
Than a house full of feasting with strife.

PROVERBS 17:1

During the Depression, many families could scarcely afford the bare essentials, much less Christmas presents. "But, I'll tell you what we can do," a father said to his six-year-old son, Pete. "We can use our imaginations and make pictures of the presents we would like to give each other."

For the next few days, each member of the family worked secretly, but joyfully. On Christmas morning, huddled around a scraggly tree decorated with a few pitiful decorations, the family gathered to exchange the presents they had created. And what gifts they were! Daddy got a shiny black limousine and a red motorboat. Mom received a diamond bracelet and a new hat. Little Pete had fun opening his gifts: a drawing of a swimming pool and pictures of toys cut from magazines.

Then it was Pete's turn to give his present to his parents. With great delight, he handed them a brightly colored crayon drawing of three people—a man, woman, and little boy. They had their arms around one another, and under the picture was one word—"us." Even though other Christmases were far more prosperous for this family, no Christmas in the family's memory stands out as more precious!

Am I GIVING THE GIFT OF MYSELF TO THOSE AROUND ME?

Giving is the thermometer of love.

151

Sticking with the Rules

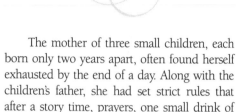

Let each one give as he purposes in his heart, not grudgingly or of necessity; for God loves a cheerful giver.

2 CORINTHIANS 9:7

Which
CONVICTIONS
DO I HAVE
THAT AREN'T
STRONG
ENOUGH
TO FOLLOW
GOD'S RULES
NO MATTER
WHAT?

The mother of three small children, each born only two years apart, often found herself exhausted by the end of a day. Along with the children's father, she had set strict rules that after a story time, prayers, one small drink of water, and a final trip to the bathroom, each child must go to bed and stay there.

One night, after a particularly trying day, all three children were finally tucked into bed, and the two parents headed to the kitchen for some cookies and milk and a little time alone together. They had just started to relax when they suddenly found themselves surrounded by three little people, all standing in silence as they watched Mom and Dad each bite into a delicious home-baked cookie. Turning to Dad, Mom asked, "Well, do we relent, or do we stick with the rules?"

Before Dad could answer, their three-year-old daughter piped up, "Stick with the rules, Mom!"

Knowing that her daughter didn't really want to be sent back to bed, Mom asked, "And what exactly are those rules, dear?"

Her daughter replied without hesitation, "Share with one another."

The persons hardest to convince they're at retirement age are children at bedtime.

Kid-Care

You, O God, provided from
Your goodness for the poor.
PSALM 68:10

Carol Porter, a registered nurse, is the cofounder of Kid-Care, Inc., a nonprofit group with volunteer staff members who deliver five hundred free meals each day to poor neighborhoods. Each meal is prepared in Porter's cramped Houston home, where extra stoves and refrigerators have been installed in what used to be the family's living room and den. Kid-Care receives no public funding, and although Carol's efforts have resulted in help from some corporations, most of her $500,000 budget comes from individual donations.

Carol credits her late mother, Lula Doe, for giving her the idea for Kid-Care. In 1984, Lula persuaded a local supermarket not to discard its blemished produce, but to let her distribute it to the poor. Then, during Christmastime in 1989, Carol saw a group of children searching for food in a McDonalds' dumpster. She says, "I saw Third World conditions a stone's throw from where I live." Kid-Care was her response.

"People ask me what's in it for me. And I tell them to go on the route with me and see the kids' faces. That's what's in it for me." She sees the meals as "better than ice cream. It's hope."

Purpose in life comes when we purpose to lift the load of another—to show God's love by doing for them what they could not do for themselves.

Whose LOAD
CAN I LIFT
TODAY?

———

A burden shared is a lighter load.

In All Things, Love

*He who covers a transgression
seeks love, but he who repeats
a matter separates friends.*

PROVERBS 17:9

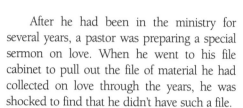

What KEEPS
ME FROM
ALLOWING
GOD'S LOVE
TO FLOW
FREELY
THROUGH ME?

*Love is like the five loaves and two fishes.
It doesn't start to multiply
until you give it away.*

After he had been in the ministry for several years, a pastor was preparing a special sermon on love. When he went to his file cabinet to pull out the file of material he had collected on love through the years, he was shocked to find that he didn't have such a file.

Thinking this to be virtually impossible, since he knew he had collected many anecdotes and quotes about love, he began searching through the cabinet, folder by folder. He fully expected to find the love folder stuck inside another folder. He searched among the folders on faith and fasting, healing and Heaven, even Christology and Christian education. But there was no folder on love.

As he sat and pondered this, he began to think back over the sermons he had preached over the years. Then he suddenly realized that he had used bits and pieces of material about love in preparing dozens of other sermons. He quickly went back to the cabinet, and sure enough, he found parts of the love file in the folders labeled patience, kindness, humility, trust, hope, loyalty, and perseverance. The greatest amount of material on love, however, was found in his file labeled forgiveness.

The Bible says that God's love is shed abroad in our hearts by the Holy Spirit. (See Romans 5:5.) When we let it flow through us, God's love can spill over into every area of our lives. The one area where that unconditional love is most vividly demonstrated is when we choose to overlook offenses and forgive those who have wronged us.

Shut Your Eyes and Hold Out Your Hand

Blessed be the Lord, who daily loads us with benefits, the God of our salvation!

PSALM 68:19

Author Elisabeth Elliot writes in *A Lamp for My Feet* about a game she played as a young girl. She relates, "My mother or father would say, 'Shut your eyes and hold out your hand.' That was the promise of some lovely surprise. I trusted them, so I shut my eyes instantly and held out my hand. Whatever they were going to give me I was ready to take." She continues, "So should it be in our trust of our heavenly Father. Faith is the willingness to receive whatever He wants to give or the willingness not to have what He does not want to give."

If your prayers aren't answered in the way you expect them to be, there may be a good reason! Several months before Christmas, Jared begged his mother to buy him a new bicycle just like his friend's—and he had to have it now! His mother was a single mom, however, and there was no extra money for a new bicycle until Christmas.

Jared's friend generously lent him his bicycle to ride, and the longer Jared rode it, the more he realized it really wasn't the right bicycle for him. For one thing, it didn't have the racing brakes he wanted.

How often do we think God has forgotten us, when He's merely giving us time to understand what we really want so He can bring us His best?

God always gives His best to those who leave the choice with Him.

What "BEST" AM I BELIEVING GOD WILL BRING TO ME?

Face Your Fear

Now the LORD my God has given me
rest on every side; there is neither
adversary nor evil occurrence.
1 KINGS 5:4

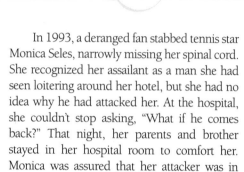

Do I TRUST
IN GOD'S
STRENGTH TO
SURMOUNT
EVERY
OBSTACLE?

In 1993, a deranged fan stabbed tennis star Monica Seles, narrowly missing her spinal cord. She recognized her assailant as a man she had seen loitering around her hotel, but she had no idea why he had attacked her. At the hospital, she couldn't stop asking, "What if he comes back?" That night, her parents and brother stayed in her hospital room to comfort her. Monica was assured that her attacker was in custody. Even so, she had flashbacks of his face, the blood-stained knife, and her own screams.

Monica did her best to stick to her physical therapy regimen, but she found it difficult to concentrate. She broke into tears at odd moments, and nightmares haunted her. Six months after the attack, her assailant was given two years probation and set free. Her fear intensified, and she sought out a psychologist to help her. Encouraged by her peers, she made a decision to return to tennis. Then came yet another blow. A German judge upheld her assailant's suspended sentence, which had been appealed. She said to herself, "Monica, you have to move on." It was time for a showdown with her fear. Three months later, she played an exhibition match and scored two wins—one on the court and one in her mind and heart.

Are you facing an obstacle that seems insurmountable? Perhaps it's time to identify its source and face it head on. The God who never leaves you nor forsakes you will be with you always, strengthening you every step of the way.

The first step on the way to victory
is to recognize the enemy.

On Being a "Sorrow Carrier"

A friend loves at all times, and
a brother is born for adversity.

PROVERBS 17:17

Although the North American Indians had no written alphabet before they met the white man, their language was anything but primitive. The vocabulary of many Indian languages was as large as that of their French and English conquerors. Often, their expressions were far more eloquent. In one Indian tongue, for example, the word "friend" is beautifully stated as "one-who-carries-my-sorrows-on-his-back."

A friend or family member who comes to you for solace, or even asking for advice, often wants nothing more than your presence, your listening ear, and your quiet caring. A young man discovered this shortly after his wedding. His new bride frequently came home from work and told him the woes of her day. His response was to offer suggestions and give solutions to her problems. His wife finally said to him, "I've already solved the problems of the day." The husband asked, perplexed, "Then why are you telling me about them?" She replied, "I don't need Mr. Fix It. I need a loving ear."

A friend who provides both physical and emotional shelter without always trying to fix things is a true haven, one who helps another weather the storms of life in safety.

Whom CAN I SHARE A LOAD WITH TODAY?

One of the best ways to demonstrate
God's love is to listen to people.

Home Sweet Home

Jesus said to her, "Did I not say to you that if you would believe you would see the glory of God?"

JOHN 11:40

How AM
I ALLOWING
GOD'S
PRESENCE
TO FILL
MY HOME?

In *Secret Strength*, Joni Eareckson Tada writes a wonderful tribute to a genuine "home, sweet home":

"Not long ago I entered a friend's home and immediately sensed the glory of God. No, that impression was not based on some heebie-jeebie feeling or super-spiritual instinct. And it had nothing to do with several Christian plaques I spotted hanging in the hallway. Yet there was a peace and orderliness that pervaded that home. Joy and music hung in the air. Although the kids were normal, active youngsters, everyone's activity seemed to dovetail together, creating the impression that the home had direction, that the kids really cared about each other, that the parents put love into action.

"We didn't even spend that much time 'fellowshipping' in the usual sense of the word—talking about the Bible or praying together. Yet we laughed. And really heard each other. And opened our hearts like family members. After dinner I left that home refreshed. It was a place where God's essential being was on display. His kindness, His love, His justice. It was filled with God's glory."

The presence of the Lord makes any home sweet!

Home, sweet home—where each lives for the other, and all live for God.

Foolproof Therapy

*A merry heart does good,
like medicine, but a broken
spirit dries the bones.*

PROVERBS 17:22

In *Growing Strong in the Seasons of Life,* Charles Swindoll writes: "Tonight was fun 'n' games night around the supper table in our house. It was wild. First of all, one of the kids snickered during the prayer (which isn't that unusual) and that tipped the first domino. Then a humorous incident from school was shared and the event (as well as how it was told) triggered havoc around the table. That was the beginning of twenty to thirty minutes of the loudest, silliest, most enjoyable laughter you can imagine. At one point I watched my oldest literally fall off his chair in hysterics, my youngest doubled over in his chair as his face wound up in his plate with corn chips stuck to his cheeks . . . and my two girls leaning back, lost and preoccupied in the most beautiful and beneficial therapy God ever granted humanity: laughter.

"What is so amazing is that everything seemed far less serious and heavy. Irritability and impatience were ignored like unwanted guests. For example, during the meal little Chuck spilled his drink twice . . . and even that brought the house down. If I remember correctly, that made six times during the day he accidentally spilled his drink, but nobody bothered to count."

What a treasure laughter is! It completely dissipates anxiety, erases stress, and relieves fears. Laughter is a precious gift from God!

What JOYS IN MY LIFE HAS GOD PROVIDED THAT I CAN THANK HIM FOR?

---

*Laughter is the brush that sweeps
away the cobwebs of the heart.*

Impatience

Hear me, O Lord, for Your lovingkindness is good; turn to me according to the multitude of Your tender mercies. And do not hide Your face from Your servant, for I am in trouble; hear me speedily.

PSALM 69:16-17

Am I
MAKING TIME
IN MY LIFE
TO HEAR
WHAT GOD
IS SAYING
TO ME?

"Have you, perchance, found a diamond pendant?" a woman phoned to ask the theater manager. "I feel certain I lost it last night in your theater."

"Not that I know of, ma'am," the manager said, "but let me ask some of my employees. Please hold the line for a minute while I make inquiry. If it hasn't been found, we certainly will make a diligent search for it."

Returning to the phone a few minutes later, the manager said, "I have good news for you! The diamond pendant has been found!"

There was no reply to his news, however. "Hello! Hello!" he called into the phone, and then he heard the dial tone. The woman who made the inquiry about the lost diamond pendant had failed to wait for his answer. She had not given her name, and attempts to trace her call were unsuccessful. The pendant was eventually sold to raise money for the theater.

We are often like this woman when we make our requests to God. We fail to wait on the Lord to hear His reply. Instead, we rush ahead impatiently, having no idea He has a great blessing to give us, if only we'd slow down long enough to receive it!

We can expect big trouble when we try to answer our own prayers.

Giving and Receiving

*If I then, your Lord and Teacher,
have washed your feet, you also
ought to wash one another's feet.*

JOHN 13:14

He received two degrees, including a master of science degree. He was elected a fellow of the Society for the Encouragement of Arts, Manufactures, and Commerce in London and won the Spingarn Medal. He received a $100,000-a-year job offer from Thomas A. Edison. He was visited by Presidents Calvin Coolidge and Franklin Roosevelt and was invited by Joseph Stalin to superintend plantations in southern Russia. Yet for all he received, George Washington Carver is best known for what he gave.

He dedicated his life to making Tuskegee Institute an instrument of ministry to the needs of rural blacks, teaching them how to become skilled farmers and useful citizens. He taught better ways of tilling the soil, the importance of a balanced diet, and called upon black farmers to grow a variety of crops, including peanuts, sweet potatoes, and cowpeas, instead of only cotton. He led the way toward the development of more than three hundred derivative food and industrial products from peanuts and more than a hundred products from sweet potatoes.

In the end, your resumé of accomplishments will mean little. Your gifts to others count the most!

How CAN I THANK GOD FOR THE PEOPLE HE HAS BROUGHT INTO MY LIFE TO BLESS ME?

*The worst moment for the atheist is
when he is really thankful and
has nobody to thank.*

Love Believes the Best

A new commandment I give to you,
that you love one another; as I have
loved you, that you also love one another.
JOHN 13:34

Whose
TRUE FRIEND
HAVE I BEEN?

One of the most noble friendships in literature is that of Melanie and Scarlett in Margaret Mitchell's classic, *Gone with the Wind*. Melanie is characterized as a woman who "always saw the best in everyone and remarked kindly upon it." Even when Scarlett tries to confess her shameful behavior toward Ashley, Melanie's husband, Melanie says, "Darling, I don't want any explanation. . . . Do you think I could remember you walking in a furrow behind that Yankee's horse almost barefooted and with your hands blistered—just so the baby and I could have something to eat—and then believe such dreadful things about you? I don't want to hear a word."

Melanie's refusal to believe, or even hear, ill of Scarlett leads Scarlett to passionately desire to "keep Melanie's high opinion. She only knew that she did not care what the world thought of her or what Ashley or Rhett thought of her, but Melanie must not think her other than she had always thought her." It is as Melanie lies dying that Scarlett faces her deep need for Melanie's pure and generous friendship: "Panic clutching at her heart, she knew that Melanie had been her sword and her shield, her comfort and her strength." In two words, Melanie had been her true friend.

A true friend loves at all times and always believes the best. Is that the kind of friend you want to have? Is that the kind of friend you aspire to be?

Real friends are those who, when
you've made a fool of yourself,
don't feel you've done a permanent job.

Relax

Whatever you ask in My name,
that I will do, that the Father
may be glorified in the Son.

JOHN 14:13

Fay Angus has said about prayer: "Without circumventing scriptural directionals, encouragements, and admonitions . . . the bottom line of prayer is to pray. When we do, the power of Heaven picks up momentum to change our lives.

"Much as we try to put Him there, God is not on trial; the good news is that neither is man. Jesus Christ stood in the docket on our behalf.

"If the answers to our prayers depended upon our worth, they would never be answered—they would never even be heard. Through the righteousness of Christ, they are.

"We tend to stroke prayer like a lucky rabbit's foot and seek God's fleece rather than His face.

"We try to manipulate His will to ours and sometimes call it faith. We push forward in the arrogance of our own stoic determination, limited by our finite vision, rather than pull back in the simple trust of His infinite plan.

"We expect Him to change the sovereignty of His omnipotent heart, instead of humbly asking Him to give us a heart willing to be changed.

"'Be still, and know that I am God' (Psalm 46:10 KJV) means, 'Relax and let God be God.'"

All I have seen teaches me to trust
the Creator for all I have not seen.

Am I SIMPLY TRUSTING IN GOD'S TOTAL LOVE FOR ME?

Loving Sacrifice

Greater love has no one than this, than to lay down one's life for his friends.

JOHN 15:13

How is
MY HEART
WILLING TO
MAKE ANY
SACRIFICE
FOR
ANOTHER'S
BENEFIT?

A number of years ago, a young mother was making her way across the hills of South Wales on foot, carrying her tiny baby in her arms. The wintry winds were blowing stronger than she anticipated and her journey was taking much longer than she had planned. Eventually, she was overtaken by a blinding blizzard.

The woman never reached her destination. When the blizzard had subsided, those expecting her arrival went in search of her. After hours of searching, they finally found her body beneath a mound of snow.

As they shoveled the snow away from her frozen corpse, they were amazed to see that she had taken off her outer clothing. When they finally lifted her body away from the ground, they discovered the reason why. This brave and self-sacrificing young mother had wrapped her own cloak and scarf around her baby and then huddled over her child. When the searchers unwrapped the child, they found to their great surprise and joy that he was alive and well!

Years later, that child, David Lloyd George, became prime minister of Great Britain and is regarded as one of England's greatest statesmen.

Is any sacrifice too great?

———∞∞∞———

Mother means selfless devotion,
limitless sacrifice, and love
that passes understanding.

Theodore?

A fool's lips enter into contention,
And his mouth calls for blows.

PROVERBS 18:6

What surely must have been one of the most frustrating conversations in history was reported in *Theatre Arts* magazine. A subscriber, desiring to report on a particular upcoming event in his community, dialed the information operator to get the magazine's telephone number.

The operator drawled, "Sorry, but there is nobody listed by the name of 'Theodore Arts.'"

The subscriber insisted, "It's not a person; it's a publication. I want Theatre Arts."

The operator responded, this time a little louder. "I told you, we have no listing for Theodore Arts in this city. Perhaps he lives in another city."

By now the subscriber was thoroughly peeved. "Confound it, the word is Theatre: t-h-e-a-t-r-e!"

The operator came back with certainty in her voice, "That is not the way to spell Theodore."

Sometimes there's just no communicating with someone who refuses to hear you, who seems unwilling to understand your point of view, or who simply "doesn't get" what you are trying to say. Rather than give that person a real kick, however, it's better to hang up and dial someone who can hear you and understand!

He who thinks by the inch and talks by
the yard deserves to be kicked by the foot.

I KNOW GOD HEARS AND UNDERSTANDS ME BY . . .

Freedom

This is eternal life, that they may know You, the only true God, and Jesus Christ whom You have sent.

JOHN 17:3

Does ANYTHING ELSE IN MY LIFE TAKE PRECEDENCE OVER MY RELATIONSHIP WITH GOD?

Kari Torjesen Malcom, the daughter of missionaries, was interned in a Chinese prison camp during World War II. Only a teenager, she found herself a nameless prisoner—number "16." She was given a small space on a bare floor and reminded daily of her lack of freedom by a wall, a moat, and an electric barbed-wire fence. She met with other prisoners daily at noon to pray for freedom, but as time passed, the enemy seemed larger and God smaller.

Kari desperately pleaded with God to reveal Himself to her. She said, "God answered my prayer and spoke to me as I searched the Bible. . . . Gradually it dawned on me that there was just one thing the enemy could not take from me. They had bombed our home, killed my father . . . but . . . they could not touch my relationship to my God."

With this revelation, Kari found it increasingly difficult to join her friends for prayer. There was more to life than just getting out of prison. The first day she missed the prayer meeting, a friend taunted her, "So we aren't good enough for you anymore, eh?" Even her peer group had been stripped away from her. Kari said, "It was only then that I was able to pray the prayer that changed my life: 'Lord, I am willing to stay in this prison for the rest of my life if only I may know You.' At that moment I was free."

We can walk through life with tremendous freedom when we remember that relationship with God is paramount. His greatest desire is to be with us always.

*I do not pray for success.
I ask for faithfulness.*

Moving On

Jesus said to Peter, . . .
"Shall I not drink the cup which
My Father has given Me?"

JOHN 18:11

Withstanding one-hundred-degree heat and tendinitis in her left knee, Monica Seles won her first tennis tournament in more than two years since she had been stabbed in the shoulder by a fanatical fan. She roared through the Canadian Open to defeat three top-twenty players en route to a finals match that lasted only fifty-one minutes. Her nightmare had truly come to an end.

To help in her recovery, Monica asked Olympic champion Jackie Joyner-Kersee and her coach/husband, Bob Kersee, to put her on a strict workout routine. While on this physical regimen, she also worked to overcome the emotional problems that accompany such an attack.

Her father and coach, Karolj, who had been stricken by prostate and stomach cancer, was a continual source of inspiration. She said, "I was down and he came into my room and said he couldn't stand to see me that way. I decided then that I had to try and put it behind me and move on."

Have you ever felt "stabbed in the back" while doing a good deed? Withdrawal is often our first temptation, but with a creative and loving God, who continually inspires us, we just can't quit! Our critics will eventually always have to say about us what was said about Monica, "She's back!"

Whom CAN I ENCOURAGE TO NOT GIVE UP ON A PROBLEM?

❧❧❧

Triumph is just "umph" added to try.

Too Close to See

He who answers a matter before he
hears it, it is folly and shame to him.
PROVERBS 18:13

Whose
GREATNESS
CAN I
RECOGNIZE
TODAY?

A six-year-old boy was sent home from school one day with a note from his teacher. The note suggested that the boy be taken out of school since he was "too stupid to learn." That boy was Thomas A. Edison.

A grandfather once gave his grandson ten shillings for writing a eulogy about his grandmother. The grandfather said as he gave him the money, "There, that is the first money you ever earned for your poetry, and take my word for it, it will be the last." The lad was Alfred Tennyson.

A woman once hesitated in letting her daughter marry a printer who had asked for her hand in marriage. She wasn't sure if he could support her daughter because the United States already had two printing offices, and she feared the nation might not be able to support a third. That printer was Benjamin Franklin.

So often we fail to recognize the greatness in those with whom we live. It's almost as if we can't see the full length and breadth of the person's life because we are standing too close. Take a few steps back. Ask God to help you see the greatness He's placed in those around you, especially your children. It's your job to help them get there.

Self-esteem isn't a lesson you teach;
it's a quality you nurture.

The Best Is Yet to Come

Blessed be the LORD God, the God of Israel, who only does wondrous things!

PSALM 72:18

John Erskine was one of the most versatile and well-educated men of his era—a true "Renaissance man."

He was an educator, considered one of the greatest teachers that Columbia University has ever had. He was a concert pianist, author of sixty books, head of the Julliard School of Music, and a popular and witty lecturer to a wide variety of groups. He had a contagious excitement for learning.

Students flocked to Erskine's courses, not because of his fame or his accomplished career, but because of what he believed about them. Erskine had a strong belief that the world did not belong to him, but to his students. He regularly told them, "The best books are yet to be written. The best paintings have not yet been painted. The best governments are yet to be formed. The best is yet to be done by you!"

It was this enthusiasm for life and optimism for tomorrow that became his greatest legacy.

Look forward and upward! Your greatest contributions in life—your best giving, your best caring, and the best of your love—are yet to be given!

Am I LOOKING FORWARD TO THE OPPORTUNI- TIES GOD HAS PLANNED TO PROVIDE FOR ME?

To be a winner in life, we must first be a winner inside.

Giving While You're Living

A man's gift makes room for him,
and brings him before great men.
PROVERBS 18:16

Have I
THANKED
ANYONE
RECENTLY
FOR THEIR
GIFTS TO ME?

A rich man once moaned to a friend, "Why is it that everybody is always criticizing me for being miserly, when everyone knows I have made provisions to leave everything I possess to charity when I die?"

The friend paused for a moment and then said, "Well, I guess it's like the pig and the cow."

"What do you mean?" the rich man asked.

The friend said, "The story goes that a pig was lamenting to a cow one day about how unpopular he was. 'People are always talking about your gentleness and your kind brown eyes,' the pig said. 'They only speak of me in degrading terms. It seems grossly unfair. Sure, you give milk and cream, but I give even more. I give bacon and ham. I give bristles. Why, they even pickle my feet! Yet nobody likes me. Why is this?'

"The cow thought for a minute and then responded, 'Well, maybe it's because I give while I'm still living.'"

Reputations and generous acts of kindness toward others receive acclaim both during and after a person's lifetime, far more than bequests. Let people see your gifts as an extension of your life, not merely as a consequence of your death.

The test of generosity is not how much
you give, but how much you have left.

The Spring of Forgiveness

If you forgive the sins of any,
they are forgiven them; if you retain
the sins of any, they are retained.

JOHN 20:23

Many of us think of springs as emerging only high in the mountains or as bubbling up in an arid desert, creating an oasis.

Some springs emerge from the earth close to salt-water seas. The water gushes up from the beach sands just as sweet as any that might burst from the rocks in the high hills. When the sea is at low tide, one can dip into the spring and drink from its clear, refreshing water.

Once the tide rolls back in and covers the spring, one might assume it would pollute the spring and cause it to become salty. Not so! When the tide again is low, the spring continues to produce fresh, sparkling water, just as sweet as before.

So, too, is it with forgiveness born of love. No wrong, cruelty, or rejection can have an impact on genuine forgiveness. We forgive no matter what—first, because it is the nature of love to forgive, and second, because our forgiveness has tremendous potential to impact the hearts of those who wrong us. This is true even if we can see no evidence of it.

Finally, forgiveness keeps our own souls fresh, clear, and sparkling. If we allow the brackish waters of unforgiveness to seep in, our spring becomes clogged, and we begin to stagnate. All we have to do to release the spring once again is to forgive. When we choose to forgive, God gives us the grace necessary to do so.

The heaviest load any man carries
on his back is a pack of grudges.

When HAVE I BEEN REFRESHED THROUGH FORGIVENESS?

The Answer Is Already Waiting

You will guide me with Your counsel,
and afterward receive me to glory.
PSALM 73:24

What
WILL I ASK
GOD FOR
GUIDANCE
IN TODAY?

It was nearly 11 P.M. by the time two women left a parents' meeting at their children's school, which was located some twenty-five miles from their homes. As they neared their car, they noticed three youths running from the parking area, laughing. "It seems we got here just in time," the driver said, glad when her engine sputtered to life. "There's a shortcut my husband takes," she said, hoping to cut some time off of their drive, since it was so late.

Forty minutes later, they were lost. Then, their headlights began to flicker, and the engine lost power. "Shall we walk and see if we can find a phone?" the driver asked. "Let's pray first," the other woman suggested. Together they prayed, "Lord, guide us to help."

They walked to a crossroad and saw a distant porch light. When a man answered their knock, they told him their problem. He said, "I'm a mechanic. Maybe I can help." When he checked the car, he said, "Some joker exchanged batteries with you. You have a golf-cart battery in your car! This may sound strange to you, but just today I brought a new battery home from my garage. I'll put it in for you if you like." Before long, the car was repaired, but the Lord had one more surprise. Friends visiting the man and his wife were from their hometown. They were just about to leave, so the two women followed them home!

God is always available to lead and guide us. All we have to do is ask!

Genuine prayer is never "good works,"
an exercise or pious attitude, but it is
always the prayer of a child to a Father.

The Four Cs

*A man who has friends must himself
be friendly, but there is a friend
who sticks closer than a brother.*

PROVERBS 18:24

Is your spouse your best friend? How privileged you are if the answer is yes. Perhaps an even more important question to ask is this: "Are you a good friend to your spouse?" In being a good friend, you often gain a best friend!

A true friend will let you empty your heart when it feels overloaded by stress, concern, or worry.

Sir Francis Bacon once wrote: "We know diseases of stoppings and suffocations are the most dangerous in the body; and it is not much otherwise in the mind: you may take sarza to open the liver, steel to open the spleen, flower of sulphur for the lungs, castoreum for the brain; but no receipt openeth the heart but a true friend, to whom you may impart griefs, joys, fears, hopes, suspicions, counsels, and whatsoever lieth upon the heart to oppress it, in a kind of civil shrift or confusion."

Listening ears are one of the best gifts you can give to your spouse and children. Such ears are invariably connected to a kind and patient heart.

Make friends with the four Cs: compassion, caring, consideration, and comfort. Those four traits will never grow old or fall out of fashion.

Do I make time to offer listening ears to others?

———

*A friend is one who comes in when
the whole world has gone out.*

No Limit on Character

*Better is the poor who walks in his
integrity than one who is perverse
in his lips, and is a fool.*

PROVERBS 19:1

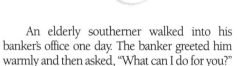

Have I
DEVOTED
MYSELF TO
FULFILLING
ALL OF MY
PROMISES?

An elderly southerner walked into his banker's office one day. The banker greeted him warmly and then asked, "What can I do for you?"

The southerner, who was a true gentleman of the "old school" replied, "Well, about thirty-five years ago, I loaned a man down South some money—not a very big sum. I told him that whenever I needed it, I would let him know and he could repay me. The time has come when I need some money, so I would like to let him know. I would like to have you conduct the transaction for me."

The banker said, "My good friend, you have no claim on that money. The statute of limitations ran out against that loan years and years ago."

"Sir," the southerner replied, "the man to whom I loaned that money is a gentleman. The statute of limitations never runs out for a gentleman."

Sure enough, when the banker made a formal request for the money, it came within a reasonable time. With it was a note, saying, "Thank you. I hope I have the privilege of returning the favor some day."

True Christian character does not seek to escape from a promise. Rather, it reflects our Master whose Word to us is always reliable and never changing.

———∞———

*Fame is vapor, popularity an accident,
riches take wing. Only one thing
endures and that is character.*

God's Presence

*You have made known to me
the ways of life; You will make
me full of joy in Your presence.*

ACTS 2:28

Dr. George Washington Carver had this to say about prayer, "My prayers seem to be more of an attitude than anything else. I indulge in no lip service, but ask the great God silently, daily, and often many times a day, to permit me to speak to Him. I ask Him to give me wisdom, understanding, and bodily strength to do His will. Hence, I am asking and receiving all the time."

One of the most magnificent truths about God is that He meets us in every moment of prayer with all the fullness of His being. He reveals Himself to us as the "I AM"—always present and available. He brings the totality of His character into each moment of our lives. He brings not just a part of Himself, but all of Himself—His undiminished majesty, power, wisdom, and love.

Our best and highest response to such marvelous access to the fullness of the holy, omnipotent, infinite King of the universe must surely be one of awe. It matters little what we say. Just to be in His presence, and to be aware of His presence, is to be put into a position of humility, need, and provision.

Rousseau once noted, "To write a good love letter, you will begin without knowing what you are going to say, and end without knowing what you have said." The same is true for prayer. To be in God's presence and to have a relationship with Him is all that matters.

How CAN I THANK GOD FOR THE PRIVILEGE OF BEING ABLE TO ENTER HIS PRESENCE?

⁂

*Prayer is essentially man standing before
his God in wonder, awe, and humility;
man, made in the image of God,
responding to his maker.*

How to Spend an Hour

Repent therefore and be converted, that your sins may be blotted out, so that times of refreshing may come from the presence of the Lord.

ACTS 3:19

What KEEPS ME FROM DEVOTING TIME EVERY DAY TO PRAYER?

A time-management expert once asked a seminar group to brainstorm a list of all the things they could do in one hour. Among the many answers written on the blackboard were the following:

- Walk the dog.
- Mow the lawn.
- Have a relaxed conversation with my spouse.
- Visit a sick or elderly friend.
- Take a nap.
- Jog through the park.
- Play ball with my son.
- Write a long-overdue letter.
- Pay the monthly bills.
- Listen to an entire CD.
- Clean the fish tank.
- Play a set of tennis.

The attendees laughed at some of their ideas and were serious about others. At the end of a two-minute session, they had listed more than a hundred ideas. When the expert asked them to identify the one activity that would have the greatest long-term impact on their lives, the great majority chose an idea that could be explained in only one word: Pray.

❈

Good endings come from prayerful beginnings.

A Legacy of Prayer

Now when they saw the boldness of Peter and John, and perceived that they were uneducated and untrained men, they marveled. And they realized that they had been with Jesus.

ACTS 4:13

In the early days of the formation of the United States, a stranger once asked how he might identify George Washington among those present at Congress. He was told, "You can easily distinguish him when Congress goes to prayer. Washington is the gentleman who kneels."

Washington had a long-standing reputation as a man of prayer. At Valley Forge, he frequently found rest and relief in prayer. One day a farmer approaching the military camp heard an earnest voice. When he drew nearer, he saw Washington on his knees, his cheeks wet with tears. The farmer returned home and said to his wife: "George Washington will succeed! George Washington will succeed! The Americans will secure their independence!"

"What makes you think so, Isaac?" his wife asked. The farmer replied, "I heard him pray, Hannah, out in the woods today, and the Lord will surely hear his prayer. He will, Hannah; thee may rest assured He will."

One person willing to humble himself and pray can leave a legacy of faith and hope, giving courage to future generations.

No Christian is greater than his prayer life.

Whose
PRAYERS HAVE
TOUCHED
MY LIFE?

177

Bless Those Who Curse You

A false witness will not go unpunished,
and he who speaks lies shall perish.

PROVERBS 19:9

Am I WILLING TO SPEND TIME INVESTIGATING THE GOOD THINGS ABOUT AN ENEMY?

The story is told that General Robert E. Lee was asked by Confederate President Jefferson Davis to give his opinion about a certain officer. Lee gave the officer a glowing report.

One of the officers in attendance was greatly astonished by his words and said to Lee, "General, do you not know that the man of whom you speak so highly to the president is one of your bitterest enemies, and misses no opportunity to malign you?"

"Yes," said Lee, "but the president asked my opinion of him; he did not ask for his opinion of me."

When we speak well of our enemies, we are doing three things: First, we increase our own value. We show that we are able to rise above cheap criticism and bestow costly praise on another.

Second, we diffuse our enemy's criticism. Any person hearing both our praise of an enemy and our enemy's disdain for us is likely to conclude that we are nothing like we have been described!

Third, we reveal to others that we are diligent investigators. It takes an effort to find something good to say about someone who hates you; it takes little effort or intelligence to respond with hate or hurtful ridicule.

The truth will always reveal itself—God will see to it!

In taking revenge a man is but even with his
enemy; but in passing it over, he is superior.

Overlooking Faults

*The discretion of a man makes
him slow to anger, and his glory
is to overlook a transgression.*

PROVERBS 19:11

The story is told of a couple at their golden wedding anniversary celebration. Surrounded by her children, grandchildren, and great-grandchildren, the wife was asked the secret to a long and happy marriage. With a loving glance toward her husband, she answered, "On my wedding day, I decided to make a list of ten of my husband's faults which, for the sake of our marriage, I would overlook. I figured I could live with at least ten faults."

A guest asked her to identify some of the faults she had chosen to overlook. Her husband looked a bit troubled at the thought of having his foibles and flaws revealed to the assembled group. However, his wife sweetly replied, "To tell you the truth, dear, I never did get around to listing them. Instead, every time my husband did something that made me hopping mad, I would simply say to myself, Lucky for him, that's one of the ten!"

Even the most devoted friends and spouses will experience storms in their relationships from time to time. Some problems are worth addressing in order to resolve them. Others are best left unspoken. With time, those issues that are of little importance tend to blow past without any need for a "blowup."

Am I
COMMITTED
TO OVER-
LOOKING THE
FAULTS OF
OTHERS?

*The art of being wise is the art
of knowing what to overlook.*

Communing with God

I call to remembrance my song in the
night; I meditate within my heart,
and my spirit makes diligent search.

PSALM 77:6

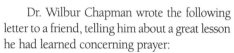

DO I MAKE
THE TIME
TO TRULY
COMMUNE
WITH GOD?

Dr. Wilbur Chapman wrote the following letter to a friend, telling him about a great lesson he had learned concerning prayer:

"At one of our missions in England the audiences were exceedingly small; but I received a note saying that an American missionary was going to pray God's blessing down on our work. He was known as Praying Hyde. Almost instantly the tide turned. The hall became packed, and at my first invitation fifty men accepted Christ as their Savior. As we were leaving I said, 'Mr. Hyde, I want you to pray for me.' He came to my room, turned the key in the door, dropped on his knees, and waited five minutes without a single syllable coming from his lips. I could hear my own heart thumping, and his beating. I felt hot tears running down my face. I knew I was with God. Then, with upturned face, down which the tears were streaming, he said, 'O God.' Then for five minutes at least he was still again; and then, when he knew that he was talking with God there came from the depths of his heart such petitions for me as I had never heard before. I rose from my knees to know what real prayer was."

True prayer is communion with God, not a one-way conversation. When we wait on God and listen to what He has to say, He will even give us the words to pray so that our prayers can be most effective. God is speaking. Are you listening?

When we serve the Lord with our whole
heart, we have confidence and joy in prayer.

Making a House a Home

I will remember the works of the
LORD; surely I will remember
Your wonders of old.

PSALM 77:11

In *Little House in the Ozarks,* Laura Ingalls Wilder writes, "I spent an afternoon a short time ago with a friend in her new home. The house was beautiful and well-furnished with new furniture, but it seemed bare and empty to me. I wondered why this was until I remembered my experience with my new house. I could not make the living room seem homelike. I would move the chairs here and there and change the pictures on the wall, but something was lacking. Nothing seemed to change the feeling of coldness and vacancy that displeased me whenever I entered the room.

"Then, as I stood in the middle of the room one day wondering what I could possibly do to improve it, it came to me that all that was needed was for someone to live in it and furnish it with the everyday, pleasant thoughts of friendship and cheerfulness and hospitality."

A homey atmosphere is not a matter of the right decorations; it emanates from the thoughts and feelings of the people who live there. Only kind, generous, and even-tempered people can create feelings of warmth and welcome. Why not determine to warm up the atmosphere where you live today?

A house is made of walls and beams;
a home is made of love and dreams.

What CAN I DO TO MAKE MY HOUSE A LOVE-FILLED HOME?

Ambassadors of Peace

Peace, peace to you, and peace to
your helpers! For your God helps you.
1 CHRONICLES 12:18

How HAVE I
TRUSTED IN
THE FATHER
AS A CHILD
TRUSTS?

Some years ago, a boy in a small Florida town heard that the Russians were our enemies. He began to wonder about the Russian children, finding it hard to believe they were his enemies, too. He wrote a short note that said, "Dear Comrade in Russia, I am seven years old and I believe that we can live in peace. I want to be your friend, not your enemy. Will you become my friend and write to me?"

He closed the letter with "Love and Peace" and signed his name. He then neatly folded the note, put it into an empty bottle, and threw it into an inland lake near his home. Several days later, the bottle and note were retrieved on a nearby beach. A story about the note appeared in a local newspaper, and a wire service picked up the story and sent it nationwide. A group of people from New Hampshire who were taking children to the Soviet Union as ambassadors of peace read the article, contacted the boy and his family, and invited them to go with them. In the end, the little boy and his father traveled to Moscow as peacemakers!

One small boy decided he could make a difference and acted on it. Jesus told us to have the faith of little children. When we have that kind of faith, nothing is impossible!

———✎———

Children are God's apostles, day by day
sent forth to preach of love and hope.

It Wasn't Luck at All

The LORD is righteous in all His ways, gracious in all His works. . . . He will fulfill the desire of those who fear Him; He also will hear their cry and save them.

PSALM 145:17,19

On a remote farm in California, a young mother was alone with her three children. The children had been swimming in the family pool when the mother suddenly noticed that her two-and-a-half-year-old son was at the bottom of it. She dove in and pulled him out as quickly as she could.

Just at that moment, a neighboring farmer came by. He immediately began mouth-to-mouth resuscitation, and after several minutes, the child stirred. The mother and farmer took him to the nearest hospital for examination. The doctors assured them that the little boy had suffered no brain damage.

In the days following, as people heard of the child's rescue, several commented to the boy's parents, "You sure were lucky!" The father said to his pastor, "When people said that to me, I replied, 'It wasn't luck at all. My wife and daughter were on their knees praying while the farmer was working on my son.'"

Those who pray can always be assured that God is at work in their particular circumstance—for their eternal benefit.

The most praying souls are the most assured souls.

DO I GO THROUGH THE MOTIONS WHEN I PRAY OR DO I TRULY BELIEVE GOD WILL ANSWER?

Shelter

Seek the LORD and His strength;
Seek His face evermore!
1 CHRONICLES 16:11

Is MY FIRST
LINE OF
RETREAT
TO RUN INTO
THE ARMS
OF GOD?

Have you ever explored a tidal pool? Low tide is the perfect time to find a myriad of creatures that have temporarily washed ashore from the depths of the sea.

Children are often amazed that they can pick up these shelled creatures and stare at them eyeball to eyeball. The creatures rarely exhibit any form of overt fear, such as moving to attack or attempting to scurry away. Usually, the children are the ones who squeal in fear, thinking themselves exposed and vulnerable to the possibility of the creatures' bites, pinches, or stings. The creatures simply withdraw into their shells, instinctively knowing they are safe as long as they remain in their nice, strong shelters.

Likewise, we are safe when we remain in Christ. We are protected from the hassles of life, the unknowns, the bites and stings of temptation and sin. Those things will come against us, but they have no power to harm us when we retreat into the shelter of Christ.

The Lord commanded us to abide in Him and remain steadfast in our faith. He tells us to trust in Him absolutely and shelter ourselves under His strong wings and in the cleft of His rock-like presence. He delights when we retreat into His arms for comfort and tender expressions of love.

Here at my office desk I ask His aid, no
matter where I am I crave His care; in
moments when my soul is sore afraid it
comforts most to know He's everywhere.

Money, Money, Money

Peter said to him, "Your money perish with you, because you thought that the gift of God could be purchased with money!"

ACTS 8:20

In 1923, several of the most powerful money magnates in the world gathered for a meeting at the Edgewater Beach Hotel in Chicago, Illinois. The combined resources and assets of these men tallied more than the U.S. Treasury that year. In the group were Charles Schwab, president of a steel company; Richard Whitney, president of the New York Stock Exchange; and Arthur Cutton, a wheat speculator. Albert Fall was a presidential cabinet member, a personally wealthy man. Jesse Livermore was the greatest Wall Street "bear" in his generation. Leon Fraser was the president of the International Bank of Settlements, and Ivan Krueger headed the largest monopoly in the nation. It was an impressive gathering of financial eagles!

What happened to these men in later years? Schwab died penniless. Whitney served a life sentence in Sing-Sing Prison. Cutton became insolvent. Fall was pardoned from a federal prison so he could die at home. Fraser, Livermore, and Krueger committed suicide. These extremely rich men ended their lives with nothing.

Money is certainly not the answer to life's ills! Only God can give us peace, happiness, and joy. When we focus on God and His goodness in our lives, whether we have money or not, we can live in contentment, knowing that God will meet all our needs.

Do I trust in God or in my own skills to supply all my needs?

In my vocabulary, there is no such word as "can't," because I recognize that my abilities are given to me by God to do what needs to be done.

Know What You Believe

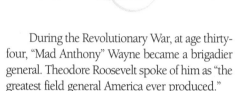

[Israel] did not believe in His wondrous works. Therefore their days He consumed in futility, and their years in fear.

PSALM 78:32-33

Do I SPEND THE TIME NECESSARY IN GOD'S WORD TO KNOW WHAT TO DO IN CHALLENG- ING CIRCUM- STANCES?

During the Revolutionary War, at age thirty-four, "Mad Anthony" Wayne became a brigadier general. Theodore Roosevelt spoke of him as "the greatest field general America ever produced."

When the British encamped at Germantown, George Washington held a council of war with his advisors. Wayne was all for attacking immediately and openly stated his views from the outset. Virtually all of the other officers sat around the table to deliberate the issue, offering innumerable excuses for holding back. After all the dissenting arguments had been made, Washington turned again to Wayne, who had been sitting quietly in a corner reading a book while the other military officers debated the issue. "What would you say, General?" Washington asked. Wayne slammed the book shut, rose slowly to his feet, and with a glare at the group of distinguished officers, declared, "I'd say nothing, Sir. I'd fight."

Wayne was not a warmonger; he was a patriot. His values about the importance of individual freedoms were rock solid, and he was willing to defend his position with his life.

Know what you believe, and you will know what to do.

———

I do not feel obliged to believe that the same God who has endowed us with sense, reason, and intellect has intended us to forgo their use.

Living Prayer

When Paul had laid hands on them, the Holy Spirit came upon them, and they spoke with tongues and prophesied.

ACTS 19:6

George Whitefield, the famous English evangelist, said, "O Lord, give me souls, or take my soul!"

Missionary Henry Martyn knelt on India's coral strands and cried out, "Here let me burn out for God."

David Brainerd, a missionary to the North American Indians, prayed, "Lord, to Thee I dedicate myself. O accept of me, and let me be Thine forever. Lord, I desire nothing else, I desire nothing more."

Thomas á Kempis prayed, "Give what Thou wilt, and how much Thou wilt, and when Thou wilt. Set me where Thou wilt and deal with me in all things, just as Thou wilt."

Dwight L. Moody prayed, "Use me then, my Savior, for whatever purpose and in whatever way Thou mayest require. Here is my poor heart, an empty vessel; fill it with Thy grace."

John McKenzie prayed as a young missionary candidate, "O Lord, send me to the darkest spot on earth!"

John Hunt, a missionary to the Fiji Islands, prayed upon his deathbed, "Lord, save Fiji, save Fiji; save these people, O Lord; have mercy upon Fiji; save Fiji."

What you pray today will determine how you live when you rise from your knees.

What IN MY LIFE NEEDS TO BE COMMITTED TO GOD?

He is no fool who gives what he cannot keep to gain what he cannot lose.

"Can-Do" Potential

Listen to advice and accept instruction,
and in the end you will be wise.
PROVERBS 19:20 NIV

What AM
I WILLING
TO INVEST
TO HELP
SOMEONE
ELSE
DISCOVER
THEIR GOD-
GIVEN
PURPOSE?

Author Phyllis Theroux writes about her father, "If there was any one thing that my father did for me when I was growing up, it was to give me the promise that ahead of me was dry land—a bright, marshless territory, without chuckholes or traps, where one day I would walk easily and as befitting my talents. . . .

"Thus it was, when he came upon me one afternoon sobbing out my unsuccesses into a wet pillow, that he sat down on the bed and . . . assured me that my grief was only a temporary setback. Oh, very temporary! Why he couldn't think of any other little girl who was so talented, so predestined to succeed in every department as I was. 'And don't forget,' he added with a smile, 'that we can trace our ancestry right back to Pepin the Stupid!'

"By the time he had finished talking, I really did understand that someday I would live among rational beings, and walk with kind, unvindictive people who, by virtue of their maturity and mine, would take no pleasure in cruelty and would welcome my presence among them. . . . There are some people who carry the flint that lights other people's torches. They get them all excited about . . . the 'can-do' potential of one's own being. That was my father's gift to me."

Determine today to give your children the same gift—the gift of knowing God created them for a purpose and they have the potential to be anything they want to be.

He climbs highest who helps another up.

Your Reputation Precedes You

They said, "Cornelius the centurion, a just man, one who fears God and has a good reputation among all the nation of the Jews, was divinely instructed by a holy angel to summon you to his house, and to hear words from you."

ACTS 10:22

Roger was a good employee—not spectacular—but reliable, punctual, even-tempered, and always willing to go the extra mile.

Brian also did good work, but he didn't mind cutting a few corners to finish a job or taking off work a few minutes early to attend to his personal needs.

When Mr. Jones, their supervisor, announced that one of the two men would be promoted, Roger counted on his record and reputation to win him the post. Brian lobbied hard for the job in an underhanded fashion by telling several of his coworkers that Roger had stolen credit for his innovative cost-saving measures, had misappropriated supplies, and was known to overextend his lunch hour. He was careful, of course, to preface all of his remarks by saying, "Just between the two of us. . . ."

The following week, when Mr. Jones announced that Roger had received the promotion, he received rousing applause from his fellow employees. No one was surprised—except Brian, of course. After all, Roger's reputation had preceded him. So had Brian's.

Consider your reputation today.

What KIND OF REPUTATION AM I BUILDING?

———

Character is like a tree, and reputation is like its shadow. The shadow is what we think of it; the tree is the real thing.

Traits of a Champion

Be strong and of good courage,
and do it; do not fear nor be dismayed,
for the LORD God . . . will be with you.
He will not leave you nor forsake you.

1 CHRONICLES 28:20

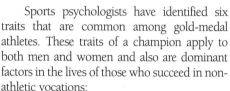

Am I
DEPENDING
ON GOD
FOR THE
STRENGTH TO
WIN RATHER
THAN TRYING
SIMPLY NOT
TO LOSE?

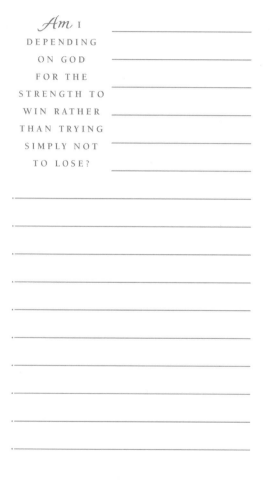

Sports psychologists have identified six traits that are common among gold-medal athletes. These traits of a champion apply to both men and women and also are dominant factors in the lives of those who succeed in non-athletic vocations:

1. *Self-analysis.* The successful athlete knows her strengths and weaknesses and engages in critical appraisal that is honest, but never negative.

2. *Self-competition.* A winner knows she can only control her own performance, so she competes against her own best effort, not others.

3. *Focus.* The champion is always in the present, concentrating on the task at hand.

4. *Confidence.* Successful athletes control anxiety by setting tough but reasonable goals. As goals are reached, confidence increases.

5. *Toughness.* This is a mental trait that involves accepting risk and trying to win, rather than trying not to lose. A winner sees change as opportunity and accepts responsibility for her destiny.

6. *Having a game plan.* Even elite athletes know talent is not enough. They have a game plan.

You don't have to be an Olympic athlete to develop these skills; they can be beneficial in every area of your life. Whether it's on the job, in the home, or at the gym, these traits can build excellence into your everyday life.

All our dreams can come true—
if we have the courage to pursue them.

The Joy of Little Cranberry Island

When he came and had seen the grace of God,
he was glad, and encouraged them all that with
purpose of heart they should continue with the Lord.

ACTS 11:23

Joy Sprague knows how to brighten the days of her customers. As the postmaster for Little Cranberry Island, Maine, she actually has customers competing to get their pictures on her post-office wall. Every twenty-fifth customer to use the U.S. Postal Service's Express Mail has a mug shot taken, which is hung on the wall (actually, a portion of the general store), and then receives a plate of Joy's home-baked cream puffs.

That's not all Joy does to make Little Cranberry, with a population of ninety, a friendlier place. She operates a mail-order stamp business that is so popular her tiny post office ranks fourth in sales out of 450 outlets in Maine. Why? Most of Joy's customers are summer visitors who want to stay in contact with the island. Joy sends a snapshot of an island scene and a handwritten note about island events along with each order.

One of the residents has said, "She invents ways to bring pleasure to others." Joy has received praise from the U.S. postmaster general and has the warm affection not only of the local residents, but friends across America who find delight in corresponding with her.

Why not ask the Lord to give you creative ideas that will brighten someone's life today? Perhaps a brief telephone call or post card will remind them how important they really are to you and to God, their heavenly Father.

Whom HAS GOD LAID ON MY HEART TO TOUCH?

A good deed is never lost; he who sows
courtesy reaps friendship, and he
who plants kindness gathers love.

The Language of the Heart

The hearing ear and the seeing eye,
the LORD has made them both.

PROVERBS 20:12

Who HAS PROVIDED ME WITH UNCONDI- TIONAL LOVE I NEED TO THANK GOD FOR?

You can win more friends with
your ears than with your mouth.

Rabbi Harold S. Kushner writes in *When All You've Ever Wanted Isn't Enough:* "A business associate of my father's died under particularly tragic circumstances, and I accompanied my father to the funeral. The man's widow and children were surrounded by clergy and psychiatrists trying to ease their grief and make them feel better. They knew all the right words, but nothing helped. They were beyond being comforted. The widow kept saying, 'You're right, I know you're right, but it doesn't make any difference.'

"Then a man walked in, a big burly man in his eighties who was a legend in the toy and game industry. He had come to this country illiterate and penniless and had built up an immensely successful company. He was known as a hard bargainer, a ruthless competitor. Despite his success, he had never learned to read or write. . . . He had been sick recently, and his face and his walking showed it. But he walked over to the widow and started to cry, and she cried with him, and you could feel the atmosphere in the room change. This man who had never read a book in his life spoke the language of the heart and held the key that opened the gates of solace where learned doctors and clergy could not."

The Bible tells us to mourn with those who mourn and rejoice with those who rejoice. As women, we often feel the need to fix whatever is wrong—to somehow make the problem go away. What hurting people need most is a listening ear, a comforting shoulder, and a sympathizing hug—unconditional love.

Changing Course

Lord God of Israel, there is no God in heaven or on earth like You, who keep Your covenant and mercy with Your servants who walk before You with all their hearts.

2 CHRONICLES 6:14

Admiral Sir Thomas Williams was in command of a ship that routinely crossed the Atlantic. His course brought him in sight of Ascension Island, which was uninhabited most of the time. It was visited only once a year for the purpose of collecting turtles.

During one crossing, the island was barely visible on the horizon when Sir Thomas felt a great urge to steer his vessel toward it. The closer he came to the island, the greater the urgency grew. When he gave the order to head for the island, his lieutenant respectfully pointed out that such a course change would greatly delay them. Even so, the admiral remained intent. The inner urging, which he had come to recognize as God's Spirit inside of him, was strong.

As the ship neared the island, his crew spotted a white flag. "It must be a signal!" Williams concluded. Sure enough, as the ship neared the beach, they found sixteen men who had wrecked on the coast many days before. They were starving and had nearly given up hope of rescue.

In prayer, yield the rudder of your soul to God, so that He might steer you toward opportunities to bless or help others.

———∞———

If your prayers are sincere, then you can be sure that [your] present life is exactly what God knows is best . . . for you!

Am I WILLING TO GIVE UP CONTROL OF MY LIFE TO GOD WHO SEES THE BIGGER PICTURE?

Bearing Fruit

*If My people who are called by My name
will humble themselves, and pray and seek
My face, and turn from their wicked ways,
then I will hear from heaven, and will
forgive their sin and heal their land.*

2 CHRONICLES 7:14

Is THERE AN
AREA OF MY
LIFE I HAVE
NOT YIELDED
TO THE HAND
OF GOD?

An Arab proverb illustrates the concept that as the tares and wheat grow, they show which of these God has blessed. The stalks of wheat bow their heads because God has blessed them with abundant grain. The more fruitful they are, the lower their heads. The tares lift their heads up high above the wheat, for they are empty of grain.

D. L. Moody once said, "I have a pear tree on my farm that is very beautiful; it appears to be one of the most beautiful trees on my place. Every branch seems to be reaching up to the light and stands almost like a wax candle, but I never get any fruit from it. I have another tree, which was so full of fruit last year that the branches almost touched the ground. If we only get down low enough, my friends, God will use every one of us to His glory. . . . The holiest Christians are the humblest."

When our prayers focus only on ourselves and our needs, they bear little fruit. When our prayers are focused on the Lord and His desires, they produce a great harvest. To yield what we want to what He wants is not only the key to prayer, but also the key to success in every area of our lives.

Humility is the principal aid to prayer.

Taking Action

They stoned Paul and dragged him out of the city, supposing him to be dead. However, when the disciples gathered around him, he rose up and went into the city. And the next day he departed with Barnabas to Derbe.

ACTS 14:19-20

In the winter of 1995, a fishing boat began to sink in the rough, cold waters off Vancouver Island, west of British Columbia, Canada. The two men on board quickly moved to a life raft that was tied to the sinking boat by a nylon rope. Unfortunately, the rope was tied so tightly that they could not untie it.

As the fishing vessel began to take on more and more water, the men knew they couldn't reboard it. Neither of them had brought a knife onto the life raft with which to cut the raft free from the sinking ship. Both men knew that if the boat went down, it would pull the life raft under—and them along with it! They were in severe danger of drowning unless they could find a way to cut the rope.

The two men began to chew the rope, taking turns as each man's jaw became exhausted. One man lost a tooth in the process. They worked steadily and feverishly for more than an hour, and minutes before the fishing boat sank, they chewed through the rope! They survived and were later rescued by another fishing vessel.

Don't let panic keep you from taking action in an adverse situation. Do whatever you find at hand to do!

———❧———

The secret of success is to be like a duck— smooth and unruffled on the top, but paddling furiously underneath.

What KEEPS ME FROM TRUSTING IN GOD FOR THE STRENGTH NECESSARY TO DEAL WITH ADVERSE SITUATIONS?

Different, but the Same

So God, who knows the heart, acknowledged them, by giving them the Holy Spirit, just as He did to us, and made no distinction between us and them, purifying their hearts by faith.

ACTS 15:8-9

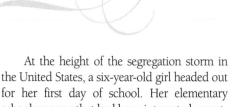

How CAN I SHOW GRATITUDE TO GOD FOR EACH UNIQUELY CREATED PERSON IN MY LIFE?

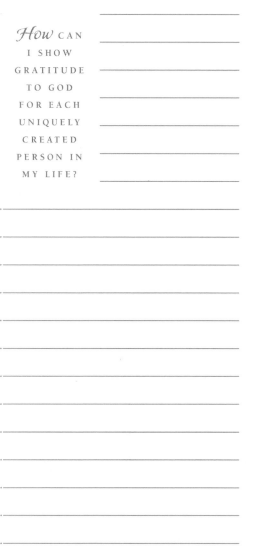

At the height of the segregation storm in the United States, a six-year-old girl headed out for her first day of school. Her elementary school was one that had been integrated recently, and the community was still full of tension. After school, her mother met her anxiously at the door, eager to hear how the day had gone. "Did everything go all right, honey?" she asked.

"Oh, Mother! You know what?" the little girl said eagerly, "A little black girl sat next to me."

With growing apprehension, the mother asked, "And what happened?"

The little girl replied, "We were both so scared about our first day at school that we held hands all day."

Often, jealousy and hate are born out of a lack of information—we simply don't know a person or an individual member of a group. Once we discover the many things that we share in common with another person—including our fears, hopes, concerns, and desires—our differences enhance our relationships. Love grows when we allow one another our unique differences.

———∞∞∞———

*Friendship doubles our joy
and divides our grief.*

Express Lane?

Wait for the LORD,
and He will save you.
PROVERBS 20:22

A woman once visited a friend in Cambridge, Massachusetts, the home of several well-known institutions of higher learning. She accompanied the friend to a supermarket on Saturday afternoon, finding it crammed with shoppers and long checkout lines.

While the two of them stood patiently in line, they noticed a young college-age man wheel an obviously full shopping cart into the cash-register lane that was clearly marked, "Express Lane—8 Items or Less."

The checkout girl looked at the loaded cart and then at the young man. He was trying to ignore her exasperated expression by fumbling in his knapsack for his checkbook.

Realizing she was stuck with a stubborn and inconsiderate customer, the girl said loudly to the high-school student who was helping her bag groceries, "This guy either goes to Harvard and can't count, or he goes to MIT and can't read!"

Although we don't always think of it in these terms, our impatience often reveals a selfish and mean spirit, while patience is really a simple act of kindness.

❧

It's easy to identify people who can't count to ten. They're in front of you in the supermarket express lane.

Whom IN MY LIFE CAN I BE PATIENT WITH TODAY?

Bound by Your Word

*It is a snare for a man to devote
rashly something as holy, and
afterward to reconsider his vows.*

PROVERBS 20:25

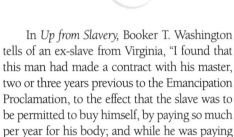

Has THERE
EVER BEEN A
TIME WHEN I
HAVE BROKEN
MY WORD?

In *Up from Slavery,* Booker T. Washington tells of an ex-slave from Virginia, "I found that this man had made a contract with his master, two or three years previous to the Emancipation Proclamation, to the effect that the slave was to be permitted to buy himself, by paying so much per year for his body; and while he was paying for himself, he was to be permitted to labor where and for whom he pleased.

"Finding that he could secure better wages in Ohio, he went there. When freedom came, he was still in debt to his master some three hundred dollars. Notwithstanding that the Emancipation Proclamation freed him from any obligation to his master, this black man walked the greater portion of the distance back to where his old master lived in Virginia and placed the last dollar, with interest, in his hands.

"In talking to me about this, the man told me that he knew that he did not have to pay his debt, but that he had given his word to his master, and his word he had never broken. He felt that he could not enjoy his freedom till he had fulfilled his promise."

Your word is the highest-valued currency you can carry, no matter what your wallet may hold.

---

*He who is slow in making
a promise is most likely to
be faithful in the keeping of it.*

The Tondelayo

The LORD said, "These have no master.
Let each return to his house in peace."

2 CHRONICLES 18:16

In *The Fall of Fortresses*, Elmer Bendiner tells of a miracle that happened to him and a few others aboard their B-17 bomber, *The Tondelayo*. During a run over Kassel, Germany, Nazi antiaircraft guns barraged the plane with flak. That was nothing unusual, but on this particular flight, the plane's fuel tanks were hit. The crew was amazed that the twenty-millimeter shell piercing the tank didn't cause an explosion. The following morning, the pilot, Bohn Fawkes, asked the crew chief for the shell as a souvenir of their unbelievable luck.

Bohn was told that not just one shell had been found in the gas tanks, but eleven! Eleven unexploded shells—it truly seemed to be a miracle.

The shells were sent to the armorers to be defused, and intelligence picked them up there. Later, they informed *The Tondelayo* crew that when they opened the shells, they found no explosive charges in any of them. They were clean and harmless. One of the shells, however, was not completely empty. It contained a carefully rolled up piece of paper. On it was scrawled in the Czech language: "This is all we can do for you now." The miracle had not been one of misfired shells, but of peace-loving hearts.

If we want peace in our homes, we need to disarm our weapons—hurtful words, prideful looks, and harmful attitudes. When we do all we can, God does all He can. He floods our home with His peace and love.

Are THERE WEAPONS IN MY LIFE I NEED TO DISARM?

Peace is not made at the council tables,
or by treaties, but in the hearts of men.

Step-by-Step

He said, "Listen, all you of Judah and you inhabitants of Jerusalem, and you, King Jehoshaphat! Thus says the LORD to you: 'Do not be afraid nor dismayed because of this great multitude, for the battle is not yours, but God's.'"

2 CHRONICLES 20:15

Have I
ASKED GOD
TO PROVIDE
STEP-BY-STEP
INSTRUC-
TIONS TO
FULFILL HIS
GOAL FOR
MY LIFE?

Several years ago, the world watched in awe as media attention was focused on three gray whales that were icebound off Point Barrow, Alaska. The battered whales floated listlessly as they gasped for breath through a small hole in the ice. They had somehow become trapped in an ice pack before they could begin their annual migration. Their only hope for survival was to be transported five miles past the ice pack to the open sea.

Rescuers began cutting a string of breathing holes about twenty yards apart in the six-inch-thick ice. Then for eight days, they coaxed the whales from hole to hole, mile after mile. Along the way, one of the whales vanished, but the other two eventually swam to freedom.

Are you feeling trapped under a heavy load today? Do you fear it may suffocate you? Do you seem to be far from the "open seas" or the free schedule you desire?

Identify where you want to go and then chart your course in a series of small steps or short-term goals. Take time for a breather as you reach each goal. God will lead and help you toward any destination that is in keeping with His good desire for you, but you need to follow. Remember: God leads us step by step, not leap by leap!

—∞∞∞—

*'Tis man's to fight, but
Heaven's to give success.*

Soar with the Eagles

*In Him we live and move and have our being,
as also some of your own poets have
said, "For we are also His offspring."*

ACTS 17:28

A farmer once caught a young eagle in the forest, brought it home, and raised it among his ducks and turkeys. Five years later, a naturalist came to visit him and saw the bird. "That's an eagle, not a chicken!" he said. "Yes," said the farmer, "but I've raised it to be a chicken." "Still," said the naturalist, "it has a wingspan of fifteen feet. It's an eagle!" "It will never fly," said the farmer. The naturalist disagreed, and they decided to put their argument to the test.

First, the naturalist picked up the eagle and said, "Eagle, thou art an eagle; thou dost belong to the sky and not to this earth; stretch forth thy wings and fly." The eagle saw the chickens and jumped down. The next day the naturalist took the eagle to the top of the house, said the same thing, and let the eagle go. Again, it spotted the chickens below and fluttered down to join them in feeding.

"One more try," said the naturalist. He took the eagle up a mountain. The trembling bird looked around, and then the naturalist made it look into the sun. Suddenly, the eagle stretched out its wings, gave a mighty screech, and flew away, never to return.

People may say you are a nobody—just a hunk of flesh—but deep inside, you have a spirit created in God's image. Look to Him and you can fly!

*Success is . . . seeking, knowing,
loving, and obeying God.*

What's KEEPING ME FROM BELIEVING THAT GOD HAS CREATED ME TO SOAR AMONG THE CLOUDS?

An Honorable Title

To do righteousness and justice is more acceptable to the LORD than sacrifice.
PROVERBS 21:3

What
ARE THE
BENEFITS
OF THE LIFE
GOD HAS
GIVEN ME?

Horace Mann is considered one of America's greatest educators. In 1837, as a lawyer, not a teacher, he entered politics and became president of the Massachusetts State Senate. A visionary, he saw vast possibilities for developing the public education system of the nation, and he pushed for improvements in education wherever he had an opportunity to speak.

Mann's pleas for education resulted in Massachusetts creating a state board of education as an experiment. The leadership position of the board was offered to Mann. His friends, who truly believed that his political career might culminate in the presidency of the United States, urged him to decline. But Mann accepted the position. His statement to his downcast friends became a classic: "If the title is not sufficiently honorable, then it is clearly left to me to elevate it."

Not only did the position have little prestige, but the $1,500 salary was only a fraction of what Mann had earned as a lawyer. About this Mann noted, "One thing is certain—if I live and have good health, I will do more than $1,500 worth of good." And he did. From his position, he gave Massachusetts a public school system that many other states adopted, benefiting millions of children through the years.

The title of "mom," or "wife," might not seem that important, but as a woman, you make it honorable by your attitude. The pay may be next to nothing, but the benefits are out of this world!

Motherhood is a partnership with God.

The Kid Who Couldn't Sit Still

*You have need of endurance, so that
after you have done the will of God,
you may receive the promise.*

HEBREWS 10:36

Nelson Diebel, a hyperactive and delinquent child, was enrolled in The Peddie School. There he met swimming coach Chris Martin, who believed that the more he practiced, the better he performed. Within a month, he had Nelson swimming thirty to forty hours a week, even though Nelson could not sit still in a classroom for more than fifteen minutes. Martin saw potential in Nelson. He constantly put new goals in front of him, trying to get him to focus and turn his anger into strength. Nelson eventually qualified for the Junior Nationals, where his times qualified him for the Olympic Trials.

Unfortunately, Nelson broke both hands and arms in a diving accident, and doctors warned he probably would never regain his winning form. Martin said to him, "You're coming all the way back. . . . If you're not committed to that, we're going to stop right now." Nelson agreed, and within weeks after his casts were off, he was swimming again. In 1992, he won Olympic gold. As he accepted his medal, he recalls thinking, *I planned and dreamed and worked so hard . . . and I did it!* The kid who once couldn't sit still and who had no ambition . . . had learned to make a plan, pursue it, and achieve it. He had become a winner in far more than swimming!

Seek God's plan for your life and don't let anything stop you from achieving it!

*We can do anything we want
to do if we stick to it long enough.*

What GOALS
DO I FEEL
GOD IS
LEADING ME
TO ACHIEVE?

Defying the Odds

*O LORD of hosts, blessed is
the man who trusts in You!*
PSALM 84:12

DO I EXPECT
TO FAIL IN
AN AREA OF
LIFE? WHY?

Joseph Strauss, the engineer responsible for building the Golden Gate Bridge, took great pride in his achievement, not only because the bridge was one of the most beautiful in the world, but because it was the safest. Strauss had heard all his life that "a bridge demands its life." At that time, it was normal to expect one death for every million dollars when building a bridge. Strauss was determined to beat that expectation.

Joseph took to heart the problems experienced by the Oakland Bay Bridge builders who were working at the same time. He kept a doctor and nurse on the construction wharf. When his suspicions about lead poisoning were confirmed, he switched from lead to iron oxide paint on the tower splices. He insisted on safety belts, hard hats, and goggles. He even put his "bridge monkeys" on special diets in hopes of helping them counteract dizziness and vertigo. He fired men who drank on the job or were reckless show-offs. And he spent $82,000 on a safety net that eventually saved the lives of nineteen men.

Although unavoidable accidents did claim lives, Strauss' bridge construction went for forty-four months with no deaths—a phenomenal record—all because he rejected negative expectations and became a wise example.

Failure is not inevitable. Put your trust in God, and let Him show you the way to succeed.

*A diamond is a piece of coal
that stuck to its job.*

Shoot for the Goal

The LORD your God is gracious and merciful, and will not turn His face from you if you return to Him.

2 CHRONICLES 30:9

When Michigan played Wisconsin in basketball early in the 1989 season, Michigan's Rumeal Robinson found himself at the foul line with just seconds left in the fourth quarter. His team was trailing by one point, and Rumeal knew that if he could sink both shots, Michigan would win. Sadly, Rumeal missed both shots. Wisconsin upset the favored Michigan, and Rumeal went to the locker room feeling devastated and embarrassed.

His dejection, however, led to a positive move on his part. He determined that for the rest of the season, at the end of each practice, he was going to shoot one hundred extra foul shots. And shoot 'em he did!

The moment came when Rumeal stepped to the foul line in yet another game, again with the opportunity to make two shots. This time there were only three seconds left in overtime, and the game was the NCAA finals! Swish went the first shot—and swish went the second. Those two points gave Michigan the victory and the collegiate national championship.

Have you just failed at something? Don't give up! Instead, work harder. Success is possible.

What AREAS OF MY LIFE DO I NEED TO PRACTICE TO SUCCEED IN?

You have to experience failure in order to understand success.

What Money Can't Buy

I have shown you in every way, by laboring like this, that you must support the weak. And remember the words of the Lord Jesus, that He said, "It is more blessed to give than to receive."

ACTS 20:35

When HAVE I TRUSTED IN MY FINANCES RATHER THAN IN GOD?

Success in the world means power, influence, money, prestige. But in the Christian world, it means pleasing God.

J. C. Macaulay once took a group of his college students, who were preparing for Christian service on the mission field, to the famous Biltmore Estate near Asheville, North Carolina. He was eager to see their response to the vast wealth of the grounds, and he was hopeful that his students would confront any materialistic desires they might have before going abroad.

He watched as the students viewed the fabulous treasures on display, moving from one luxurious room to another. Several of the students commented on the value of various items. Others remarked about the exquisite perfection of various artifacts and pieces of furniture. All demonstrated a great appreciation for the upkeep of the spacious and beautiful grounds.

As they returned from the trip, his heart was warmed, though, when the students spontaneously began to sing the words of an old hymn:

> *When you look at others*
> *with their lands and gold,*
> *Think that Christ has promised you*
> *His wealth untold;*
> *Count your blessings—money cannot buy*
> *Your reward in Heaven nor your home on high.*

When the allure of materialism threatens to pull you in, recount to yourself the marvelous blessings God has given you—blessings that cannot be bought or sold, lost or stolen, broken or used up. God's blessings are eternal.

Help Me!

Be merciful to me, O LORD,
For I cry to You all day long.

PSALM 86:3

In an article written for *America* magazine entitled, "Praying in a Time of Depression," Jane Redmont wrote:

"On a quick trip to New York for a consulting job, a week or two into the anti-depressant drug and feeling no relief, I fell into a seven-hour anxiety attack with recurring suicidal ideations. On the morning after my arrival, I found I could not focus my attention; yet focus was crucial in the job I was contracted to do for twenty-four hours, as recorder and process observer at a conference of urban activists that was beginning later that day. I felt as if I were about to jump out of my skin—or throw myself under a truck.

"An hour away from the beginning of the conference, walking uptown on a noisy Manhattan street in the afternoon, I prayed . . . perhaps out loud, I am not sure. I said with all my strength, 'Jesus, I don't usually ask You for much, but I am asking You now, in the name of all those people whom You healed, in the name of the man born blind and the bent-over woman and the woman who bled for years, in the name of the man with the demons and the little girl whom You raised up, help me.'

"Within an hour, I was calm again."

God is our high tower—a refuge in times of trouble. When we pray in the midst of anxiety and depression, God can fill us with His peace that passes understanding, sheltering us from the torment of our worry, and restoring us to wholeness once again.

What FEARS OR PROBLEMS WILL I TURN OVER TO GOD TODAY?

I do not always bend the knee to pray;
I often pray in crowded city street in
some hard crisis of a busy day—prayer
is my sure and comforting retreat.

Begin with Prayer

Give ear, O LORD, to my prayer; and attend to the voice of my supplications. In the day of my trouble I will call upon You, for You will answer me.

PSALM 86:6-7

Has A DAY IN MY LIFE EVER BEEN CHANGED THROUGH BEGINNING IT IN PRAYER?

Pope John Paul II has made no secret of his daily schedule in the Vatican. He begins his day at 5:30 A.M., while most of Rome is still asleep. By 6:15 he is in his private chapel, meditating and praying before its altar, over which hangs a large bronze crucifix. Also within sight is a copy of Poland's most cherished Catholic icon, the Black Virgin of Czestochowa.

Those who have seen the Pope in prayer say that at times he prostrates himself before the altar. At other times he sits or kneels and with closed eyes, cradles his forehead in his hands.

This early-morning prayer session is his time to bring before God his prayer requests for others. It is not uncommon for the stack of intentions to have more than two-hundred sheets, with many names written on each one.

The Pope considers prayer, more than liquid or food, to be the sustaining force of his life. Says Monsignor Diarmuid Martin, secretary of the Vatican's Justice and Peace Commission, the Pope makes all his decisions "on his knees."

Prayer—there's no better way to start a day or to begin and end the decision-making process.

He who runs from God in the morning will scarcely find Him the rest of the day.

Age Doesn't Matter

The God of our fathers has chosen you that you should know His will, and see the Just One, and hear the voice of His mouth.

ACTS 22:14

One of the marks of maturity is the ability to accept the responsibility for a talent—to diligently develop the inherent, God-given abilities and make the most of them with joy and thanksgiving. A person who does this can become a success at any age.

- Victor Hugo wrote his first tragedy at age fifteen.

- John de Medecci was fifteen when he became a cardinal.

- Raphael painted his masterpieces before he died at age thirty-seven.

- Tennyson wrote his first volume of poetry at age eighteen.

- Pascal wrote his great works between the ages of sixteen and his death at thirty-seven.

- Joan of Arc was burned at the stake at nineteen.

- Romulus founded Rome at twenty.

- Calvin joined the Reformation at age twenty-one and wrote his famous Institutes at age twenty-seven.

- Alexander the Great had conquered his world by the time he was twenty-three.

- Isaac Newton was twenty-four when he introduced the Law of Gravity.

Age has nothing to do with genius. These great people merely took full responsibility for their God-given gifts and wasted no time as they maximized every opportunity to its fullest potential.

What GOD-GIVEN GIFT HAVE I NOT FULLY DEVELOPED?

Have a purpose in life, and having it, throw into your work such strength of mind and muscle as God has given you.

The Smile Parade

The following night the Lord stood by him and said, "Be of good cheer, Paul; for as you have testified for Me in Jerusalem, so you must also bear witness at Rome."

ACTS 23:11

What CAN I DO TO BRIGHTEN THE LIFE OF ANOTHER TODAY?

A pastor tells the story of how during the twelve years of his pastorate at one particular church, he had a custom of calling the children forward just before his Sunday-morning sermon so that they could go to children's church and hear a sermon geared especially for them. During the processional to their assembly hall, the children marched past the pulpit, and the pastor made it a point to smile at each child. He always received their smiles in return. "It was one of the high points of the service," he recalled.

One day, however, the pastor apparently missed smiling at one child. A curly-headed, four-year-old ran out of the procession and threw herself into the arms of her mother, sobbing as if her heart were broken.

After the service, the pastor sought out the mother to find out what had happened. The mother explained that after her child had quieted, she asked what caused the tears. The child had said, "I smiled at God, but He didn't smile back!" The pastor reflected, "To that child, I stood for God. I had failed with my smile, and the world went dark."

Smile at each person you meet today. You may never know how much you have brightened a life!

———

What sunshine is to flowers, smiles are to humanity. They are but trifles, to be sure, but, scattered along life's pathway, the good they do is inconceivable.

Found: Black Derby

This being so, I myself always strive
to have a conscience without
offense toward God and men.

ACTS 24:16

What "OLD
WRONG" CAN I
RIGHT TODAY?

In the 1890s, a man drove by the farm of Mrs. John R. McDonald. A sudden gust of wind caught his black derby hat and whirled it onto the McDonald property. He searched in vain for the hat and finally drove off with a bare head.

Mrs. McDonald retrieved the hat, and for the next forty-five years, various members of her family wore it. Finally, the old derby was completely worn out and beyond repair. At long last, Mrs. McDonald went to the local newspaper and advertised for the owner of the hat. She noted in her ad that while the hat had been on the heads of the menfolk in her family, it had been on her conscience!

Is something nagging your heart today— an awareness that you have committed a wrong against another person or a feeling that something has gone amiss in a relationship? Don't ignore those feelings. Seek to make amends.

A guilty conscience is a heavy load to carry through life. Jesus died on the cross so you wouldn't have to bear that burden. He did His part; now you do yours. Strive to obtain and maintain the freedom and peace He purchased for you!

A lot of people mistake a short
memory for a clear conscience.

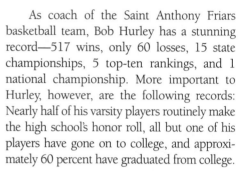

Dedication

JULY 22

*He covets greedily all day long, but the
righteous gives and does not spare.*
PROVERBS 21:26

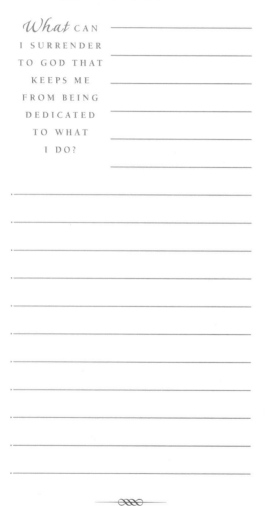

What CAN
I SURRENDER
TO GOD THAT
KEEPS ME
FROM BEING
DEDICATED
TO WHAT
I DO?

*Success is to be measured not by wealth,
power, or fame, but by the ratio between
what a man is and what he might be.*

As coach of the Saint Anthony Friars basketball team, Bob Hurley has a stunning record—517 wins, only 60 losses, 15 state championships, 5 top-ten rankings, and 1 national championship. More important to Hurley, however, are the following records: Nearly half of his varsity players routinely make the high school's honor roll, all but one of his players have gone on to college, and approximately 60 percent have graduated from college.

Hurley has a reputation for helping his players choose a college based on academics first and athletics second. He declares players ineligible if their grades suffer. "If you're not committed to your education," he says, "how committed can you be to this team?" On the court, he is tough, impatient, and noisy. On the other hand, players who honestly struggle in their studies are often treated to dinner and private tutoring at Hurley's home.

Hurley has been offered numerous opportunities to leave his high-school position in Jersey City, but for him, that's home. It's the place where he has invested his life. In 1992, he was honored by his city with a major banquet and rousing accolades. The next day he was back to work, out hunting summer jobs for his players.

If you're truly dedicated to what you do, don't change anything. Enjoy the accolades you receive, then go on and do what you do best.

The World Won't Make You Happy

The sacrifice of the wicked is an abomination; how much more when he brings it with wicked intent!

PROVERBS 21:27

When the great golfer Babe Didrikson Zaharias was dying of cancer, her husband, George Zaharias, came to her bedside. Although he desired to be strong for her sake, he found he was unable to control his emotions and began to cry. Babe gently said to him, "Now honey, don't take on so. While I've been in the hospital, I have learned one thing. A moment of happiness is a lifetime, and I have had a lot of happiness."

Happiness does not come wrapped in brightly colored packages as a gift given to us by others. Happiness comes when we uncover the gifts that lie within us and begin to use them to please God and bless others.

Happiness flows from within. It is found in the moments of life we label as "quality" rather than "quantity." It rises up in life's greatest tragedies when we choose to smile at what we know to be good and lasting, rather than cry at what temporarily hurts us. George Bernard Shaw once said, "This is the true joy in life, the being used for a purpose recognized by yourself as a mighty one . . . being a force of nature instead of a feverish selfish little clod of ailments and grievances complaining that the world will not devote itself to making you happy."

The only person who can truly make you happy is yourself. You simply have to decide.

───∞∞∞───

The heart is the happiest when it beats for others.

How WILL I MAKE MYSELF HAPPY TODAY?

Keep Swimming!

They all were trying to make us afraid,
saying, "Their hands will be weakened in
the work, and it will not be done." Now
therefore, O God, strengthen my hands.

NEHEMIAH 6:9

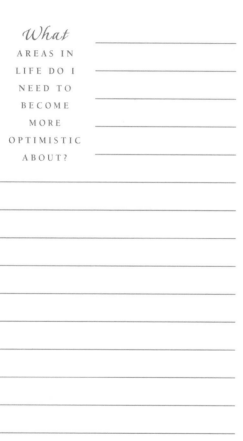

What
AREAS IN
LIFE DO I
NEED TO
BECOME
MORE
OPTIMISTIC
ABOUT?

The pessimist sees a glass that is filled half way with water as being half empty; the optimist sees it as half full. The optimistic and creative person will see it as a vase for a rosebud, the optimistic pragmatist as a means of quenching thirst, the optimistic priest as holy baptismal water!

Consider the benefits of choosing the optimistic route as described in this poem:

Two frogs fell into a deep cream bowl,
One was an optimistic soul;
But the other took the gloomy view,
"I shall drown," he cried, "and so will you."
So with a last despairing cry,
He closed his eyes and said, "Good-bye."
But the other frog, with a merry grin
Said, "I can't get out, but I won't give in!
I'll swim around till my strength is spent.
For having tried, I'll die content."
Bravely he swam until it would seem
His struggles began to churn the cream.
On the top of the butter at last he stopped
And out of the bowl he happily hopped.
What is the moral? It's easily found.
If you can't get out—keep swimming around!

—Anonymous

Some people complain because God put
thorns on roses, while others praise
Him for putting roses among thorns.

Is the Door Really Locked?

Do not sorrow, for the joy
of the LORD is your strength.

NEHEMIAH 8:10

Harry Houdini, the early twentieth-century escape artist, issued a challenge wherever he went. He claimed he could be locked in any jail cell in the country and set himself free within minutes. He had a long track record of proving himself!

One time, however, something seemed to go wrong. Houdini entered a jail cell in his street clothes. The heavy metal doors clanged shut behind him, and he took from his belt a concealed piece of strong, but flexible metal. He set to work on the lock to his cell, but something seemed different about this particular lock. He worked for thirty minutes without results. An hour passed. This was long after the time that Houdini normally freed himself, and he began to sweat and pant in exasperation. Still, he could not pick the lock.

Finally, after laboring for two hours, Houdini—feeling a sense of failure close in around him—leaned against the door in frustration. To his amazement, as he collapsed against the door, it swung open! It had not been locked in the first place!

How many times are challenges impossible—or doors locked—only because we think they are? When we put our minds and energy toward them, we often find impossible tasks turn into achievements.

———— ∞ ————

Four steps to achievement: plan
purposefully, prepare prayerfully,
proceed positively, pursue persistently.

What
"LOCKED
DOORS" WILL
I TRY TO
OPEN TODAY?

_____
_____
_____
_____
_____
_____
_____
_____
_____
_____
_____
_____
_____
_____
_____
_____
_____
_____
_____
_____
_____
_____
_____
_____
_____
_____

Taking the First Step

A good name is to be chosen rather than great riches, loving favor rather than silver and gold.

PROVERBS 22:1

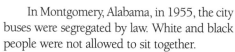

Where DO I NEED TO STAND MY GROUND?

In Montgomery, Alabama, in 1955, the city buses were segregated by law. White and black people were not allowed to sit together.

On December 1 of that year, Mrs. Rosa Parks was riding the bus home from her job at a tailor shop. As the section for whites filled up, the black people were ordered to move to the back to make room for the white passengers who were boarding. Three blacks in Mrs. Parks' row moved, but she remained in her seat. Later she said, "Our mistreatment was just not right, and I was tired of it. I knew someone had to take the first step. So I made up my mind not to move."

The bus driver asked her if she was going to stand up. "No, I am not," she answered him. Mrs. Parks was arrested and taken to jail. Four days later, sympathizers—black and white—organized a boycott of the city bus line that lasted until a year later, when the Supreme Court declared the segregation ordinance unconstitutional.

Today, Mrs. Parks is known as the "mother of the modern-day civil-rights movement." Her name inspires others to take courage and continue taking steps toward justice despite often overwhelming opposition. She made a name for herself, but not because of her great talent, wisdom, or education. Like Rosa Parks did, stand your ground for righteousness' sake. It's something you can do every day and everywhere you go.

If you were given a nickname descriptive of your character, would you be proud of it?

Measure of Success

He who pursues righteousness and
love finds life, prosperity and honor.

PROVERBS 21:21 NIV

Steve's father was passed over for promotion time after time because he wasn't willing to play political games and use other people to get ahead. As a teenager, Steve promised himself that when he grew up, he would make it to the top, and that is exactly what he did. By the age of thirty-five, Steve was second in command in a large corporation with a significant salary and a generous yearly bonus.

Steve once asked his dad, "Does it bother you that you have worked hard all your life and have so little to show for it? I mean, you've lived in the same house all your life. You've never gotten away for more than a week at a time. Your pension isn't going to let you really enjoy your retirement. Do you ever regret not getting ahead more?"

After some silence, his father responded, "Steve, maybe I use a different measure than you do. There's never been a night in my life that I couldn't put my head down and go to sleep knowing I have lived my life with honor. I raised a son who is successful, and I have a wife whom I love. I have what I need and what makes me happy. How much farther ahead should I be?"

His dad's answer made Steve realize the immeasurable wealth he had been given by a man whom he thought had nothing.

———

You may give without loving, but
you cannot love without giving.

What IMMEASURABLE WEALTH HAVE I BEEN GIVEN BY THE PEOPLE IN MY LIFE?

Carrying Our Precious Possessions

God is my witness, whom I serve with
my spirit in the gospel of His Son,
that without ceasing I make mention
of you always in my prayers.

ROMANS 1:9

What

AREAS DO

I NEED TO

ASK GOD FOR

FORGIVE-

NESS IN?

Before the surrender of Weinsberg in 1140 to the new German king, the women of that besieged city asked the enemy to allow them to leave, carrying their most precious possessions with them. Permission was granted. To their astonishment, the women of Weinsberg, displaying both shrewdness and love, came plodding through the city gates with their husbands, sons, and brothers on their shoulders!

How wise we are to carry our dear ones out of sin and away from evil on the shoulders of our prayers. During one of D. L. Moody's services in London, this was demonstrated in a profound way. A father and mother voiced great distress about their son, who had given up God's ways and run away to the bush of Australia. They asked the vast congregation to pray for their son. That night, some twenty thousand believers voiced prayers on his behalf.

Later, the parents learned that at the very hour of that prayer, their son had been riding through the Australian bush into town, a day's ride from his camp. As he rode, the Spirit of the Lord convicted him of his sin. Dismounting, he knelt and asked God for forgiveness. When he reached town, he wired the news of his repentance to his mother and asked if he might come home. Her reply was cabled immediately, "Come home at once!"

———

Men may spurn our appeals, reject
our message, oppose our arguments,
despise our persons, but they are
helpless against our prayers.

The Attitude Diet

Train up a child in the way he
should go, and when he is old
he will not depart from it.

PROVERBS 22:6

Several years ago, a man was asked to give a commencement address. After he had given his speech, he sat on the platform, watching the graduates receive their college degrees. Suddenly, the entire audience began applauding for a student who had earned a perfect 4.0 grade-point average. During the applause, a faculty member seated next to the speaker leaned over and said to him, "She may be Miss Genius, but her attitude stinks." The speaker later said, "Without even thinking, my hands stopped clapping in midair. I couldn't help but think, *How sad.*"

No matter how beautiful, intelligent, talented, or athletic a child may be, there's no substitute for a positive, loving attitude toward others! The foremost architects of that attitude are a child's parents.

The attitudes you feed your children every day are the diet of their minds, just as food is the diet of their bodies. Don't feed your children junky ideas, sour opinions, rotten theology, poisoned feelings, or wilted enthusiasm. Instead, feed your children with the best positive ideas, emotional expressions, and thoughtful opinions you have!

Who NEEDS TO BENEFIT FROM MY LOVING ATTITUDE TODAY?

⬦⬦⬦

Our children are like mirrors—
they reflect our attitudes in life.

Daily Deposit

*Make the most of your chances
to tell others the Good News.*
COLOSSIANS 4:5 TLB

How CAN I
BEST SPEND
GOD'S GIFT
OF TIME
TODAY?

A woman once had a dream that an angel was giving her this message: "As a reward for your virtues, the sum of $1,440 will be deposited into your bank account every morning. There is only one condition. At the close of each business day, any balance that has not been used will be canceled. It won't carry over to the next day or accrue any interest. Each morning, a new $1,440 will be credited to you."

The dream was so vivid, she asked the Lord to show her what it meant. He led her to realize she was receiving 1,440 minutes every morning, the total number of minutes in a 24-hour day. What she did with this deposit of time was important, because 1,440 minutes per day was all she would ever receive!

Each of us has a similar account. At the close of each day, we should be able to look over our ledger and see that these golden minutes were spent wisely.

Time is God's gift to you. What you do with your time is your gift to God.

---

*Time is a precious gift of God—
so precious that He only gives
it to us moment by moment.*

The Lady with the Lamp

He who has a generous eye
will be blessed, for he gives
of his bread to the poor.

PROVERBS 22:9

One night in 1837, she believed she heard the voice of God telling her that she had a mission. Nine years later, that mission began to take shape when a friend sent her information about the Institution of Protestant Deaconesses in Germany. She later entered the institution to learn how to care for the sick. In 1853, she became superintendent of a women's hospital in London. But then in 1854, the Crimean War broke out, and she volunteered at once to care for British soldiers, leaving for Constantinople almost immediately.

Once in Turkey, she was put in charge of nursing at the military hospital. Even though doctors were hostile toward her because she was a woman, and the hospital itself was deplorably filthy, she dug in her heels and began caring for her patients. She first used the provisions she had brought with her, then undertook a correspondence campaign to restock the hospital. She spent many hours each day in the wards, touching virtually every man who ever entered the hospital. The comfort she gave on night rounds earned her the nickname, "The Lady with the Lamp."

Her selfless giving eventually made her name, Florence Nightingale, synonymous with compassionate nursing care.

What KEEPS ME FROM GIVING TO OTHERS SELFLESSLY?

The Lord can do great things through those who don't care who gets the credit.

Even Cockroaches?

We also glory in tribulations, knowing that tribulation produces perseverance; and perseverance, character; and character, hope.
ROMANS 5:3-4

What PROBLEMS IN MY LIFE CAN I BEGIN TO VIEW AS "CHARACTER BUILDING" FROM GOD?

A pastor's wife was accustomed to uninvited guests and was usually delighted to have them, but not when the guests were cockroaches. She was appalled when they made their appearance in her new parsonage. The very word, "cockroaches," sounded dirty to her. She immediately sought a way to get rid of them. Spraying pesticides in the house was impossible due to the physical condition of one of her children. The only solution seemed to be the use of roach traps—a safe, but slow process. It took almost a year before the house was free of the dirty insects.

During that year, the pastor's wife encountered Romans 8:28: "We know that all things work together for good to those who love God." She laughed and said, "Well, Lord, if you say so!" She couldn't imagine what good might come from battling cockroaches month after month, but she trusted God.

Several weeks after the disappearance of the last cockroach, she received a letter from her daughter, who had gone to Paraguay as a missionary. She wrote, "Mom, do you remember all those awful cockroaches we had? Well, we have huge, flying ones here! I'm glad I was able to get used to them at home before coming to Paraguay!"

God is in the process of perfecting you. His greatest aim is to build His character in you. He doesn't send the "cockroaches" into our lives, but He will use them for our benefit. He always has your ultimate good in mind!

When God does not immediately respond to the cries of His children, it is because He wants to accomplish some gracious purpose in their lives.

Inside Information

*He who dwells in the secret place of
the Most High shall abide under
the shadow of the Almighty.*

PSALM 91:1

How CAN
I BEST
SEEK GOD'S
PRECEPTS FOR
MY LIFE?

Down through the years, a number of famous quotes about character have focused on one attribute: the hidden nature of character. Character is what you are in the dark. The measure of someone's real character is what he would do if he knew he never would be found out.

The difference between personality and character: Personality is what you are when lots of people are around; character is what you are when everybody goes home.

Ultimately, you are the only person who truly knows the nature of your character. It's like the little boy who once came crying to his mother with the pronouncement, "Mommy, eating too many green apples can make a person sick." His mother tried to comfort him and asked, "Where did you learn this?" The little boy replied, "I have inside information."

Only you know what you would do in any given situation. As you formulate the "coulds," "shoulds," and "woulds" of your life in accordance with God's Word, your character grows. Look within, and see what kind of person you find!

*Prayer is a rising up and a drawing near
to God in mind, and in heart, and in spirit.*

Improvising under Pressure

*The LORD is my strength and my
shield; my heart trusts in him,
and I am helped.*

PSALM 28:7 NIV

When HAVE
I GIVEN UP
IN THE FACE
OF DIFFICULT
CIRCUM-
STANCES?

Nicolò Paganini was a well-known and gifted nineteenth-century violinist. His most memorable concert, however, was one marked by a difficult test rather than easy success. The concert was performed with a full orchestra before a packed house in Italy. Those who heard him play say that Paganini's technique was incredible and his tone fantastic. Toward the end of the concert, Paganini was astounding his rapt audience with an intricate composition when one string on his violin suddenly snapped and hung limply from his instrument. Paganini frowned only briefly, shook his head, and continued to play, improvising beautifully.

Then to everyone's surprise, including Paganini's, a second string broke. Shortly thereafter, a third string snapped. It seemed like a slapstick comedy routine as Paganini stood before the awed crowd with strings dangling from his Stradivarius violin. Instead of leaving the stage to repair his instrument, he stood firm. He calmly completed the difficult number on the one remaining string—a performance that won him applause, admiration, and enduring fame.

Your best work may be performed under tough and unusual circumstances. So don't give up. Just keep playing!

※

*To follow, without halt, one aim:
There's the secret of success.*

Peace from Prayer

*He shall call upon Me, and I will answer
him; I will be with him in trouble;
I will deliver him and honor him.*

PSALM 91:15

It was two o'clock in the morning when a weary traveler landed in Tahiti. Her flight from Hawaii had been a turbulent one, causing a delay in her arrival on the island. The stormy skies had also forced her connecting flight to a nearby island to be canceled, requiring her to make plans to spend at least a day near the airport. An hour later, she found herself standing with her luggage in a small but clean motel room, totally exhausted after more than twenty-four hours of travel. Her mind, however, refused to stop racing with concern about whom to call and what to do.

The woman was on a short-term missionary trip to help set up a clinic on a remote South Seas island. Now she was beginning to wonder if she had heard God correctly! At that hour, and as weary as she was, she felt alone at the edge of the world. Glancing down at her watch, she saw it was 11 A.M.—the time her Bible study group said they would be in prayer for her. *They're praying right now!* she thought, and suddenly, she felt deep peace and comfort. Within minutes, she was sound asleep.

When you are about to unravel inside, turn to prayer. The travel route of prayer is never misdirected or put off schedule—nor is it dangerous! On the contrary, prayer gives peace and helps us avoid danger.

———※———

*A day hemmed in prayer
is less likely to unravel.*

How CAN I USE PRAYER TODAY TO DEAL WITH A DIFFICULT SITUATION?

Expressions of Divine Exactness

What then shall we say to these things?
If God is for us, who can be against us?
ROMANS 8:31

How HAVE
I SEEN
GOD'S TRUTH
PREVAIL IN
THE PAST?

Cardinal von Faulhaber of Munich is reported once to have had a conversation with the famed physicist, Albert Einstein.

"Cardinal von Faulhaber," Einstein said, "I respect religion, but I believe in mathematics. Probably it is the other way around with you."

"You are mistaken," replied the cardinal. "To me, both are merely different expressions of the same divine exactness."

"But, Your Eminence, what would you say if mathematical science should someday come to conclusions directly contradictory to religious beliefs?"

"Oh," the cardinal answered with ease. "I have the highest respect for the competence of mathematicians. I am sure they would never rest until they discovered their mistake."

Regardless of how ardently some people try to suppress it, God's truth will always prevail!

Before God created the universe,
He already had you in mind.

Finish Big

*Though your beginning was
small, yet your latter end
would increase abundantly.*

JOB 8:7

Scott McGregor worked for a company that rented cellular phones to business travelers. The phones were not designed to produce itemized bills, however, and some corporations refused to reimburse their employees without one. Each phone needed a computer chip to keep a billing record of calls made.

McGregor quit his job and began to pursue the idea full-time. He felt sure it was a winner. But despite two years of effort, he met with little success and faced being evicted from his home. At the eleventh hour, he found an investor willing to help him turn his idea into a reality.

McGregor used part of the money to hire a consulting engineer, but after several months, the engineer said the system McGregor wanted was impossible. He already had an appointment to demonstrate a prototype to BellSouth, so he called his twenty-two-year-old son, Greg, who was a computer science major. Greg began working up to eighteen hours a day to create an automated circuit that would defy the experts. He and his dad flew to Atlanta to meet with BellSouth, and his solution worked.

Today, the McGregor family firm, Telemac Cellular Corporation, is an industry leader worth millions of dollars.

A slow start diligently pursued can result in a big finish.

---

*To climb steep hills
requires slow pace at first.*

What WILL
I DILIGENTLY
PURSUE
TODAY?

Lasting Treasures

"Naked I came from my mother's womb, and naked I will depart."

JOB 1:21 NIV

Who NEEDS
TO RECEIVE
LOVE FROM
ME TODAY?

Paula doesn't have any dolls from her childhood. The quilts her grandmother made are nowhere to be found. The boxes in her attic are few, mostly seasonal things she packs back up with each holiday. There are no heirlooms, hand-me-downs, or pieces of furniture from a previous generation.

If you ask her why, Paula will tell you about a fire that destroyed her home when she was a teenager. She'll tell you about walking through the blackened outline of her bedroom and weeping over the hope chest that was charred—the contents destroyed.

Paula doesn't hold tightly to her possessions since the fire. Instead, she holds tightly to the people in her life and to each moment as it comes.

"We embrace our belongings as if they are ours forever," she says. "But one day we'll be gone and nothing will be like we once knew it. I'm glad to have nice things in my house, but I don't think of them as 'mine' anymore. They are toys I get to borrow for this life. All that is really mine is the love I've received and the love I've given. That can never be destroyed or taken away."

---

*Life is not a problem to be solved,
but a gift to be enjoyed.*

Hand of Comfort

Lord, when doubts fill my mind, when my heart is in turmoil, quiet me and give me renewed hope and cheer.

PSALM 94:19 TLB

On the first of June, John Alexander spent the evening playing basketball at the gym. When his wife was late picking him up, he began to worry. Within an hour, he received some horrible news. On their way to the gym, his wife and daughter had been killed in a collision with a drunken driver.

John's life became a tailspin of grief and anger. After a few weeks, however, he began to exude a calmness that baffled those closest to him.

When he returned to work, the team members he led were uncomfortable and afraid of doing or saying the wrong thing. In order to dispel the awkwardness, John called a meeting on a Friday afternoon. He reviewed the facts of the accident, then before closing the meeting gave an opportunity for questions. Their question: What had enabled him to move from intense grief to the calm they sensed from him now?

"Well, first of all, don't mistake my calm for a lack of grief. I will miss my family every day for the rest of my life. But about two weeks after their deaths, I woke up one morning with the distinct sensation of a hand on my shoulder. I couldn't escape the feeling. It became a comfort. I felt less alone. As crazy as it sounds, I think it is God's presence with me, helping me through. It's been there ever since. It gives me hope that I will get through this and God won't leave me alone."

No matter what you may be going through, let God comfort you and bring you His peace.

When HAVE I FELT GOD'S PEACE IN MY LIFE?

Being at peace with yourself is a direct result of finding peace with God.

Cattle for Sale

He does great things past finding out,
yes, wonders without number.

JOB 9:10

What
MIRACLES
WILL I
EXPECT GOD
TO PERFORM
IN MY LIFE?

Soon after Dallas Theological Seminary opened in 1924, it faced a major financial crisis. Creditors banded together and announced that they intended to foreclose. On the morning of the threatened foreclosure, the leadership of the seminary met in the president's office to pray that God would meet their need. One of the men present was Harry Ironside, who prayed in his characteristic style, "Lord, the cattle on a thousand hills are Thine. Please sell some of them and send us the money."

While they were praying, a tall Texan walked into the outer office and said to the secretary, "I just sold two carloads of cattle. I've been trying to make a business deal but it fell through, and I feel compelled to give the money to the seminary. I don't know if you need it, but here's the check."

Knowing the financial need, the secretary took the check and timidly tapped on the door of the office where the prayer meeting was being held. When Dr. Chafer saw the check, he was amazed. The gift was exactly the amount of the debt! Recognizing the name on the check as that of a prominent Fort Worth cattleman, he announced with joy, "Harry, God sold the cattle!"

❦

I know not by what methods rare,
but this I know: God answers prayer.

Level Ground

Do not make friends with a hot-tempered man,
do not associate with one easily angered, or you
may learn his ways and get yourself ensnared.

PROVERBS 22:24-25 NIV

Amy can tell you the exact moment she fell in love with Brian. One cold, rainy night they were on a date, and Brian's car stalled. When they couldn't get it started, Brian asked her to steer while he pushed the car off the road. Amy was an inexperienced driver and began to steer the car toward a rising incline that would have been impossible to climb with a dead motor and one man pushing.

"Amy, if you'll turn the wheel to the right, we'll be on level ground," was all she heard from Brian at the rear of the automobile.

For someone like Amy who had been berated for the smallest of mistakes, the moment was monumental. When all she expected was anger and impatience, and all she received was gentle instruction, she knew she'd found a man with whom she could spend the rest of her life.

Times of inconvenience and adversity give us a window into our truest selves. It is in those times we show our truest colors. Brian showed Amy she could depend on him for more than a hot-tempered response when the going got rough. That simple window into his soul let love shine through.

What CHARACTERISTICS DO I DISPLAY WHEN TIMES GET HARD?

It is with trifles, and when he is off guard,
that a man best reveals his character.

231

Quiet Communication

Oh, that you would be silent,
and it would be your wisdom!

JOB 13:5

What ARE
MY ACTIONS
COMMUNI-
CATING?

Author and pastor's wife Colleen Townsend Evans has written, "Silence need not be awkward or embarrassing, for to be with one you love, without the need for words, is a beautiful and satisfying form of communication.

"I remember times when our children used to come running to me, all of them chattering at once about the events of their day—and it was wonderful to have them share their feelings with me. But there were also the times when they came to me wanting only to be held, to have me stroke their heads and caress them into sleep. And so it is, sometimes, with us and with God our Father."

Don't force your children to talk to you. Give them the respect and space to remain silent. Sometimes children need to work out their own ideas and opinions in quiet before voicing them. On the other hand, when they do talk, take time to listen intently, carefully, and kindly. In so doing, your children will know that they can talk to you whenever they want or need to, and you can rest assured that their silence is not rooted in suspicion or fear.

Communication goes far beyond words. We communicate to our children, and others, through our attitudes and actions as well.

———

People may doubt what you say, but
they will always believe what you do.

Entrance Exam

*Serve wholeheartedly, as if you were serving
the Lord, not men, because you know that
the Lord will reward everyone for whatever
good he does, whether he is slave or free.*

EPHESIANS 6:7-8 NIV

The order from the head teacher was abrupt: "The classroom needs sweeping. Take the broom and sweep it."

Young Booker T. Washington knew this was his chance. He swept the room three times and then dusted the furniture four times. When the head teacher came back to evaluate his work, she inspected the floor closely and then used her handkerchief to rub the woodwork around the walls, the table, and the student benches. When she could not find one speck of dust anywhere in the room, she said quietly, "I guess you will do to enter this institution."

Cleaning a classroom was Booker T. Washington's entrance examination to Hampton Institute in Virginia. In later years, he would recall this as the turning point in his life. He wrote in his autobiography, *Up from Slavery,* "I have passed several examinations since then, but I have always felt that this was the best one I ever passed."

Slacking off, goofing off, and dozing off rarely open doors of opportunity. Those doors are best opened and entered into by consistent, excellent effort. Give your family, your job, your world, and your God your best effort today!

*Opportunities are usually
disguised as hard work.*

What WILL
I SACRIFICE
TO GIVE GOD
MY BEST
EFFORTS?

Saints in Circulation

I beseech you therefore, brethren, by the mercies of God, that you present your bodies a living sacrifice, holy, acceptable to God, which is your reasonable service.

ROMANS 12:1

What AREA
OF MY LIFE
AM I
HOLDING
BACK FROM
GOD?

_____

_____

_____

_____

_____

_____

_____

_____

_____

_____

_____

_____

_____

_____

_____

During the reign of Oliver Cromwell, the British government ran low on the silver they used to make their coins. Lord Cromwell sent his men to a local cathedral in search of silver. "The only silver we could find is in the statues of the saints standing in the corners," they reported. "Good!" Cromwell replied, "We'll melt down the saints and put them into circulation."

Circulating melted-down saints? It's an unusual metaphor but good theology! The Lord never intended for us to be silver-plated, highly polished ornaments solely for liturgical use. He intends for us to give our all—our very life's blood, talent, sweat, resources, time, and, yes, silver—to wage war against evil in the trenches of life.

A man once prayed, "Lord, I want to be Your man, so I give You my money, my car, and my home." Then he added, "I bet it's been awhile since someone gave so much." The Lord replied, "No. Not really."

The Lord wants far more than our material possessions. He wants our hearts, our prayers, and our tears. He wants to be the object of our desire. The blood of Jesus can't be bought. It can only be received—by giving nothing less than our all.

───✺───

Beware of placing the emphasis on what prayer costs us; it cost God everything to make it possible for us to pray.

The Secret of His Happiness

Owe no one anything except to love one another, for he who loves another has fulfilled the law.

ROMANS 13:8

A fable is told of a young orphan boy who had no family and no one to love him. Feeling sad and lonely, he was walking through a meadow one day when he saw a small butterfly caught in a thorn bush. The more the butterfly struggled to free itself, the deeper the thorns cut into its fragile body. The boy carefully released the butterfly, but instead of flying away, right before his eyes the butterfly transformed into an angel.

The boy rubbed his eyes in disbelief as the angel said, "For your wonderful kindness, I will do whatever you would like." The little boy thought for a moment and then said, "I want to be happy!" The angel replied, "Very well," and then leaned toward him, whispered in his ear, and vanished.

As the little boy grew up, there was no one in the land as happy as he was. When people asked him the secret of his happiness, he would only smile and say, "I listened to an angel when I was a little boy."

On his deathbed, his neighbors rallied around him and asked him to divulge the key to his happiness before he died. The old man finally told them: "The angel told me that everyone, no matter how secure they seemed, no matter how old or young, how rich or poor, had need of me."

You have something to give to everyone with whom you come into contact today. It may be as simple as a friendly smile or a kind word. Whatever it is, know that you are needed by God to spread His love. There's not a person in the world who doesn't need it.

What CAN I DO TODAY TO SPREAD THE LOVE OF GOD?

The heart that loves is always young.

Little Annie

As he thinks in his heart, so is he.
"Eat and drink!" he says to you,
But his heart is not with you.

PROVERBS 23:7

How CAN I
POUR MYSELF
INTO OTHERS
TODAY?

A number of years ago, a young girl known as Little Annie was locked in the dungeon of a mental institution outside Boston—the only place, said the doctors, for the hopelessly insane. At times, Annie behaved like an animal, attacking anyone who came close to her cage. At other times, she just sat in a daze.

An elderly nurse held hope for all God's children, and she began taking her lunch break in the dungeon, just outside Little Annie's cage. She hoped to somehow communicate love to her. One day she left her dessert—a brownie— next to Annie's cage. There was no response from Annie, but the next day, the nurse found the brownie had been eaten. Every Thursday thereafter, she brought a brownie to Annie.

As the weeks passed, doctors noticed a change in Little Annie. After several months, they moved her upstairs. And eventually, the day came when this supposedly hopeless case was told she could return home. By that time, Annie was an adult, however, and she chose to stay at the institution to help others. One of those for whom she cared, taught, and nurtured was Helen Keller. Little Annie's full and proper name was Anne Sullivan.

Your children become the embodiment of the love you pour into them. Pour generously!

———

Children are likely to live up
to what you believe of them.

Listen

*I would know the words which He
would answer me, and understand
what He would say to me.*

JOB 23:5

One day, an old woman went to Anthony Bloom and told him that while she had recited the prayer of Jesus for many years, she had never really experienced the presence of God.

Bloom replied, "How can God get a word in edgeways if you never stop talking? Give Him a chance. Keep quiet."

"How can I do that?" she asked. He then gave her this advice, which he subsequently gave to many others. He advised her to tidy her room each day after breakfast, making it as pleasant as possible, and then sit down in a position where she could see the entire room, including the window that looked out on the garden. "When you have sat down, rest for a quarter of an hour in the presence of God, but take care not to pray," Bloom said. "Be as quiet as you can and as you obviously can't do nothing, knit before the Lord and tell me what happens." She returned several days later, happy to report that at long last she had felt the presence of God!

The Lord most often speaks gently—in a still, small voice—therefore, it takes a still, quiet heart to hear Him.

∞

If you would have God hear you when you pray, you must hear Him when He speaks.

What WILL
I GIVE UP
TO HEAR
THE VOICE
OF GOD?

Pea Soup Prayers

*Apply your heart to instruction, and
your ears to words of knowledge.*

PROVERBS 23:12

What PART
OF MY WILL
NEEDS TO BE
ABANDONED
IN ORDER
FOR GOD'S
WILL TO
TAKE
PRECEDENCE?

Many of us show up for prayer times with a long list of things that we want God to do for us. In addition, we often include instructions about how we want Him to accomplish these things.

Ruby Johnson has referred to such prayers as "pea soup prayers." She has said, "Curt taught us about 'pea soup prayers.' When he was in grade school, he walked home for lunch every day. As he walked, he would pray something like, 'Please Lord, don't let Mom fix pea soup today.'

"Why did he pray like that? The answer is probably obvious: He hated pea soup. No matter how hungry he was, a bowl of that 'green goop' just didn't appeal to him at all. He knew it was nutritious and good for him, but that did not change his view in the least. Nutritious or not, he wanted no part of pea soup."

According to Johnson, a "pea soup prayer" is when, "instead of allowing Him to intervene and solve the problem in His own way . . . we tell Him how to provide the solution. . . . [Curt] recognized God's superior abilities, but on the other hand he played the superior role by advising God. Absurd, isn't it?"

If we are praying for God's will to be done, we must first dismiss our own will from the room.

———⊗⊗⊗———

*Don't bother to give God instructions;
just report for duty.*

True Beauty

> *The LORD does not look at the things man looks at. Man looks at the outward appearance, but the LORD looks at the heart.*
>
> 1 SAMUEL 16:7 NIV

Many years ago, a boy was born in Russia who thought himself to be so ugly, he was certain there would be no happiness for him in life. He bemoaned the fact that he had a wide nose, thick lips, small gray eyes, and big hands and feet. He was so distraught about his ugliness, he asked God to work a miracle and turn him into a handsome man. He vowed that if God would do this, he would give Him all he possessed, as well as all he might possess in the future.

That Russian boy was Count Leo Tolstoy, one of the world's foremost twentieth-century authors, perhaps best known for his epic *War and Peace*. In one of his books, Tolstoy admits that through the years, he discovered that the beauty of physical appearance he had once sought was not the only beauty in life. Indeed, it was not the best beauty. Instead, Tolstoy came to regard the beauty of a strong character as the greatest beauty.

Today, so many people spend enormous sums of money on their physical appearance. Character, in contrast, is not a matter of money or beauty. It is a matter of doing what is right in spite of money and of standing up for what is right in spite of appearances.

It's still true and always will be—true beauty comes from the inside. Let your beauty shine today!

Beauty without virtue is like a flower with no perfume.

What PART OF MY CHARACTER IS THE MOST BEAUTIFUL? THE LEAST BEAUTIFUL?

Father Knows Best

The foolishness of God is wiser than men, and the weakness of God is stronger than men.

1 CORINTHIANS 1:25

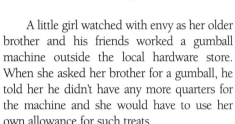

Have I EVER OVERLOOKED A BLESSING FROM GOD BECAUSE IT WASN'T WHAT I WAS LOOKING FOR?

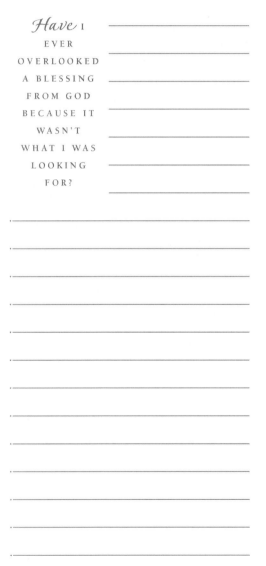

A little girl watched with envy as her older brother and his friends worked a gumball machine outside the local hardware store. When she asked her brother for a gumball, he told her he didn't have any more quarters for the machine and she would have to use her own allowance for such treats.

When her father arrived at home that evening, the little girl approached him to make her request, "Daddy, can I have a quarter?" Feeling generous, the father pulled out his wallet and offered his daughter a crisp new twenty-dollar bill.

Not realizing what the bill was, the little girl refused the paper money. As far as she was concerned, it was useless—it wouldn't fit into the gumball machine. She said, "No, I don't want that. I want a quarter."

Are there times when we deal with our heavenly Father as this little girl dealt with her father? Do we sometimes ask for some small favor, refusing His offer of a blessing that is a hundred times more valuable?

God may not answer our prayers precisely as we would desire, but we can know He will always answer our prayers in the way that is best for us.

———⊗⊗⊗———

God's answers are wiser than our prayers.

Trust Your Instruments

Your faith should not be in the wisdom
of men but in the power of God.

1 CORINTHIANS 2:5

Richard E. Byrd spent the winter of 1934 at Bolling Advance Weather Base in Antarctica, where the temperature ranged from minus fifty-eight degrees to minus seventy-six degrees Fahrenheit. By the time he was rescued, he was suffering from frostbite and carbon-monoxide poisoning. He wrote in his book, *Alone:* "I had hardly strength to move. I clung to the sleeping bag, which was the only source of comfort and warmth left to me, and mournfully debated the little that might be done.

"Two facts stood clear. One was that my chances of recovering were slim. The other was that in my weakness I was incapable of taking care of myself. But you must have faith—you must have faith in the outcome, I whispered to myself. It is like a flight . . . into another unknown. You start and you cannot turn back. You must go on . . . trusting your instruments, the course you have plotted."

With faith as his only guidance instrument, Byrd forced himself to do the necessary things for survival slowly and with great deliberation. At times he felt as if he were living a thousand years any given minute. But at each day's end, he could say he was still alive. And that was enough.

Sometimes the only thing left to do in an impossible situation is to press on in faith. God still makes the impossible possible!

———

Feed your faith and your doubts
will starve to death.

IS THERE AN AREA IN MY LIFE WHERE I HAVE STOPPED PRESSING ON?

Dial 911

*They caused the cry of the poor
to come to Him; for He hears
the cry of the afflicted.*

JOB 34:28

IS THERE
ANYTHING
THAT KEEPS
ME FROM
FULLY
TRUSTING
IN THE ALL-
KNOWING
GOD?

In recent years, nearly every community in the United States has been equipped with a 911 emergency phone system. The newest versions of this system are state of the art. All a person has to do is dial those three numbers to be instantly connected to a dispatcher.

The dispatcher's computer screen identifies the number from which the call is being made, the address, and the name under which the telephone number is listed. The system is simultaneously connected to the police department, fire department, and paramedics. A person using the 911 system doesn't even need to utter a word in order for help to be activated and dispatched to the scene.

God has His own 911 system—a system more foolproof, fail-safe, and faithful than anything man could ever hope to design. When we send up 911 prayers, we are sometimes hysterical, or we don't know the right words to convey our deepest needs. But God hears. He already knows our name and all about our circumstances. He knows the precise answer to our prayer even before we voice it. His help is on the way the moment we turn to Him.

*When we depend on man, we get
what man can do; when we depend
on prayer, we get what God can do.*

Life Is a Gift, Not a Right

If they obey and serve Him, they
shall spend their days in prosperity,
and their years in pleasures.

JOB 36:11

At age fourteen, Andrea Jaeger won her first professional tennis tournament. At eighteen, she reached the finals at Wimbledon. Then at nineteen, a bad shoulder problem all but ended her career. Many a world-class athlete may have become bitter or discontented with life at that point. Jaeger, however, turned her competitive spirit to a new endeavor—a nonprofit organization called Kids' Stuff Foundation that attempts to bring joy to children suffering from cancer and other life-threatening illnesses. Her work there also has inspired her to take correspondence courses in nursing and child psychology.

Jaeger not only created the program, but runs it full-time, year-round, unpaid. "I'm inspired by these brave kids, and humbled," she has said. "They lose their health, their friends, and sometimes their lives. And yet their spirit never wavers. They look at life as a gift. The rest of us sometimes look at ourselves as a gift to life."

"You get very spoiled on the tour," she adds with a twinkle in her eye. "The courtesy cars, the five-star hotels, the thousands of people clapping for you when you hit a good shot. It's easy to forget what's important in life. . . . I forget it a lot less lately."

Today, remember that your life is a gift. Your children are a gift. Your spouse is a gift. Your extended family and friends are a gift. And don't miss the other gifts God sends your way—those in need. The opportunity to make a difference in someone's life is truly a gift from God.

Whom CAN I GIVE THE GIFT OF MY LIFE TO TODAY?

~∞~

The secret of contentment is the
realization that life is a gift, not a right.

Maintaining Love

Serve the LORD with gladness; come
before His presence with singing.
PSALM 100:2

What
ACTS CAN I
DO TODAY
THAT WILL
COMPLEMENT
ANOTHER'S
TALENTS?

A woman once went away on a long weekend retreat with a group of women from her church. About halfway through the final session, she suddenly jumped to her feet and left the room. Concerned, a friend followed her to see what had caused her to leave the meeting so abruptly. She found her friend just as she was hanging up a telephone in the lobby.

"Is everything all right?" she asked urgently.

"Oh, yes," the woman responded. "I didn't mean to cause you alarm." A bit sheepishly, she added, "I suddenly remembered that it's Monday morning—trash day."

"Trash day? Your husband is still at home. Surely. . . ."

"Yes," the woman interrupted, "but it takes two of us to put out the trash. I can't carry it. And he can't remember it."

Marriages are meant to be complementary—two pulling together as one, not in competition, but in mutual association. Learning how to work and live together is the best way to maintain love.

———✺———

A marriage may be made in Heaven, but
the maintenance must be done on earth.

Seeds of Self-Respect

*Do you not know that your body is
the temple of the Holy Spirit
who is in you?*

1 CORINTHIANS 6:19

A businessman hurriedly plunked a dollar into the cup of a man who was selling flowers on a street corner and rushed away. Half a block down the street, he suddenly whirled about and made his way back to the beggar. "I'm sorry," he said, picking out a flower from the bunch that the beggar had in a canister beside him. "In my haste I failed to make my purchase. After all, you are a businessman just like me. Your merchandise is fairly priced and of good quality. I trust you won't be upset with my failure to take more care in my purchase." And with that, the businessman smiled and walked away, flower in hand.

At lunch a few weeks later, the business-man was approached by a neatly dressed, well-groomed man who introduced himself and then said, "I'm sure you don't remember me, and I don't even know your name, but your face is one I will never forget. You are the man who inspired me to make something of myself. I was a vagrant selling wilted flowers until you gave me back my self-respect. Now I believe I am a businessman."

Self-respect is vital to every person. Purpose in your heart to build up the respect and self-esteem of others. In so doing, you'll be building more respect for yourself!

———⟨∞∞⟩———

*Those who deserve love
the least need it the most.*

Whom CAN I BUILD UP THE SELF-RESPECT OF TODAY?

Standing in the Gap

The LORD restored Job's losses when he prayed for his friends. Indeed the LORD gave Job twice as much as he had before.

JOB 42:10

Whom CAN
I PRAY
FOR TODAY?

A young woman lay in a hospital, far from home and family, drifting in and out of consciousness. Several times she became aware of a woman's voice praying for her salvation, as well as for her physical healing. At one point, a physician described her condition as critical, warning those present in the room that she might not survive. She heard all of this as if she were in a stupor, unable to respond. Then she heard a second voice, one that spoke in faith: "Doctor, I respect what you say, but I cannot accept it. I've been praying and I believe she will not only recover, but she will walk out of here and live for God."

Before long, the young woman did walk out of that hospital and return to work. It was then she learned that it had been her boss' wife (whom she had met only twice) who had stood in the gap, interceding for her at her hospital bed. When she attempted to thank this woman for her prayers, she replied, "Don't thank me, thank God. Others have prayed for me. Their prayers changed my life. I believe God has great plans for you."

It was five more years before she gave her life to Christ, but all the while, she never forgot how a faithful woman of God had believed He would answer prayer.

Have the prayers of another brought about a change in your life? Be assured—your prayers for others will, too!

Prayer changes everything:
It changes the one who prays,
and it changes the one prayed for.

Search Me, O God

Hear my prayer, O Lord,
and let my cry come to You.

PSALM 102:1

One day during her morning devotions, Jeannie found herself weeping as she read Psalm 139:23: "Search me, O God, and know my heart." She cried out to the Lord to cleanse her of several bad attitudes she had been harboring. Later that morning as she boarded an airplane, she sensed God asking her, "Are you ready?" She had a strong feeling that God was confirming to her that He had forgiven her and could now use her for a special assignment. She whispered a prayer, "Lord, help me to stay awake."

Jeannie usually took motion-sickness medication before flying, and therefore, often slept from takeoff to landing. On this flight, however, she forced herself to stay awake. A woman took the seat next to her, and as they began to talk, the woman asked, "Why do you have so much joy?" Jeannie replied, "Because of Jesus." And for the next three hours, she had a wonderful opportunity to witness to the woman. Later, she sent her a Bible, and they exchanged letters. Then late one evening, the woman called, and Jeannie led her to the Lord over the phone.

God will not only hear your heart's cry today, but His answer will bring a blessing to your life that you will be able to share with others.

Prayer is the wing wherewith
the soul flies to Heaven.

What ATTITUDES DO I NEED GOD TO CLEANSE ME OF?

The Common Law of Life

Do you not know that those who run in a race all run, but one receives the prize? Run in such a way that you may obtain it.

1 CORINTHIANS 9:24

What PROBLEMS WILL I CONSIDER TO BE "GROWING ASSISTANCE" FROM GOD?

The tree that never had to fight
For sun and sky and air and light,
That stood out in the open plain
And always got its share of rain,
Never became a forest king,
But lived and died a common thing.
The man who never had to toil,
Who never had to win his share
Of sun and sky and light and air,
Never became a manly man,
But lived and died as he began.
Good timber does not grow on ease
The stronger wind, the tougher trees,
The farther sky, the greater length,
By sun and cold, by rain and snows,
In tree or man good timber grows.
Where thickest stands the forest growth,
We find the patriarchs of both,
And they hold converse with the stars
Whose broken branches show the scars
Of many winds and much of strife,
This is the common law of life.

—Anonymous

You may have to fight a battle more than once to win it.

Unexpected Beauty

He has made everything beautiful in its time.
Also He has put eternity in their hearts,
except that no one can find out the work
that God does from beginning to end.

ECCLESIASTES 3:11

Karen had been volunteered to take some Christmas gifts to the children's home for the mentally handicapped. Her plan was to drop them at the door and be on her way. Places "like that" made her uncomfortable.

She put down the packages, but before she could make her getaway, a voice called out behind her, "Oh thank you so much!" It was a middle-aged woman with a name tag that read "Lily" and who wore nurse-type shoes. Karen explained who she was and where the gifts were from, keeping one eye on the clock and the other on the door.

Lily seemed unaware of Karen's exaggerated hurry. She invited Karen to take part in giving the children their gifts. Karen wasn't sure she could bear to witness such pitiful little people in the midst of such a festive season.

Going from room to room, the ice and fear in Karen's heart began to melt. She did have to clean up a few messes, but she also saw happy, shining eyes and grateful hearts beneath the confusion and curiosity.

On her way out, she noticed the sign by the door: "God makes everything beautiful in its time" and said, "I wouldn't have believed this sign before because I thought of these children as pitiful and even, I'm ashamed to say, ugly. But now that I've spent time with them, I know I have truly seen the beauty that only God can create."

Lily just smiled an understanding smile, for Karen was not the first to have her heart won with surprise by what God makes beautiful.

What
UNLOVELY
CIRCUM-
STANCES IN
MY LIFE HAS
GOD MADE
BEAUTIFUL?

It's not your outlook but
your "uplook" that counts.

Visualization

I applied my heart to know, to search and seek out wisdom and the reason of things, to know the wickedness of folly, even of foolishness and madness.

ECCLESIASTES 7:25

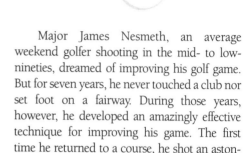

What

GOALS DO I HAVE THAT WOULD BENEFIT FROM VISUALIZING SUCCESS?

_____

_____

_____

_____

_____

_____

_____

_____

_____

_____

_____

_____

_____

_____

_____

Major James Nesmeth, an average weekend golfer shooting in the mid- to low-nineties, dreamed of improving his golf game. But for seven years, he never touched a club nor set foot on a fairway. During those years, however, he developed an amazingly effective technique for improving his game. The first time he returned to a course, he shot an astonishing seventy-four! He had cut twenty strokes off his average.

What was his secret? Visualization. For seven years, Major Nesmeth was a prisoner of war in North Vietnam. He was imprisoned in a cage 4 ½ feet high and 5 feet long. Most of those years, he saw no one, talked to no one, and had no physical activity. He knew he had to find some way to occupy his mind, or he would lose his sanity, so he began to visualize playing golf. Each day, he played eighteen holes at the imaginary country club of his dreams. He imagined every detail . . . every shot. And not once did he miss a shot or putt. Seven days a week, four hours a day, he played eighteen holes in his mind.

Your dreams for the future will be much more likely to come true if you visualize your goals and imagine reaching them. You will be training your mind to produce successful thoughts and ideas.

———⟨⟨⟩⟩———

On the clarity of your ideas depends the scope of your success in any endeavor.

Investing the Best

Whatever your hand finds to do,
do it with your might; for there is no
work or device or knowledge or wisdom
in the grave where you are going.

ECCLESIASTES 9:10

On a December evening in 1995, the employees of Malden Mills in Lawrence, Massachusetts, thought their jobs had gone up in smoke. The mill had been destroyed by fire. But when morning came, the company leader, Aaron Feuerstein, told his more than three thousand employees that he had decided to rebuild—immediately. Not only that, he intended to keep everyone on the payroll for thirty days. That decision cost him millions of dollars a week.

It was not the first time Feuerstein had disregarded the obvious. When other textile mills in the area moved south to take advantage of lower taxes and cheaper labor, Feuerstein felt he had a responsibility to the people he employed and stayed put.

When paychecks were handed out two days after the fire, each employee received a Christmas bonus and a note from the boss that read, "Do not despair. God bless each of you."

By January 2, the mill had reopened, and within ninety days, 75 percent of the workers were back on the job. Experts had said it could never be done. The mill was able to fill 80 percent of its orders in spite of the fire. Feuerstein's investment in his employees had been returned to him in miracle-working effort and loyalty.

When we give our best to others, we inspire them to give their best in return.

What "BEST" IN MYSELF WILL I GIVE TO OTHERS TODAY?

The gent who wakes up and finds
himself a success hasn't been asleep.

Experiencing Leadership

My son, eat honey because it is good, and the honeycomb which is sweet to your taste; so shall the knowledge of wisdom be to your soul; if you have found it, there is a prospect, and your hope will not be cut off.

PROVERBS 24:13-14

What AREAS OF MY LIFE DO I CONSIDER MYSELF TO BE A LEADER IN?

Earl Reum has written these thought-inspiring words about experience:

"I wish you could know how it feels 'to run' with all your heart and lose—horribly!

"I wish that you could achieve some great good for mankind, but have nobody know about it except for you.

"I wish you could find something so worthwhile that you deem it worthy of investing your life within it.

"I hope you become frustrated and challenged enough to begin to push back the very barriers of your own personal limitations.

"I hope you make a stupid mistake and get caught red-handed and are big enough to say those magic words: 'I was wrong.'

"I hope you give so much of yourself that some days you wonder if it's worth all the effort.

"I wish for you a magnificent obsession that will give you reason for living and purpose and direction and life.

"I wish for you the worst kind of everything you do, because that makes you fight to achieve beyond what you normally would.

"I wish you the experience of leadership."

———⁂———

Do not follow where the path may lead—go instead where there is no path and leave a trail.

Starting Over

*A righteous man may fall seven
times and rise again, but the
wicked shall fall by calamity.*

PROVERBS 24:16

In 1991, Anne Busquet was general manager of the Optima Card division for American Express. When five of her two thousand employees were found to have hidden $24 million in losses, she was held accountable. Busquet had to face the fact that, because she was an intense perfectionist, she apparently came across as intimidating and confrontational to her subordinates—so much so, they were more willing to lie than to report bad news to her!

Busquet lost her Optima job, but was given a second chance by American Express— an opportunity to salvage one of its smaller businesses. Her self-esteem shaken, she nearly turned down the offer. However, she decided this was her chance to improve the way she related to others. She took on the new job as a personal challenge to change.

Realizing she had to be much more understanding, she began to work on being more patient and listening more carefully and intently. She learned to solicit bad news in a reassuring way.

Four years after she was removed from her previous position, Anne Busquet was promoted to an executive vice-president position at American Express.

Failure is not the end; it is a teacher for a new beginning and a better life!

❧

*Failure isn't falling down.
It's staying down.*

What AREAS
OF FAILURE IN
MY LIFE CAN I
LEARN FROM?

The Power of a Hug

Scarcely had I passed by them,
When I found the one I love.
SONG OF SOLOMON 3:4

Who IN MY
LIFE CAN
BENEFIT
FROM MY
TOUCH
TODAY?

Our ability to become emotionally involved with and vulnerable to others is directly related to our having been stroked, caressed, and cuddled as children. We learn how to give and receive affection from the tender models in our lives. We learn security from the warmth of being held close.

Before birth, a baby is enveloped in the soft, warm embrace of the womb. After birth, a child who is not touched and cuddled will form a bond with anything it can touch, even a stuffed toy. If all human contact is denied, the baby will die.

Our need for touch continues throughout our lifetime. In fact, our body chemistry changes when we are physically close to another person. When a person is touched, the amount of hemoglobin in the blood—which carries oxygen and helps prevent disease and speed recovery from illness—increases significantly. In one animal study, rabbits that were held close and stroked often developed less hardening of the arteries than those rabbits that were deprived of touch.

You've heard the question a thousand times, but it bears repeating: Have you hugged your child today?

Children spell "love" . . . T-I-M-E.

Love Never Fails

[Love] bears all things, believes
all things, hopes all things,
endures all things. Love never fails.

1 CORINTHIANS 13:7-8

Napoleon went to school in Brienne, France, with a young man named Demasis, who greatly admired him. After Napoleon quelled the mob in Paris and served at Toulon, his authority was stripped from him, and he became penniless. We rarely think of Napoleon as struggling through hard times. However, with thoughts of suicide, he proceeded toward a bridge to throw himself into the waters below. On the way, he met his old friend Demasis, who asked him what was troubling him.

Napoleon told him bluntly that he was without money, his mother was in need, and he despaired of his situation ever changing. "Oh, if that is all," Demasis said, "take this; it will supply your wants." He put a pouch of gold into his hands and walked away. Normally Napoleon would have never taken such a handout, but that night he did, and his hope was renewed.

When Napoleon came to power, he sought far and wide to thank his friend and promote him, but he never found him. It was rumored that Demasis lived and served in one of Napoleon's own armies, but never revealed his true identity. He was content to quietly serve in support of the leader he admired.

Sometimes our simple words or deeds can make all the difference in the world to someone who doesn't know where to turn. Sometimes the opportunities God sends your way are so simple they could easily be missed. Today, keep your eyes, ears, and heart open.

What OPPORTUNI-
TIES WILL I
PRAY GOD
WILL SEND
MY WAY?

A good man makes no noise over
a good deed, but passes on to another
as a vine to bear grapes again in season.

Show Me How to Live

What is the conclusion then? I will pray with the spirit, and I will also pray with the understanding. I will sing with the spirit, and I will also sing with the understanding.

1 CORINTHIANS 14:15

What

"HOPELESS"
SITUATION
WILL I
TURN OVER
TO GOD?

Joni Eareckson Tada lives such an inspirational life of ministry today that it is often difficult for others to accept the fact that in the wake of her paralyzing accident, Joni experienced nearly three years of depression and suicidal despair. She finally reached the point where she prayed, "God, if I can't die, show me how to live, please!"

Things didn't change for Joni overnight, but they did begin to change. Her situation changed little, but her outlook—her attitude, her mind, her perspective, her spirit—began to change and grow. She knew with an increasing assurance that God would help her learn how to do what seemed to be impossible: handle life in a wheelchair.

Are you facing a seemingly impossible situation today? Do you feel as if any option you might have is really no option at all? Perhaps it's time to pray, "God, show me how to live in the midst of this situation." Accepting God's help in coping with the despair and hopelessness of a situation is often the first step God uses in preparing us to live a new way—a way that is far beyond mere coping. His way is always one of true fulfillment and joy.

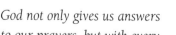

*God not only gives us answers
to our prayers, but with every
answer gives us something of Himself.*

Knowing God

"Come now, and let us reason together," says the LORD, "though your sins are like scarlet, they shall be as white as snow; though they are red like crimson, they shall be as wool."

ISAIAH 1:18

At times, we are tempted to think that because we are Christians, read our Bibles, and know a great deal about God, we know God. Nothing could be further from the truth. The only way we can know God is by experiencing Him. Many of those experiences come in prayer as we listen quietly. It is then that we can truly hear God whispering in our hearts.

Søren Kierkegaard noted that most of us are so busy that we are unwilling to wait patiently for God. We might consider an appointment with a hairdresser to be inviolable, but when God lays claim to our time, we balk. Rather than spend time with God and allow ourselves to bask in His presence and soak up His love, we manufacture substitutes—things to do to take the place of simply being with Him. We offer praise, do good works, memorize Bible verses—all good activities, but unequal to resting quietly before Him.

The highest value of prayer is found in developing a relationship with God. That takes both our time and our willingness to receive from Him. There is no substitute for either.

The value of persistent prayer is not that He will hear us . . . but that we will finally hear Him.

What AM I WILLING TO GIVE UP IN ORDER TO TRULY EXPERIENCE GOD?

Old Friends

Prepare your outside work,
Make it fit for yourself in the field;
And afterward build your house.

PROVERBS 24:27

How CAN I
REARRANGE
MY SCHEDULE
IN ORDER
TO HELP
SOMEONE
ELSE?

_____

Every word and deed of a parent is
a fiber woven into the character of a
child that ultimately determines how
that child fits into the fabric of society.

All of their lives, Mary and Walt worked hard. One would have thought they'd be ready to relax when they hit retirement years. They had good health, sufficient income, a home and cars that were paid for, and children who were happily married and self-sufficient. "You ought to travel some," their friends advised them. But Mary's response was always, "What would our old friends do?"

Mary and Walt's "old friends" were several elderly neighbors who lived nearby. Mary was in the habit of getting up at five in the morning and making her rounds, helping these neighbors with their showers and breakfasts. Then in the afternoon, she and Walt would return to help them with laundry, housework, and grocery shopping. In the evenings, Mary would bake bread and make casseroles to take to her neighbors. "Old people need someone to help them so they can stay in their own homes," Mary would tell her concerned friends. "Mother always said to me, 'Go see if Mrs. So-and-so needs anything.' And that's still what I'm doing! I'd feel bad if something happened to one of these old people because I failed to help them."

"But Mary," her friends protested, "your 'old' people are in their late seventies. You're eighty-three!"

You're never too old (or too young) to help someone. Model this principle for your children, like Mary's mother did. There's nothing so rewarding in life as helping someone else. Give the gift of compassion to your children, and they will pass it to their children.

Working for Your Dreams

My beloved brethren, be steadfast, immovable, always abounding in the work of the Lord, knowing that your labor is not in vain in the Lord.

1 CORINTHIANS 15:58

All her life, Veronica worked in jobs that served other people but gave her little personal satisfaction. As a young girl, she missed a lot of school to take care of her younger siblings and help with the family business. Consequently, she never learned to read.

After getting married, she worked as a cook in a restaurant, memorizing ingredient labels and recipes to conceal her illiteracy. Every day she lived in fear of making a mistake, while dreaming of one day being able to read.

Then, a serious illness put Veronica in the hospital, and she spent an extended period at home in recovery. Her health improved some, but not enough for her to go back to work. She saw this time as her opportunity to learn to read and enrolled in an adult reading program.

Veronica's new reading skills boosted her self-confidence, and she became involved in her church and in organizing community activities. Eventually, she wrote a prize-winning cookbook and became a local celebrity.

While working hard wherever she found herself, Veronica never let go of her dream. In the end, her dreams were realized far beyond her imagination!

Where you are may not be where you want to be, but the Bible says that if you're faithful in the small things, God will make you ruler over bigger things. (See Matthew 25:21.) It also has been said, "Diligence is the mother of all good fortune."

What SMALL THINGS WILL I GIVE MY ATTENTION TO TODAY?

Be like a postage stamp— stick to one thing 'till you get there.

Success Takes Wisdom

Wisdom is the principal thing;
therefore get wisdom. And in
all your getting, get understanding.
PROVERBS 4:7

In WHAT
AREAS OF
MY LIFE DO
I NEED GOD
TO GIVE ME
WISDOM?

Charles Goodyear had no formal education. At the age of twenty-one, he went into partnership with his father in a hardware business that soon failed. It was the first of many losses. Failure and poverty characterized much of his life, and more than once, he spent time in debtor's prison. His family frequently existed on the charity of neighbors. Six of his twelve children died in infancy. By the time he was forty, his health was poor. He could not get around without the aid of crutches.

Most of Goodyear's troubles stemmed from his obsession with rubber. He had a fanatical determination to transform raw rubber into a useful material. To pursue his experiments, he sold his watch, the living-room furniture, and the dishes off the table. Even while in jail, he experimented with rubber, trying to discover its unique properties and mold it to his satisfaction.

Quite by accident, he stumbled upon the process of vulcanizing rubber when he dropped a piece of the material that had been treated with sulfur on a hot stove. He refined this process, which opened the development of an entire industry. While he might have amassed a fortune, his own bad judgment resulted in a pauper's death.

It takes more than effort and goals to gain and keep success. It also takes wisdom.

———∞∞∞———

Lasting success rarely comes to
those who do not first decide to succeed.

Why to Live

> *Who can utter the mighty acts of the
> LORD? Who can declare all His praise?*
>
> PSALM 106:2

During World War II, the Nazis stripped Victor Frankl of everything he owned after his arrest. He arrived at Auschwitz with only his manuscript—a book he had been researching and writing for years—sewn into the lining of his coat. Upon arrival, even that was taken from him. He later wrote, "I had to undergo and overcome the loss of my spiritual child. . . . It seemed as if nothing and no one would survive me. I found myself confronted with the question of whether under such circumstances my life was ultimately void of any meaning."

Days later, the Nazis forced the prisoners to give up their clothes. In return, Frankl was given the rags of an inmate who had been sent to the gas chamber. In the pocket of the garment, he found a torn piece of paper—a page from a Hebrew prayer book. On it was the foremost Jewish prayer, "Shema Yisrael," which begins, "Hear, O Israel! The Lord our God is one God."

Frankl says, "How should I have interpreted such a 'coincidence' other than as a challenge to live my thoughts instead of merely putting them on paper?" He later wrote in his classic masterpiece, *Man's Search for Meaning*, "He who has a why to live for can bear almost any how."

What IS MY
"WHY" TO
LIVE FOR?

*A coincidence is a small miracle where
God prefers to remain anonymous.*

261

No Limits

Behold, God is my salvation, I will trust and not be afraid; "For YAH, the LORD, is my strength and song; He also has become my salvation."

ISAIAH 12:2

What IS
HINDERING
ME FROM
BEING ALL
GOD CREATED
ME TO BE?

_____

_____

_____

_____

_____

_____

_____

_____

_____

_____

_____

_____

_____

_____

_____

_____

As a senior in high school, Jim batted .427 and led his team in home runs. He also quarterbacked the football team to the state semifinals. Later, Jim went on to pitch professionally for the New York Yankees.

That's a remarkable achievement for any athlete. But it's an almost unbelievable one for Jim, because he was born without a right hand.

Once a little boy who had only parts of two fingers on one of his hands came to Jim in the clubhouse after a Yankees game and said, "They call me crab at camp. Did kids ever tease you?"

"Yeah," Jim replied. "Kids used to tell me that my hand looked like a foot." And then he asked the boy an all-important question, "Is there anything you can't do?" The boy wisely answered, "No."

"Well, I don't think so either," Jim responded.

What others see as your limitation is only a limitation if you think it is. God certainly doesn't see you as limited; He sees you as having unlimited potential. When you begin to see yourself the way God sees you, there truly are no limits to what you can do!

―――――∞∞∞―――――

If God be your partner, make your plans large.

Transformation

We all, with unveiled face, beholding as in a mirror the glory of the Lord, are being transformed into the same image from glory to glory, just as by the Spirit of the Lord.

2 CORINTHIANS 3:18

Two friends, who loved men with deep-seated problems, decided to meet weekly to fast and pray. Over the weeks and months that followed, they prayed for every possible cause that could have contributed to their loved one's difficulties—from physiology to prenatal memories, from early childhood experiences to lack of ability to communicate, and from physical problems to addictions. One of the women said, "We were praying for a total healing in their lives. Looking back, I realize we were also asking God to transform them into the men we thought they should be and which we genuinely thought God wanted them to be."

After nearly a year, both of the women thought they had prayed all they could and must then trust God. "Nothing happened to improve our relationships," one of the women said. "Both men went their own way and we know of no change in their attitudes or behavior. What did happen was that my friend and I were transformed. We were healed of broken hearts and shattered dreams. We had our faith renewed and our hope restored. God surely will work in their lives, but the real miracle happened in us!"

When we pray for change in others, we may not get what we expect. As a result of spending time with God and caring for others enough to spend time praying on their behalf, we are changed.

In WHAT AREAS OF MY LIFE DO I NEED GOD TO HELP ME TO CHANGE?

Prayer does not change God, but changes him who prays.

Preparing for Eternity

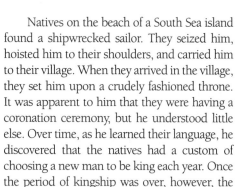

Our light affliction, which is but for a moment, is working for us a far more exceeding and eternal weight of glory.

2 CORINTHIANS 4:17

What IS
KEEPING
ME FROM
FOCUSING
ON GOD'S
ULTIMATE
GOAL FOR
MY LIFE?

Natives on the beach of a South Sea island found a shipwrecked sailor. They seized him, hoisted him to their shoulders, and carried him to their village. When they arrived in the village, they set him upon a crudely fashioned throne. It was apparent to him that they were having a coronation ceremony, but he understood little else. Over time, as he learned their language, he discovered that the natives had a custom of choosing a new man to be king each year. Once the period of kingship was over, however, the man was banished to a nearby island where he starved to death.

Not particularly looking forward to this outcome, the sailor decided to take full advantage of his position as king. Rather than sitting around idle and being waited upon, he put his carpenters to work making boats, his farmers to work transplanting trees and growing crops, and his masons to work building houses on the nearby island. When the year was over and he was exiled, the formerly barren island had become an abundant paradise.

As you live your life here on earth, never lose sight of eternity. Remember that with each trial or affliction through which you walk with God's grace, you are adding to your future glory.

Don't wait for your ship to come in;
swim out to it.

Buzzards and Bees

A word fitly spoken is like apples
of gold in settings of silver.

PROVERBS 25:11

Buzzards and bees have a major difference in their feeding habits. Buzzards fly overhead searching for dead animals. When they spy a decaying carcass, they swoop down to gorge themselves on it, stripping it to the bare bones. Honeybees, by comparison, look for the sweetest nectar. They are discriminating as they search through the flowers in a garden.

Buzzards produce nothing, except fear in those who behold them at work. Honeybees produce honeycombs, dripping with honey, for the health and delight of others.

Just as the bees and buzzards always find what they are seeking, so a spouse can generally find what he or she is looking for. If you focus on your partner's faults and mistakes, you'll find them. Your relationship will become one to be avoided, not cherished. On the other hand, if you seek out the goodness in your spouse, you can find that, too! And you may be surprised at how sweet your relationship can become.

Unlike buzzards and bees, creatures that cannot choose their own instincts and behavior, we have a choice in what we elect to perceive and comment upon. Choose affirmation and virtue.

———❦———

Good words are worth much and cost little.

What
VIRTUES CAN
I FIND IN THE
PERSON WHO
IS CLOSEST
TO ME?

By Kindness

By purity, by knowledge, by longsuffering, by kindness, by the Holy Spirit, by sincere love.

2 CORINTHIANS 6:6

How CAN
I BE A
KINDNESS
GIVER
TODAY?

After two years of marriage, Pete no longer saw his wife as interesting, fun, or attractive. In his mind, he regarded her as an overweight, sloppy housekeeper with a faultfinding personality. He visited a divorce attorney, who advised him, "Pete, if you really want to get even with your wife, start treating her like a queen! Do everything in your power to serve her, please her, and make her feel special. Then, after a couple of months of this royal treatment, pack your bags and leave. That way you'll disappoint her as much as she has disappointed you." Pete could hardly wait to enact the plan! He picked up a dozen roses on his way home, helped his wife with the dinner dishes, brought her breakfast in bed, and began complimenting her on her clothes, cooking, and housekeeping. He even treated her to an out-of-town trip.

After three months, the attorney called and said, "Well, I have the divorce papers ready for you to sign. In a matter of minutes, you can be a happy bachelor."

"Are you crazy?" Pete said. "My wife has made so many changes that I wouldn't think of divorcing her now!"

Kindness extended toward another person may or may not change the other person, but it certainly changes the perspective of the kindness giver!

Kindness is the oil that takes the friction out of life.

Tool of Togetherness

Since we have these promises, dear friends,
let us purify ourselves from everything
that contaminates body and spirit,
perfecting holiness out of reverence for God.

2 CORINTHIANS 7:1 NIV

Many years ago, Sheila watched from her window as her neighbor tried to train a new pup to walk on a leash. Pulling and pushing and straining to run, that pup had no idea of what walking on a leash was all about. Through the days and weeks that followed, the pup slowly learned what was expected of him. Sheila's neighbor spent time each day with the dog to practice its skills.

More recently, Sheila has watched her neighbor bring out the leash and the now-aging, adult dog. The leash seemed almost a redundancy. It seemed now that the dog was pleased and happy to stay by his master's side and walk together with him. What had once been a restriction of obedience had become a tool of togetherness.

That is how it is with us as we obey God. At first we feel restricted in conforming our will to His. But after years of alternately trusting and straining at His presence, our obedience is rewarded by a sense of closeness to Him. We can then rejoice as He leads us through life.

You can accomplish more in one hour
with God than one lifetime without Him.

Are THERE ANY AREAS OF MY LIFE IN WHICH I AM NOT TOTALLY OBEDIENT TO GOD?

Winning Friends

Love your neighbor as yourself.
MATTHEW 22:39 NIV

Who NEEDS
ME TO TRULY
LISTEN TO
THEM TODAY?

*God has given each of us one
tongue and two ears that we may
hear twice as much as we speak.*

Dale Carnegie, author of *How to Win Friends and Influence People,* is considered one of the greatest friend winners of the century. He taught, "You can make more friends in two months by becoming interested in other people than you can in two years by trying to get other people interested in you."

To illustrate, Carnegie would relate how dogs have learned the fine art of making friends better than most people. He would point out that when you get within ten feet of a friendly dog, it will begin to wag its tail, a visible sign that the dog welcomes and enjoys your presence. If you take time to pet the dog, it will become excited, lick you, and jump all over you to show how much it appreciates you. The dog became man's best friend by being genuinely interested in people.

One of the foremost ways, of course, in which we show our interest in others is to listen to them—to ask questions, pay attention to their answers, and ask further questions based upon what they say. The person who feels heard is likely to seek out the friendly listener again and again and to count that person as a great friend.

If you feel alone and in need of friendship, learn how to listen. If you sow the seeds of friendship by listening, you'll reap a harvest of friendship and an available ear when you really need it.

He'll Catch You

The eternal God is your refuge, and
underneath are the everlasting arms.

DEUTERONOMY 33:27

When Walter Wangerin was a boy, he told all of his friends that his father was the strongest man alive. Then came the day when Wally climbed to the top of the backyard cherry tree. A storm blew up suddenly, and Wally was trapped. Wind ripped through the tree with such velocity that it was all Wally could do to hang on to a branch about ten feet above the ground. "Daddy!" he shouted, and instantly his father appeared. "Jump," he yelled. "Jump, and I'll catch you."

Wally was frozen in fear. His big, strong dad looked quite small and frail down there on the ground, two skinny arms reaching out to catch him. Wally thought, *If I jump and Dad doesn't catch me, I'll hit the ground and die!* "No!" he screamed back. At that moment, the limb Wally was clinging to cracked at the trunk. Wally surrendered. He didn't jump—he fell—straight into his dad's ready arms. Crying and trembling, Wally wrapped his arms and legs around his father. Dad was strong after all. Up to that point, it had only been a theory. Now, it was a reality to him.

Prayer is about surrendering our will to God's will, yielding our strength to God's strength, giving up our desires to take on God's desires, and surrendering when He asks us to jump into His waiting arms.

⸺⸺◦∞∞◦⸺⸺

Just when I need Him, He is my all,
answering when upon Him I call;
tenderly watching lest I should fall.

Are THERE AREAS OF MY WILL THAT NEED TO BE SURRENDERED TO GOD?

269

The Thundering Legion

*The weapons of our warfare are
not carnal but mighty in God for
pulling down strongholds.*

2 CORINTHIANS 10:4

ISN THERE A
SITUATION IN
MY LIFE THAT
I HAVE TRIED
TO HANDLE
INSTEAD OF
ALLOWING
GOD TO
HANDLE IT?

The Militine Legion was one of the two most famous legions in the Roman army. It was also known as the Thundering Legion. Emperor Marcus Aurelius bestowed the nickname on his men in AD 176, during a military campaign against the Germans.

In their march northward, precipitous mountains occupied by their enemies encircled the Romans. In addition, due to a drought, they were tormented by great thirst. Then a member of the Praetorian Guard informed the emperor that the Militine Legion was made up of Christians who believed in the power of prayer. Although he himself had been a great persecutor of the Church, the emperor said, "Let them pray then." The soldiers bowed on the ground and earnestly sought God to deliver them in the name of Jesus Christ.

They had scarcely risen from their knees when a great thunderstorm arose. The storm drove their enemies from their strongholds and into the Romans' arms, where they pleaded for mercy. The storm also provided water to drink and ended the drought. The emperor renamed them the Thundering Legion and subsequently abated some of his persecution of the Christians in Rome.

Let prayer be your first resort, instead of your last. Prayer and deliverance go hand in hand!

*We possess a divine artillery that silences
the enemy and inflicts upon him the
damage he would inflict upon us.*

My Left Foot

Shall the thing made say of him who made it,
"He did not make me"? Or shall the thing formed say
of him who formed it, "He has no understanding"?

ISAIAH 29:16

Christy Brown was born in Ireland in 1932 and was raised in a Dublin slum. Born with a severe form of cerebral palsy, he could not walk, talk, eat, or drink without help. He never went to school.

One day, one of his siblings was on the floor drawing letters on a piece of paper with crayons. Christy suddenly moved his left foot, managed to pick up and hold the crayon with his toes, and tried to copy the letters. From that day until his death in 1981, he was able to write using his left foot, typing with his little toe. That was enough, however, for him to write his autobiography, *My Left Foot,* which became a major motion picture. He also wrote two works of fiction. It took him fifteen years to type one of them, *Down All the Days,* but his effort resulted in his being hailed "a man of genius" by the *New York Times.*

Christy Brown never moved from the slums and eventually fell in love and married. He was a man who learned to accept his limitations and then rise above them.

Accept who you are and what you have today. Then use what you have. You will find it's enough to bring you to a place of fulfillment in life.

What HAS
GOD GIFTED
ME WITH
THAT I'M
NOT USING?

The doors of opportunity are
marked "Push" and "Pull."

271

Start Somewhere

A generous man devises
generous things, and by
generosity he shall stand.
ISAIAH 32:8

What
GOALS DO I
DREAM OF
ACHIEVING
BUT HAVE
NEVER BEGUN
WORKING
TOWARD?

Sue had fairly serious health problems. An invalid since childhood, she had a birth defect that left a hole in one of the chambers of her heart. The births of five children, a number of surgeries, and weight gain all took their toll. She lived in almost constant pain. Then she decided that one of the things she wanted to do most in life was to run a marathon, a feat her friends and husband thought was totally unrealistic. She became committed to her goal, however, and began running—slowly—in the subdivision where they lived. Each day she ran just a little further. Soon she was running one mile, then three, then five. Finally, Sue registered to run her first marathon.

Sue ran a smart race, stopping regularly to stretch, drinking plenty of water, and pacing herself. The race was run mostly in the rain, however, and when no more runners were seen crossing the finish line, Sue's family became concerned. Her husband went in search of her. He found her a couple of miles from the finish, encouraging a group of friends with whom she was running. She crossed the finish line five hours after starting the race, but she finished! Her goal had been reached!

Having goals changes us. Working toward them develops us. Reaching them establishes us.

Success is achieving the goals
you have set for yourself.

In the Thick of It

O LORD, be gracious to us; we have waited
for You. Be their arm every morning,
our salvation also in the time of trouble.

ISAIAH 33:2

Does it seem to you that the only stories you hear about miracles occur in remote African villages or obscure Chinese provinces? Do you wonder if God is visibly active only on the mission field? Steven Mosley, author of *If Only God Would Answer,* believes the reason we hear more stories from missionary ventures than local churches is, "God is most active when we are reaching out most. He stretches out when we stretch out.

"Consider the life of George Müeller. He wrote an entire book of answers to specific prayer requests he made while living in complacent Victorian England. Müeller was stretched—he was seeking to meet the needs of two thousand orphans. In remote China, Hudson Taylor was given needed funds or had personal needs met without ever making an appeal to any human being. Taylor was stretched—sharing the Gospel where it had not been preached before. Brother Andrew, 'God's Smuggler,' had an abundance of answered prayers. He, too, was stretched—devoting his life to taking Bibles behind the iron curtain."

Mosley has concluded, "God is most active in the thick of it."

Are you asking God to help you meet your heart's desires today, or are you asking Him how you might help Him meet His heart's desires?

—⚬⚬⚬—

Don't pray for tasks suited to your
capacity. Pray for capacity
suited to your tasks.

What DO I SEE GOD WORKING ON THAT I COULD JOIN IN?

273

Pressed, but Not Crushed

That is why, for Christ's sake, I delight
in weaknesses, in insults, in hardships,
in persecutions, in difficulties. For
when I am weak, then I am strong.

2 CORINTHIANS 12:10 NIV

What KEEPS
ME FROM
ALLOWING
GOD'S
POWER TO
STRENGTHEN
ME IN A
DIFFICULT
CIRCUM-
STANCE?

Bathyspheres are amazing inventions. Operating like miniature submarines, they have been used to explore the ocean in places so deep the water pressure would crush a conventional submarine as easily as if it were an aluminum can. Bathyspheres compensate for the intense water pressure with plates of steel several inches thick. The steel keeps the water out, but it also makes a bathysphere heavy and difficult to maneuver. The space inside is cramped, allowing for only one or two people to survey the ocean floor by looking through a tiny plateglass window.

What divers invariably find at every depth of the ocean are fish and other sea creatures. Some of these creatures are quite small and appear to have fairly normal skin. They look flexible and supple as they swim through the inky waters. How can they live at these depths without steel plating? They compensate for the outside pressure through equal and opposite pressure on the inside.

Spiritual fortitude works in the same way. The more negative the circumstances around us, the more we need to allow God's power to work within us to exert an equal and opposite pressure from the inside. With God on the inside, no pressure on earth can crush us!

⎯⎯ ⤫ ⎯⎯

It is not enough to begin;
continuance is necessary.
Success depends upon staying power.

Being a Great Mom

They glorified God in me.
GALATIANS 1:24

When Rose Kennedy died at age 104, the world lost one of the most dedicated and famous mothers of the twentieth century. She was mother to nine children, among them a former United States president, an attorney general, and a current U.S. senator.

In spite of her own marital challenges, the birth of a mentally challenged child, and the early deaths of four of her children, Rose Kennedy lived a life of faith and strength before her children and grandchildren. At her funeral, her son Ted put into perspective the considerable impact she had on the lives of her family members—with actions both great and small—conveying to her children her love and care and God's love and care: "She sustained us in the saddest times. . . . Her faith in God was the greatest gift she gave us. . . . She was ambitious not only for our success but for our souls. From our youth we remember how, with effortless ease, she could bandage a cut, dry a tear, recite from memory 'The Midnight Ride of Paul Revere,' and spot a hole in a sock from a hundred yards away."

Great mothers don't always bear children who achieve greatness in the eyes of the world, but great mothers always convey great love.

❦

Each loving act says loud and clear, "I love you. God loves you. I care. God cares."

Whom CAN I CONVEY GREAT LOVE TO TODAY?

275

The Harvest Is Ripe

Those who wait on the LORD shall
renew their strength; they shall mount up
with wings like eagles, they shall run and
not be weary, they shall walk and not faint.

ISAIAH 40:31

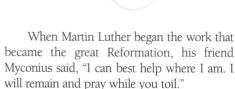

IS THERE
SOMEONE
WHO NEEDS
ME TO BE
OF ACTIVE
HELP IN
THEIR LIFE?

When Martin Luther began the work that became the great Reformation, his friend Myconius said, "I can best help where I am. I will remain and pray while you toil."

Then, one night Myconius dreamed that Jesus approached him and showed him His hands and feet wounded by His crucifixion. He looked into the eyes of his Savior and heard Jesus say to him, "Follow Me." Jesus led him to a mountaintop and pointed eastward. Myconius looked and saw a plain stretching away to the horizon. It was dotted with thousands and thousands of white sheep. One man was trying to shepherd the great flock. Myconius recognized him as his friend, Luther. The Savior then pointed westward, and Myconius saw a great field of standing corn. Only one reaper was trying to harvest it all. The lonely laborer was obviously exhausted, but he persisted. Myconius recognized the solitary reaper. Again, it was Luther.

"It is not enough that I should pray," said Myconius when he awoke. "The sheep must be shepherded; the field must be reaped. Here am I; send me." He immediately sought out Luther and volunteered to serve in whatever capacity Luther desired.

Today, are you praying to help, or to be of help?

Oh, do not pray for easy lives.
Pray to be stronger men.

Set an Extra Place

*Have you suffered so many things
in vain—if indeed it was in vain?*

GALATIANS 3:4

One day a businessman called his wife to ask if he might bring home a visiting foreigner as a dinner guest that night. At the time, the wife had three children in school and one preschooler at home, so she had a full workload on any given day, apart from entertaining strangers. Still, she agreed, and the meal she prepared was both delicious and graciously served. The foreigner, an important official in Spain, had a delightful time and thanked the couple repeatedly for inviting him into their home and treating him to a home-cooked meal and an evening of family warmth and fellowship.

Years later, friends of this family went to Spain as missionaries. However, their work was brought to a standstill by government regulations. This particular Spanish official got word that the missionaries were friends of the couple who had hosted him in such a loving manner, and he used his influence to clear away the restrictions on their behalf. Today in that province of Spain, a church exists, due in part to the setting of one extra place at the dinner table!

As busy as you may be today, take time for the people whom God may bring across your path. Only God knows what His plan may be for the future.

What CAN
I DO TO
RECOGNIZE
THE PEOPLE
IN NEED
GOD BRINGS
TO ME?

---

*A man's work is from sun to sun,
but a mother's work is never done.*

A Way in the Sea

*Thus says the LORD, who makes
a way in the sea and a path
through the mighty waters.*

ISAIAH 43:16

Am I
OVERLOOK-
ING STEPS
GOD WOULD
HAVE ME
TAKE TO
ACHIEVE
A GOAL?

*Don't wait for your ship to
come in; swim out to it.*

Don played the tambourine in junior high, and that seemed about the extent of his musical ability—at least in the opinion of his peers. They recall that he couldn't carry a tune in a bucket. However, Don considered himself a musician.

When his friends graduated and went on to college, Don packed his things and moved to Nashville. He bought a used car and slept in it, took a job working nights so he could visit record companies during the day, and learned to play the guitar. For years, he practiced, wrote songs, and knocked on doors, with virtually no breaks. Then one day, his old friends heard a song on the radio. It was a good song by a good singer who was rising on the country charts. It was Don Schlitz singing a song he had written and recorded.

A short time later, Kenny Rogers recorded one of Don's songs. "The Gambler" became the title song for one of the best-selling, country-music albums of the eighties. Don has since written twenty-three number-one hits.

Don didn't wait for fame and fortune to come to him. He went in search of them.

There's an old saying among business planners that can apply to virtually every area of your life: Plan your work, then work your plan. Go for your goals. Don't expect them to arrive on your doorstep in a neatly packaged bundle. God will direct your steps, but He can't take them for you.

Gentleness

The fruit of the Spirit is love, joy, peace,
longsuffering, kindness, goodness,
faithfulness, gentleness, self-control.

GALATIANS 5:22-23

George Washington and General Lafayette were walking together one morning when they were greeted on their path by a slave. The old man paused, tipped his hat, and said, "Good mo'nin', Gen'l Washin'ton."

Immediately, George Washington removed his hat, bowed, and answered, "Good morning to you, and I hope you have a pleasant day."

General Lafayette was shocked, but when he recovered his composure, he exclaimed, "Why did you bow to a slave?"

Washington smiled and replied, "I would not allow him to be a better gentleman than I."

Gentleness is a character trait that results from the indwelling Spirit of God in our lives. Consider this approach in evaluating yourself as a gentleperson:

G—Gracious and good
E—Engaging, willing to listen
N—Nice to others, regardless of who they are
T—Taking the time to move at another's pace
L—Loving
E—Endearing by acts of kindness and goodwill

Have I BEEN PRAYING FOR GOD TO GIVE ME GENTLENESS OF SPIRIT?

Nothing is so contagious as an example.
We never do great good or great evil
without bringing about more of
the same on the part of others.

It Can't Be Done

Let us not grow weary while doing good, for in due season we shall reap if we do not lose heart.

GALATIANS 6:9

IS THERE
SOMEONE IN
MY LIFE WHO
NEEDS TO
HEAR FROM
ME THAT
THEY CAN
ACHIEVE
THEIR
GOALS?

Somebody said that it couldn't be done,
But he with a chuckle replied,
That "maybe it couldn't" but he would be one
Who wouldn't say so till he'd tried.

So he buckled right in with the trace of a grin
On his face. If he worried, he hid it.
He started to sing as he tackled the thing
That couldn't be done. And he did it.

Somebody scoffed: "Oh, you'll never do that,
At least no one ever has done it."
But he took off his coat and took off his hat
And the first thing he knew he'd begun it.

With the lift of his chin and a bit of a grin,
If any doubt rose he forbid it;
He started to sing as he tackled the thing
That couldn't be done, and he did it.

There are thousands to tell you
*   it cannot be done,*
There are thousands to prophesy failure;
There are thousands to point out to you,
*   one by one,*
The dangers that wait to assail you,

But just buckle right in with a bit of a grin,
Then take off your coat and go to it.
Just start in to sing as you tackle the thing
That cannot be done, and you'll do it.

—Anonymous

In trying times, don't quit trying.

Mother Hen

*The lazy man buries his hand
in the bowl; it wearies him to
bring it back to his mouth.*

PROVERBS 26:15

Hard work means nothing to a hen. Regardless of what business prognosticators say about the price of eggs, regardless of what others expect of her, regardless of fluctuations in the commodities market, she keeps on digging worms and laying eggs.

If the ground is hard, she scratches harder.

If it's dry, she digs deeper.

If it's wet, she digs where it is dry.

If she strikes a rock, she digs around it.

If she gets a few more hours of daylight in the barnyard, she digs a few more hours.

Have you ever seen a pessimistic hen?

Have you ever seen a hen cackle in disgust at the prospect of her job?

Did you ever hear one cluck because the work was hard, the conditions were poor, and some of her eggs were taken from her before they hatched?

No.

Hens save their breath for digging and their cackles for the eggs that are hatched!

What DO I NEED TO CHANGE IN ORDER TO HAVE AN OPTIMISTIC NATURE?

*The secret of success is to start from
scratch and keep on scratching.*

Tea Party

*A good man deals graciously
and lends; he will guide
his affairs with discretion.*

PSALM 112:5

How CAN
I BENEFIT
THOSE
WHO COME
BEHIND ME?

In the mid-nineteenth century, tea cost about a dollar a pound, making it an expensive staple. George Hartford and George Gilman came up with a simple but revolutionary plan to lower the price. They bought tea directly from the ships in New York Harbor. Then, taking a low-percentage profit, they worked for high-volume sales. Their tactics worked. They soon turned their mail-order business into a chain of stores called the Great Atlantic and Pacific Tea Company—A&P.

From the outset, even with a family of five children, Hartford generously gave thousands of dollars a year to charitable causes. As his fortune increased, he established a foundation as a conduit for his giving. Hartford's desire was that his contributions benefit people such as those whose purchases at A&P stores had built his fortune. Later, he reorganized the foundation to receive his estate, so that by the time he died, bequests to individuals totaled $500,000, with $55 million going to the foundation, including $40 million in A&P stock. Thus, a portion of every dollar spent at an A&P store would eventually be donated. In many ways, Hartford is still giving his fortune away!

Live your life in such a way that your legacy continues to the next generation.

⸺∞⸺

*You can't take your money with you,
but you can send it on ahead.*

Barbedwire Fences

Like a madman shooting firebrands or
deadly arrows is a man who deceives
his neighbor and says, "I was only joking!"

PROVERBS 26:18-19 NIV

When HAVE
I PUSHED
SOMEONE
AWAY WITH
MY WORDS?

Tom has been angry most of his life. You can tell it from his conversation, his actions, and his words. When he first comes into a new group, he is the jokester—the loudmouth—but then as you get to know him, you find out that being the loudmouth is the only way he knows how to communicate. His manner may be joking, but his words often cut like a knife.

The puzzling thing about Tom is how lonely he is. He holds everyone at bay with his verbal barbs and emotional fences, yet he longs for companionship and connection. That is why Tom is angry.

The sad thing is, Tom is like a lot of us. We protect ourselves to the point of hurting ourselves, and too often, we hurt each other as well.

Tom needs people—he needs friends. Yet he pushes them away with his words and demeanor. Sometimes, we all act like Tom. But within God's grace, there is hope for us all.

You never saw a fish on
the wall with its mouth shut.

Forgive and Forget

Be kind to one another, tenderhearted,
forgiving one another, even as
God in Christ forgave you.

EPHESIANS 4:32

Is THERE
SOMEONE IN
MY LIFE I
NEED TO
FORGIVE?

A man once had too much to drink at a party. First, he made a foolish spectacle of himself—even to the point of wearing the proverbial lampshade as a hat—and then he passed out. Friends helped his wife take him home and put him to bed. The next morning he was remorseful and asked his wife to forgive him. She agreed to forgive and forget the incident.

As the months went by, however, the wife referred to the incident from time to time, always with a hint of ridicule and shame in her voice. Finally, the man grew weary of being reminded of his bad behavior and said, "I thought you were going to forgive and forget."

"I have forgiven and forgotten," the wife argued, "but I just don't want you to forget that I have forgiven and forgotten."

Once we have confronted an offender, we need to remember that nothing is gained from harboring unforgiveness in our hearts. True forgiveness releases a healing process, and eventually, the memory of what the other person did or said to injure us no longer causes us pain.

When you make a commitment to forgive another person, ask the Lord to heal you of the impact of that person's behavior on your life. Forgive, forget, and go on living in peace.

Despair is the sin which cannot find—
because it will not look for it—forgiveness.

A Matter of Perspective

*I complained, and my
spirit was overwhelmed.*

PSALM 77:3

Mary Smith went to church one Sunday morning and winced when she heard the organist play a wrong note during the processional. She noticed a teenager talking during the opening prayer. She also couldn't help but notice that the altar bouquets were looking wilted. She felt the usher passing the offering plate was scrutinizing what every person put in, which made her angry. To top it all off, the preacher made at least five grammatical errors in his sermon. After the closing hymn, as she left the church through the side door, she thought, *What a careless group of people!*

Amy Jones went to church one Sunday morning and was thrilled by the arrangement of "A Mighty Fortress" that was performed. Her heart was touched at hearing a teenager read the morning Scripture lesson. She was delighted to see the church take up an offering to help hungry children in Nigeria. In addition, the preacher's sermon answered a question that had been bothering her for some time. During the recessional, she felt radiant joy from the choir members. She left the church thinking, *What a wonderful place to worship God!*

Mary and Amy went to the same church, on the same Sunday morning. Which service would you have attended?

───── ∞∞∞ ─────

*Some people are always grumbling
because roses have thorns;
I am thankful that thorns have roses.*

Have I EVER BEEN OVERLY CRITICAL AND MISSED A BLESSING OF GOD?

Digging Ditches

*Whatever you do, whether in word or deed,
do it all in the name of the Lord Jesus, giving
thanks to God the Father through him.*

COLOSSIANS 3:17 NIV

What
OUTLOOK OF
MINE NEEDS
TO BE
CHANGED BY
THE HANDS
OF GOD?

Richard Foster has written, "I had come to Kotzebue on the adventure of helping to 'build the first high school above the Arctic Circle,' but the work itself was far from an adventure. It was hard, backbreaking labor.

"One day I was trying to dig a trench for a sewer line—no small task in a world of frozen tundra. An Eskimo man whose face and hands displayed the leathery toughness of many winters came by and watched me for a while. Finally he said simply and profoundly, 'You are digging a ditch to the glory of God.'

"He said it to encourage me, I know. And I have never forgotten his words. Beyond my Eskimo friend no human being ever knew or cared whether I dug that ditch well or poorly. In time it was to be covered up and forgotten. But because of my friend's words, I dug with all my might, for every shovelful of dirt was a prayer to God.

"Even though I did not know it at the time, I was attempting in my small and unsophisticated way to do what the great artisans of the Middle Ages did when they carved the back of a piece of art, knowing that God alone would see it."

When life gets tough and all our hard work seems to be for naught, our tendency is to ask the Lord to change our circumstances. Perhaps we should ask God to change our outlook instead.

Life's best outlook is a prayerful uplook.

Be Strong and Courageous

Take up the whole armor of God, that you may be able to withstand in the evil day, and having done all, to stand. Stand therefore, having girded your waist with truth, having put on the breastplate of righteousness.

EPHESIANS 6:13-14

Napoleon called Marshall Ney the bravest man he had ever known. Yet Ney's knees trembled so badly one morning before a battle that he had difficulty mounting his horse. When he was finally in the saddle, he shouted contemptuously down at his limbs, "Shake away, knees. You would shake worse than that if you knew where I am going to take you."

Courage is not a matter of not being afraid. It is taking action even when you are afraid!

Courage is more than sheer bravado, shouting, "I can do this!" and launching out with a do-or-die attitude over some reckless dare. True courage is exhibited when a person chooses to take a difficult or dangerous course of action because it is the right thing to do. Courage is looking beyond yourself to what is best for others.

The source of all courage is the Holy Spirit, our Comforter. It is His nature to remain at our side and help us. When we welcome Him into our lives and He compels us to do something, we can confidently trust Him to be right there, helping us to get the job done!

What DO I STRUGGLE TO GIVE UP FOR THE GOOD OF OTHERS?

Courage is resistance to fear, mastery of fear, not absence of fear.

Positioned for Prayer

I know that this will turn out for my deliverance through your prayer and the supply of the Spirit of Jesus Christ.

PHILIPPIANS 1:19

When I PRAY, DO I EXPECT GOD TO HEAR ME?

Three ministers were talking about prayer one day, and they began debating among themselves about the most appropriate and effective positions for prayer. As they talked, they were totally oblivious to a telephone repairman working on the phone system in a corner of the room where they were sitting.

One minister contended that the key to prayer was in the hands. He always held his hands together to show a firmness of commitment and then pointed his hands upward as a symbolic form of worship. The second minister countered that real prayer could only be made if a person was on his knees. The third suggested that the best position for prayer was to stretch out flat with one's face to the ground, the position of supreme surrender.

By this time, the telephone repairman could no longer refrain from adding his opinion: "Well, I have found that the most powerful prayer I ever made was while I was suspended forty feet above the ground, dangling upside down by my heels from a telephone pole."

The real power of prayer lies in the One who hears our prayers, not in the form of the prayer.

―❦―

God looks not at the oratory of your prayers, how elegant they may be; nor at the geometry of your prayers, how long they may be; nor at the arithmetic of your prayers, how many they may be; nor at the logic of your prayers, how methodical they may be; but the sincerity of them.

Thou Shalt Not Whine

*Do all things without
complaining and disputing.*

PHILIPPIANS 2:14

Rather than whining because we don't have certain things in our lives or because we think something is wrong, we should take positive action. Here are four steps for turning whining into thanksgiving:

1. *Give something away.* When you give, you create both a physical and a mental space for something new and better to come into your life.

2. *Narrow your goals.* Don't expect everything good to come into your life all at once. When you focus your expectations toward specific, attainable goals, you are more apt to direct your time and energy toward reaching them.

3. *Change your vocabulary from "I need" to "I want."* Most of the things we think we need are actually things we want. When you receive them, you will be thankful for even small luxuries, rather than seeing them as necessities you can't live without.

4. *Choose to be thankful for what you already have.* Thanksgiving is a choice. Every one of us has more things to be thankful for than we could even begin to recount in a single day.

Each time you catch yourself whining, apply one or more of these steps to the situation. As you put them into practice, you will find yourself whining less and thanking God more. Living a life of gratitude and thanksgiving to God is the best antidote for stress.

What CAN I
THANK GOD
FOR TODAY?

*Jesus can turn water into wine, but
He can't turn your whining into anything.*

Only the Strong

Brethren, I do not count myself to have apprehended; but one thing I do, forgetting those things which are behind and reaching forward to those things which are ahead.

PHILIPPIANS 3:13

Am I LOOKING TO GOD FOR THE STRENGTH TO LIVE ACCORDING TO HIS WILL?

Many people are good starters but poor finishers. When things start getting tough, they listen to the little imp on their shoulder who whispers, "You can't do it" and "You'll never make it." Others don't even start.

While doing something requires risk, so does doing nothing. The risk of action may be failure, but the risks of a failure to act can be stagnation, dissatisfaction, and frustration.

The story of the covered wagon crossing the plains toward the Golden West began with a song:

> *The Coward never started;*
> *The Weak died on the way;*
> *Only the Strong came through!*

That's the way it is in life. Being strong does not refer only to physical strength. True strength flows from a strong spirit—a spirit made powerful by a close relationship with God. He gives us the will to succeed, dreams that will not die, and wisdom to turn evil into blessing.

Lean on God for direction and keep leaning on Him for the wisdom and courage to finish what you've begun.

Step by step, little by little, bit by bit—
that is the way to wealth, that is the way
to wisdom, that is the way to glory.

The Wind Blows

The peace of God, which surpasses all understanding, will guard your hearts and minds through Christ Jesus.

PHILIPPIANS 4:7

Tom Dooley was a young doctor who gave up an easy, prosperous career in the States to organize hospitals in Southeast Asia and pour out his life in service to the afflicted people there. As he lay dying of cancer at age thirty-four, Dooley wrote to the president of Notre Dame, his alma mater:

"Dear Father Hesburgh: They've got me down. Flat on the back, with plaster, sand bags, and hot water bottles. I've contrived a way of pumping the bed up a bit so that, with a long reach, I can get to my typewriter. . . . Two things prompt this note to you. The first is that whenever my cancer acts up a bit . . . I turn inward. Less do I think of my hospitals around the world or of ninety-four doctors, fund-raisers, and the like. More do I think of one Divine Doctor and my personal fund of grace. . . . I have monstrous phantoms; all men do. And inside and outside the wind blows. But when the time comes, like now, then the storm around me does not matter. The winds within me do not matter. Nothing human or earthly can touch me. A peace gathers in my heart. What seems unpossessable, I can possess. What seems unfathomable, I can fathom. What is unutterable, I can utter. Because I can pray. I can communicate. How do people endure anything on earth if they cannot have God?"

The storms of life will come and go, vary in their intensity, and hit us at our worst moments, but the peace of God remains the same—constant, enduring, and comforting. When we choose His peace over worry, fear, and anxiety, our hearts and minds abide secure in Him.

What WORRY, FEAR, OR ANXIETY IN MY LIFE IS DROWNING OUT THE PEACE GOD PROVIDES?

God takes life's pieces and gives us unbroken peace.

An Old-Fashioned Working

His merciful kindness is great toward
us, and the truth of the LORD
endures forever. Praise the LORD!

PSALM 117:2

Whom
AROUND ME
CAN I HELP
TODAY?

"I often have thought that we are a little old-fashioned here in the Ozark hills," writes Laura Ingalls Wilder in *Little House in the Ozarks*. "Now I know we are, because we had a 'working' in our neighborhood this winter. That is a blessed, old-fashioned way of helping out a neighbor.

"While the winter was warm, still it has been much too cold to be without firewood; and this neighbor, badly crippled with rheumatism, was not able to get up his winter's wood. . . . So the men of the neighborhood gathered together one morning and dropped in on him. With cross-cut saws and axes, they took possession of his wood lot. . . . By night there was enough wood ready . . . to last the rest of the winter.

"The women did their part, too. All morning they kept arriving with well-filled baskets, and at noon a long table was filled with a country neighborhood dinner. . . . When the dishes were washed, they sewed, knit, crocheted, and talked for the rest of the afternoon. It was a regular old-fashioned good time, and we all went home with the feeling expressed by a newcomer when he said, 'Don't you know I'm proud to live in a neighborhood like this where they turn out and help one another when it's needed.'"

What kind of neighbor are you?

＊＊＊

Kindness is a language which the
deaf can hear and the blind can see.

Vision, Risk, and Courage

Be of good courage, and let us be strong
for our people and for the cities of our God.
And may the LORD do what is good in His sight.

2 SAMUEL 10:12

In 1990, Bill and Gina Ellis were living a comfortable life in Los Angeles. Then just before Christmas, Bill was laid off from his job. To distract themselves from the loss during the holiday season, they reviewed sketches of a sofa Gina had seen in Spain. The style lent itself to washable slipcovers that could be changed with the seasons. They made slight variations in the design and had the sofa custom built. Their friends raved.

Bill took a long hard look at drawings he had of other pieces of furniture. He said impulsively, "We could sell these." Gina agreed, and within a week they had launched Quatrine Washable Furniture. Using equity from their home, they leased a small shop and paid a craftsman to construct their first five sofas and chairs. Customers loved their furniture, but felt it was too expensive.

Three months later, a woman came into their shop, selected several pieces of furniture, and wrote a check for $14,000. With that profit, they were able to create a line of more reasonably priced furniture. By summer, the new pieces were ready. They moved their business to Detroit and eventually opened branches in Dallas, Chicago, and Denver. By 1996, their sales totaled more than $5 million a year.

Reward cannot be separated from vision, risk, and courage. If you want to grow and develop in any area of life, you have to pay the price. The benefits, however, far outweigh the cost.

When HAVE I BEEN AFRAID TO RISK IN ORDER TO ACHIEVE A BENEFIT?

Success requires the vision to see,
the faith to believe, and the courage to do.

Slides, Swings, and Monkey Bars

OCTOBER 12

Whatever you do, do it heartily,
as to the Lord and not to men.
COLOSSIANS 3:23

What's
KEEPING ME
FROM WHAT
I DESIRE?

A man once dreamed of building a playground in a ghetto neighborhood. He approached the owners of an apartment complex who gave him permission to build, but offered no help. As he walked through the complex one day, he met a little girl. He shared his dream of a playground with her, and she immediately ran to her apartment. She returned with a thick stack of crayon sketches. She already shared his vision! Her drawings showed him the playground she wanted—one with two slides, lots of swings, and monkey bars. She showed him the exact spot where she wanted it built, and then she said, "I've been praying for this a long time!"

The man told her he would need lots of help to turn the dream into a reality, and the little girl nodded in agreement. In the coming weeks, she tirelessly slipped flyers under doors and made appointments for the man to speak to parents and teachers. Word of the project quickly spread. Several companies donated materials. The little girl convinced architects and fund-raisers to help. When construction began, hundreds of volunteers showed up to help. In no time at all, the playground the man and the young girl had dreamed of became a reality!

Are you willing to work for what you desire? It may be the key to receiving God's best.

———✦———

Pray to God, but row for the shore.

The Grand Adventure

Walk in wisdom toward those who
are outside, redeeming the time.

COLOSSIANS 4:5

In *A Closer Walk*, Catherine Marshall writes about a neighbor, "Cynthia felt she was losing her identity in an endless procession of social events and chauffeuring of children. During one cocktail party, Cynthia decided to limit herself to ginger ale and made some discoveries—not especially pleasant: 'I saw our crowd through new eyes,' she told me. 'No one was really saying anything. . . . All at once I began to ask questions about what we call "the good life."'"

"In a search for answers, Cynthia set aside an hour each day for meditation. As she did this over a period of weeks, there came to her the realization that she was being met in this quiet hour by something more than her own thoughts and psyche . . . by Someone who loved her and insisted this love be passed on to her family and friends."

Cynthia made changes in her life as the result of her hour spent with God. She turned mealtime into time for family sharing. A family game night became a substitute for television once a week. She and her husband joined a Bible study that met twice a month. In all, Cynthia concluded, "God . . . the Author of creativity, is ready to make a dull life adventure-some the moment we allow His Holy Spirit to go to work."

Does your life seem dull and monotonous? Join the grand adventure! It's as simple as letting God lead you.

What GRAND ADVENTURE DO I FEEL GOD LEADING ME TO?

Open your eyes and the
whole world is full of God.

Offspring Day

Remember the days of old; consider the generations long past. Ask your father and he will tell you, your elders, and they will explain to you.

DEUTERONOMY 32:7 NIV

What ONE THING ABOUT MYSELF DO I HOPE TO IMPROVE IN THE COMING YEAR?

On the fourth Sunday of July, the descendants of Roberto and Raquel Beaumont celebrate Offspring Day. They have been doing this since 1956, when Raquel gathered her five preteen children around the dinner table at their home in Lima, Peru. She placed a rose by the napkin of each daughter and a carnation by the napkin of each son.

Knowing that in a few years her children would be going their separate ways, she told her children that the gifts she gave them on Offspring Day were not mere flowers, but a token of her true gifts to them—time and love. Furthermore, she expected them to pass on those same gifts to their children. Through the years, Raquel was the best example of her message. She always made time for each of her children, who regularly sought her advice and encouragement.

On Offspring Day each year, the elders who gather offer words of wisdom to their children. The young are encouraged to pick one thing about themselves they hope to improve in the coming year. It is a time for the generations to hear from one another and to set new goals for relationships. They do it all in the spirit of Raquel's example.

A pint of example is worth a barrelful of advice.

The Flowers

This is the day the LORD has made;
we will rejoice and be glad in it.

PSALM 118:24

The fictional character Sherlock Holmes is known for his keen powers of observation in solving crimes. But Holmes also used his skills for renewing his faith. In *The Adventure of the Naval Treaty,* Dr. Watson says of Holmes, "He walked past the couch to an open window and held up the drooping stalk of a moss rose, looking down at the dainty blend of crimson and green. It was a new phase of his character to me, for I had never before seen him show an interest in natural objects.

"'There is nothing in which deduction is so necessary as in religion,' said he, leaning with his back against the shutters. . . . 'Our highest assurance of the goodness of Providence seems to me to rest in the flowers. All other things, our powers, our desires, our food, are really necessary for our existence in the first instance. But this rose is an extra. Its smell and its color are an embellishment of life, not a condition of it. It is only goodness which gives extras, and so I say again that we have much to hope from the flowers.'"

Life is filled with little extras—gifts from a loving God that enrich our lives. Take time to notice them today!

❦

The teacher asked the pupils to tell the meaning of loving-kindness. A little boy jumped up and said, "Well, if I was hungry and someone gave me a piece of bread that would be kindness. But if they put a little jam on it, that would be loving-kindness."

What "LITTLE EXTRAS" HAS GOD GIVEN ME LATELY?

Rah! Rah! Rah!

And sent Timothy, our brother and minister of God, and our fellow laborer in the gospel of Christ, to establish you and encourage you concerning your faith.

1 THESSALONIANS 3:2

Who IN MY LIFE CAN USE ENCOURAGE-MENT TODAY?

Part of your role as a family member is to be a fan of those with whom you live. God created you to be a cheerleader for your spouse and children.

E-N-C-O-U-R-A-G-E-M-E-N-T is perhaps the best cheer you can learn!

E is for enthusiasm and energy in support-ing causes important to your family members.

N is for saying, "Next time you'll succeed."

C is for compassion.

O is for open lines of communication.

U is for understanding.

R is for rooting on the team.

A is for arranging your schedule to make time for others in your family.

G is for going the second mile.

E is for entertaining your children's friends.

M is for modeling a positive attitude.

E is for empowering your child with God's Word.

N is for never giving up.

T is for taking time out for hugs and praise.

"E-N-C-O-U-R-A-G-E" your family today, and let them know you "M-E-N-T" it!

We cannot hold a torch to light another's path without brightening our own.

Friend in Need

Wounds from a friend can be trusted,
but an enemy multiplies kisses.

PROVERBS 27:6 NIV

The Moores and the Lamberts have been friends for years. They went to some of the same schools. They had children about the same time. They've known each other through the important times and during the everyday events. They've served on PTA and played on softball leagues together.

It was Brenda Moore that let Coleen Lambert know that her oldest son was taking drugs. It was Ben Lambert that let Bob Moore know that his daughter was in trouble at school. They wouldn't have trusted the news from anyone else. They might not have believed it from anyone else. They saw the pain in each other's eyes and knew they could trust the wounds of their friends.

Many people have come and gone in their town, but these families have remained friends and probably always will. They have stood by each other in every circumstance, and they have grieved their losses together.

That's the kind of friends we all need to have. That's the kind of friends we all need to be—friends who can be trusted in any kind of weather and with any kind of message.

Be a good friend today.

Is THERE SOMEONE WHO NEEDS MY LOVING INTERCESSION TODAY?

A friend is someone with
whom you dare to be yourself.

For Love

*You yourselves are taught
by God to love one another.*
1 THESSALONIANS 4:9

Who IN MY
LIFE HAS
EXHIBITED
GOD'S LOVE
FOR ME?

Perhaps the most famous "mother" in the world was Mother Teresa. In 1948, as Sister Teresa, she was given permission to leave her order of nearly twenty years and travel to India. On her first day in Calcutta, Teresa picked up five abandoned children and brought them to her "school." Before the year ended, she had forty-one students learning about hygiene in her classroom in a public park. Shortly thereafter, a new congregation was approved. Mother Teresa quickly named it "Missionaries of Charity." Within two years, their attention had become focused on the care of the dying.

Once, a poor beggar was picked up as he lay dying in a pile of rubbish. Reduced by suffering and hunger to a mere specter, Mother Teresa took him to the Home for the Dying and put him in bed. When she began to wash him, she discovered his body was covered with worms. Pieces of skin came off as she washed him. For a brief moment, the man revived. In his semiconscious state, he asked, "Why do you do it?" Mother Teresa responded with the two words that became her hallmark: "For love."

Ask any mother why she does what she does, and you are likely to receive the same answer. Love is both a mother's work—and a mother's reward.

*Being a full-time mother is one of
the highest salaried jobs in my field
since the payment is pure love.*

All Things Are for the Best

Rejoice always.

1 THESSALONIANS 5:16

Bernard Gilpin was falsely accused of heresy before Bishop Bonner and shortly thereafter was sent to London for trial. Gilpin's favorite saying was: "All things are for the best." He set out on his journey with that attitude, but on his way fell from his horse and broke his leg.

"Is all for the best now?" a mocker asked, scorning Gilpin for his optimism. "I still believe so," he replied.

He turned out to be right. During the time he was convalescing from the accident and unable to resume his journey, Queen Mary died. Consequently, the case against him was dropped. Instead of being burned at the stake, Gilpin returned home in triumph.

While God never leads us into accidents or causes illness, He can take those things our enemy intends for evil and use them for our ultimate good. Therefore, rather than spending our energy railing against bad times, perhaps we should direct our efforts toward praising the One who promises to work all things together for our good.

―――∞∞∞―――

It is good to remember that the tea kettle,
although up to its neck in hot water,
continues to sing.

Have I ALLOWED GOD TO GIVE ME JOY TO OVERCOME ANY OBSTACLE?

One Thing at a Time

If any of you lacks wisdom, he should ask God,
who gives generously to all without finding
fault, and it will be given to him.

JAMES 1:5 NIV

Am I
ASKING GOD
FOR HIS
LEADERSHIP
IN PLANNING
MY EVERYDAY
LIFE?

Charles Schwab, one of the first presidents of Bethlehem Steel Company, once told efficiency expert Ivy Lee, "If you can give us something to pep us up to do the things we ought to do, I'll gladly pay you anything you ask within reason."

"Fine," Lee said, "I can give you something in twenty minutes that will step up your 'doing' by at least 50 percent." He then handed Schwab a piece of paper and said, "Write down the six most important tasks you have to do tomorrow and number them in the order of their importance." Then Lee said, "Now put this paper in your pocket and first thing tomorrow morning, look at item one and start working on it until it is finished. Then tackle item two in the same way; then item three and so on. Do this until quitting time. . . . Do this every working day. After you've convinced yourself of the value of this system, have your men try it . . . and then send me a check for what you think it is worth." A few weeks later, Schwab sent Lee a check for $25,000, calling his advice the most profitable lesson he had ever learned.

What are the six most important tasks you have to do today?

❧

Success in life is a matter not so
much of talent or opportunity as of
concentration and perseverance.

Playing in Harmony

*As iron sharpens iron, so a man
sharpens the countenance of his friend.*

PROVERBS 27:17

Leonard Bernstein, the famous orchestra conductor, was once asked by an admirer, "What is the hardest instrument to play?"

Bernstein responded without hesitation, "Second fiddle. I can always get plenty of first violinists, but to find one who plays second violin with as much enthusiasm or second French horn or second flute, now that's a problem. And yet if no one plays second, we have no harmony."

Leaders cannot lead without followers, contributors, and supporters—those willing to help without fanfare. Without leadership, an institution or organization of any size fails to move forward. Without those who follow enthusiastically, an institution has no strength. Envy can kill both progress and stability!

A true friend chooses to rejoice with those who succeed rather than envy them. This can be difficult at times, but when the glow of the success or blessing grows dim, the friendship remains brighter and more satisfying than ever.

*He who considers his work beneath him
will be above doing it well.*

Am I WILLING TO SUBORDINATE MY WANTS TO PLAY SECOND FIDDLE TO SOMEONE ELSE WHO NEEDS SUPPORT?

Then Comes the Harvest

As for you, brethren, do not grow weary in doing good.
2 THESSALONIANS 3:13

What's
KEEPING
ME FROM
EXPECTING
MY HARVEST?

In *Traveling Hopefully,* Stan Mooneyham writes, "Early on I learned that it is a lot more fun to harvest than to hoe. Or, for that matter to plant. Few rewards can compare with that of plucking the bounty of the earth which represents the fruit of your labor. Harvesting is dramatic, fulfilling. You see what you get and you get what you see.

"Not that harvesting isn't hard work, too; but it's different. That's the payoff. The sense of reward represented by autumn's harvest can cause you to forget the less satisfying work of spring and summer. . . .

"Of course, it goes without saying that there would be no autumn harvest if there was no drudgery of spring and summer. Full barns require soil preparation, planting, and hoeing. The 'winning run' in baseball may top off all the prior runs, but the first was as necessary as the final one, even if the crowds didn't leap to their feet and tear the stadium apart early in the game."

If you find yourself feeling that your marriage has turned into drudgery and work, remember that life has a wonderful reward ahead. You may not see it today, but the harvest is growing!

Prayer is profitable wherever it is invested.

On Her Knees

Then you will call upon Me and go and
pray to Me, and I will listen to you.
And you will seek Me and find Me, when
you search for Me with all your heart.

JEREMIAH 29:12-13

Fanny Crosby, the eminent hymn writer, said she never attempted to write a hymn without first kneeling in prayer. Given the fact that she wrote more than eight thousand songs, she was obviously a woman of considerable prayer!

Like many creative people, Miss Crosby was often under pressure to meet deadlines. One such time came in 1869 as she tried to write lyrics for a tune composer, W. H. Doane. She couldn't seem to find the words, and then she remembered she had forgotten to pray. As she rose from her knees, she dictated—as fast as her assistant could write—the words for the famous hymn, "Jesus, Keep Me Near the Cross."

Another time, she had run short of money and needed exactly five dollars for a particular purpose. There was no time to call upon her publishers, so she simply prayed for the money. As she ended her prayer, she began to pace back and forth in her room, trying to get in the mood to write. Just at that time, an admirer called upon her. The two chatted briefly, and in parting, the woman pressed something into her hand. It was a five-dollar bill! Fanny fell to her knees in a prayer of thanksgiving and upon rising, wrote, "All the Way My Saviour Leads Me."

Jesus does not just give us answers, He gives us Himself—He is the answer.

❈❈❈

God not only gives us answers to our
prayers, but with every answer
gives us something of Himself.

How HAS
JESUS BEEN
MY ANSWER?

Boulders and Pebbles

Ah, LORD GOD! Behold, You have made the heavens and the earth by Your great power and outstretched arm. There is nothing too hard for You.

JEREMIAH 32:17

What PROBLEMS IN MY LIFE HAVE I THOUGHT "TOO SMALL" TO TURN OVER TO GOD?

In *He Still Moves Stones*, Max Lucado writes, "What matters to you matters to God. You probably think that's true when it comes to the big stuff. When it comes to the major-league difficulties like death, disease, sin, and disaster—you know that God cares. But what about the smaller things? What about grouchy bosses or flat tires or lost dogs? What about broken dishes, late flights, toothaches, or a crashed hard drive? Do these matter to God?

"I mean, he's got a universe to run. He's got the planets to keep balanced and presidents and kings to watch over. He's got wars to worry with and famines to fix. Who am I to tell him about my ingrown toenail? I'm glad you asked. Let me tell you who you are . . . you are God's child. . . . As a result, if something is important to you, it's important to God."

In labeling something as a big problem, we are implying that it will take God more effort to resolve it. To say something is a little problem implies less effort. The fact is, there are no degrees of difficulty to One who is omnipotent. God is all-powerful, and therefore, all-capable. He knows all the solutions, even as He knows all the problems. No problem, big or small, is beyond His love, concern, and ability. He removes the boulders from our path and the pebbles from our shoe.

Make every matter of care a matter of prayer.

The Gasoline Is Prayer

Call to Me, and I will answer you,
and show you great and mighty
things, which you do not know.

JEREMIAH 33:3

Mother Teresa once said, "Prayer feeds the soul—as blood is to the body, prayer is to the soul—and it brings you closer to God. It also gives you a clean and pure heart. A clean heart can see God, can speak to God, and can see the love of God in others."

This view has been echoed by Sister Kateri, who is affiliated with the Sisters of Charity (the order founded by Mother Teresa) in the Bronx, New York. She has said:

"The most important thing that a human being can do is pray, because we've been made for God and our hearts are restless until we rest with Him. And it's in prayer that we come into contact with God. . . .

"I used to share this with the men at the prison I visited. I'd give them the example: If you had to go on a trip, what would you need? And the men would say, 'You'd need a car and you'd need gasoline.' We used to have a good time because we usually decided that the gasoline was prayer, the car was our life, the journey was to Heaven, you had to have a map, you had to know where you were going, and so on. My point really is that the gasoline of our life is prayer and without that we won't reach our destination, and we won't reach the fulfillment of our being."

Is your tank running on empty today? Maybe it's time to get off the expressway and stop for a fill-up.

⸻

The Christian life without prayer is like
computer hardware without the software.

IS THERE ANYTHING THAT KEEPS ME FROM FILLING MY GAS TANK UP WITH PRAYER EVERY DAY?

A Close Family

Let no one despise your youth, but be an
example to the believers in word, in conduct,
in love, in spirit, in faith, in purity.
1 TIMOTHY 4:12

Who HAS
PROVIDED
ME WITH
UNCONDI-
TIONAL LOVE?

The daughter of missionaries to India, Wendy resented being held to the high expectations of others. As a teenager in boarding school, she rebelled against those expectations. Her parents returned to Canada so the family might be together, but Wendy continued to rebel. Her mother and father, however, didn't judge or condemn her. She says, "They just kept on loving me. I discovered that I could fight rules and people who criticized me, but I couldn't put up walls against love. Because of my parents' patient love for me, I stopped rebelling, and . . . I recommitted my life to Christ."

As a young adult, Wendy herself became a missionary to India. One of her students, Anne, had a negative attitude toward Christianity. Wendy said, "I prayed diligently for Anne, and decided that I would treat her with the same loving-kindness with which my parents had treated me. I accepted Anne as she was, without placing spiritual expectations on her. When Anne realized that I didn't intend to judge her . . . she began opening up to me." Finally, Anne accepted Christ into her life. Wendy concludes, "A 'close family' has little to do with geography and being together physically. But [it] has everything to do with loving . . . supporting . . . and communicating with each other."

Is there an Anne in your life? Reach out in love.

———— ✕ ————

Children have more need
of models than of critics.

Seed Money

*Let, I pray, Your merciful kindness
be for my comfort, according
to Your word to Your servant.*

PSALM 119:76

It was almost planting season, and a farmer found himself without any money to buy seed. He had prepared his fields for planting, assuming that the bank would lend him money for seed as they had for several years. This year, however, the bank had changed its policy—no more seed money.

The farmer didn't know what to do, except to talk to God about the problem. As he prayed, the idea came to him, *Perhaps the co-op will advance me the seed.* He knew the co-op rule: credit for fertilizer, chemicals, and fuel—but seed had to be paid for in cash. Even so, he decided to go talk to the co-op manager. Upon arriving at the office, the secretary greeted him warmly and handed him an envelope as she ushered him into the manager's office. "What's this?" he asked. "Your payment for last year's crop," the manager replied.

"I didn't think it was due for several months," the farmer said as he opened the envelope. The manager smiled and said, "This year we decided to do it earlier."

"Thank you!" the farmer blurted out as he saw the amount of the check—it was $10,000 more than he needed for seed.

"Now, what did you want to talk to me about this morning?" the manager asked. "Not a thing," the farmer replied thinking to himself, *Talking to God has already taken care of it.*

If you're facing a difficult situation today, talk to God about the problem.

What
PROBLEMS
WILL I TURN
OVER TO
GOD TODAY?

Daily prayers lessen daily cares.

The Gift of Life

Now godliness with
contentment is great gain.
1 TIMOTHY 6:6

What GIFT
HAS GOD
PLACED IN
MY LIFE THAT
I'VE BEEN
OVERLOOKING?

Once a nationally syndicated columnist and now an author, Anna Quindlen (a Pulitzer Prize winner in 1992) seems to have enjoyed success at everything she has attempted. However, in taking a fellow commentator to task after he made light of teenage problems, Anna was reminded of the two attempts she had made to end her own life at age sixteen. She writes, "I was really driven through my high school years. I always had to be perfect in every way, ranging from how I looked to how my grades were. It was too much pressure."

In the early 1970s, Anna's mother died from ovarian cancer. This tragedy cured Anna from any desire to commit suicide. Her attitude toward life changed. "I could never look at life as anything but a great gift. I realized I didn't have any business taking it for granted."

When we are faced with the realization that life is only temporary, we can finally come to grips with what is important. Our priorities quickly come into focus when we face our own immortality. Life is God's gift, and we need to cherish every precious moment. It will help us to find purpose and meaning for each day.

Life is the childhood of our immortality.

Go

*I know whom I have believed and am
persuaded that He is able to keep what
I have committed to Him until that Day.*

2 TIMOTHY 1:12

Do I TRUST
IN MY OWN
EFFORTS
RATHER THAN
IN GOD'S
PLAN?

From childhood, two sisters had desired to go to the mission field together. As they approached midlife, they realized they were both well established in their professions, and they began to investigate where they might go to serve God. After several months of talking to various missionary agencies, one of the sisters quit her job and moved to South America, where she became involved in pioneering churches.

The other sister, however, decided the hazards of the mission field were too great. She would remain at home and make even more money. "I'll go later," she said as she bid her sister good-bye. Two years later, she died in an accident on the job. She had saved her life, only to lose it.

Apart from God, safety is an illusion. Many people trust in their jobs, unaware that their companies are on the brink of bankruptcy. Others trust in the government, unaware that funds are diminishing and laws are subject to change. Still others trust in their own abilities, never considering the possibility of accident or illness.

If the Lord has spoken to your heart to go, be swift to respond when He opens the door for you. The safest place to dwell is in the shelter of His will.

*I have held many things in my hands and
lost them all; but the things I have placed
in God's hands, those I always possess.*

Wars and Rumors of Wars

Shun profane and idle babblings,
for they will increase to
more ungodliness.
2 TIMOTHY 2:16

IS THERE AN
ATTITUDE IN
MY LIFE
THAT NEEDS
CHANGING?

A little girl once asked her father how wars got started.

"Well," said her father, "suppose America persisted in quarreling with England, and. . . ."

"But," interrupted her mother, "America must never quarrel with England."

"I know," said the father, "but I am only using a hypothetical instance."

"But you are misleading the child," protested Mom.

"No, I am not," replied the father indignantly, with an edge of anger in his tone.

"Never mind, Daddy," the little girl interjected, "I think I know how wars get started."

Most arguments don't start over major differences, but are rooted in small annoyances, breaches, or trespasses. It's like the mighty oak that stood on the skyline of the Rocky Mountains. The tree had survived hail, heavy snows, bitter cold, and ferocious storms for more than a century. It was finally felled not by a great lightning strike or an avalanche, but by an attack of tiny beetles.

A little hurt, neglect, or insult can be the beginning of the end for any relationship. Therefore, take care what you say, check your attitude, and be quick to ask for forgiveness when you've been wrong.

People can alter their lives
by altering their attitudes.

Plan B

Stand fast and prepare yourselves.

JEREMIAH 46:14

In the 1984 Olympics, heavyweight boxer Henry Tillman planned a careful strategy. He decided he would fight defensively, simply warding off his opponent's blows until he saw an opening for a strike of his own. Minutes into the fight, it became obvious to Tillman that his opponent had planned the same strategy! After the bell sounded ending the first round, Tillman stepped back, dropped his hands, and mentally shifted gears. He recognized that his initial game plan might not work, but he had come prepared with a second plan. He switched to an offensive mode of fighting, won the match, and ultimately won a gold medal.

Figure skater Kristi Yamaguchi also had a "plan B" for her Olympic bid. Originally, she had planned to perform her most difficult jump—three revolutions in the air and a graceful single-skate landing known as the triple salchow. A slight stumble in the early portion of her routine led her to make a change. She cut the triple salchow to a double, regained her balance, caught up with her music, and then went on to perform another triple jump—the lutz.

No matter how much we rehearse or plan, things don't always go as we desire. True champions are those who are prepared to adapt if necessary and switch to what works. Be flexible. You'll have much more peace and a lot less stress if you don't expect things to always go the way you planned.

What KEEPS ME FROM BEING FLEXIBLE?

One important key to success is self-confidence. An important key to self-confidence is preparation.

They Shall Take Up Serpents

*Do not fear, for I am with you; do not
be dismayed, for I am your God.*
ISAIAH 41:10 NIV

What SITUATIONS HAVE I ENCOUNTERED THAT GOD HAS HANDLED?

A woman was sitting in her den one day when a small black snake suddenly appeared, slithered across the floor, and made its way under the couch. Being deathly afraid of snakes, the woman promptly ran to the bathroom to get her husband, who was taking a shower. He came running from the shower, wearing only a towel, grabbed an old broom handle from the closet, and began poking under the couch.

At this point, the sleeping family dog woke up. Curious to see what was happening, he came up behind the husband and touched his cold nose to the back of the man's heel. The man, surmising that the snake had outmaneuvered him and had bitten him on the heel, fainted dead away. The wife concluded that her husband had overexerted and collapsed with a heart attack. She called the hospital just one block away, and the ambulance drivers promptly arrived to place the man on a stretcher. As they were carrying him out of the house, the snake reappeared from beneath the couch. One of the drivers became so excited that he dropped his end of the stretcher and broke the husband's leg. Seeing her husband's twisted leg, the wife passed out.

Meanwhile, the snake slithered quietly away!

When you face a frightening situation, don't lose your cool. Keep your wits about you. God is there with you in the midst of it, and He will deliver you!

*Even a woodpecker owes his success
to the fact that he uses his head.*

The Hallmark of Integrity

*Better is the poor who walks in
his integrity than one perverse
in his ways, though he be rich.*

PROVERBS 28:6

Dwight L. Moody's father died when Dwight was only four. A month later, Mrs. Moody gave birth to twins. With nine mouths to feed and no income, the widow Moody was dogged by creditors. In response to such a dire and impoverished situation, the eldest son ran away from home. Few would have criticized Mrs. Moody for seeking institutional assistance or letting others help raise her children. However, she was determined to keep her family together.

On a nightly basis, Mrs. Moody placed a light in the window, certain her son would return home. Dwight wrote of those days, "When the wind was very high and the house would tremble at every gust, the voice of my mother was raised in prayer." In time, her prayers were answered. Moody recalls that no one recognized his older brother when he came to the door, a great beard flowing down his chest. It was only as the tears began to soak his beard that Mrs. Moody recognized her son and invited him in. He said, "No, Mother, I will not come in until I hear first that you have forgiven me." She was only too willing to forgive, of course, and threw her arms around her son in a warm embrace.

Mrs. Moody didn't change just because her circumstances did. That is the hallmark of integrity.

Keep praying and trust God to answer.

Is THERE A
LONG-TERM
PROBLEM IN
MY LIFE I'VE
GIVEN UP ON?

*Success isn't measured by the position
you reach in life; it's measured by
the obstacles you overcome.*

In Every Circumstance

In all things showing yourself to be a
pattern of good works; in doctrine showing
integrity, reverence, incorruptibility.
TITUS 2:7

Is THERE A
CIRCUM-
STANCE IN
MY LIFE THAT
GOD NEEDS
ME TO
CREATE
GOOD IN?

During World War II, Max had one of the worst jobs in the camp—carrying stones and planks through the mud to build a crematorium. Daily, he was under the lash of the camp's infamous guard, "Bloody Krott." Yet all the while, Father Maximillian Kolbe kept smiling. One prisoner recalled, "Because they were trying to survive at any cost, all the prisoners had wildly roving eyes watching in every direction for trouble or the ready clubs. Kolbe, alone, had a calm straightforward look, the look of a thoughtful man. . . . In spite of his physical suffering, he was completely healthy, serene . . . extraordinary in character." Another said, "Those eyes of his were always strangely penetrating. The SS men couldn't stand his glance and used to yell at him, 'Look at the ground, not at us!'"

Kolbe often let others take his food ration. He said to those who questioned this, "Every man has an aim in life. Most of you men want to return to your wives . . . your families. My part is to give my life for the good of all men." Kolbe encouraged others to keep hope—to lift their voices in songs of praise. One recalled, "He made us see that our souls were not dead."

Good circumstances don't create great people. Great people create good in every circumstance.

—————

Choice, not chance,
determines human destiny.

Imprisoned by Hatred

We ourselves were also once foolish, disobedient, deceived, serving various lusts and pleasures, living in malice and envy, hateful and hating one another.

TITUS 3:3

On February 9, 1960, Adolph Coors III was kidnapped and held for ransom. His body was found seven months later on a remote hillside. He had been shot to death. Adolph Coors IV, who was fifteen years old at the time, lost not only his father but also his best friend. For years, young Coors hated Joseph Corbett, the man who was sentenced to life for the slaying.

Then in 1975, Adolph Coors IV became a Christian. He knew his hatred for Corbett impeded his growth in faith and also alienated him from other people. Still, resentment seethed within him. He asked God to help him stop hating Corbett.

Coors eventually felt led to visit Corbett in the maximum security unit of Colorado's Canon City penitentiary. Corbett refused to see him, but Coors left a Bible with this inscription: "I'm here to see you today and I'm sorry that we could not meet. As a Christian I am summoned by our Lord and Savior, Jesus Christ, to forgive. I do forgive you, and I ask you to forgive me for the hatred I've held in my heart for you." Coors later confessed, "I have a love for that man that only Jesus Christ could have put in my heart." Coors' heart, imprisoned by hatred, was at last set free.

Today, check your heart. Is there anyone you need to forgive?

Who HAS FORGIVEN ME WHEN I NEEDED IT?

Life lived without forgiveness becomes a prison.

The Lord Is My Pacesetter

I rise before the dawning of the
morning, and cry for help;
I hope in Your word.

PSALM 119:147

Do I ALLOW
THE LORD
TO SET THE
PACE FOR ME
EACH DAY?

Not one of us automatically has time to pray. We have to make time for prayer, carving a time out of our day and setting it aside as a sacred appointment that cannot be changed and must not be delayed. As you set aside your prayer time for today, consider this Japanese version of the twenty-third Psalm:

> *The Lord is my pacesetter . . . I shall not rush.*
> *He makes me stop for quiet intervals.*
> *He provides me with images of stillness that restore my serenity.*
> *He leads me in the way of efficiency through calmness of mind, and His guidance is peace.*
> *Even though I have a great many things to accomplish each day, I will not fret, for His presence is here.*
> *His timelessness, His all importance will keep me in balance.*
> *He prepares refreshment and renewal in the midst of my activity by anointing my mind with the oils of tranquillity.*
> *My cup of joyous energy overflows.*
> *Truly harmony and effectiveness shall be the fruits of my hours for I shall walk in the pace of my Lord and dwell in His house forever.*

I have so much to do today that I shall
spend the first three hours in prayer.

The Passions of Life

When the righteous rejoice,
there is great glory.
PROVERBS 28:12

In his autobiography, Bertrand Russell identified the passions that he believed had fueled his long life. "Three passions," he wrote, "simple but overwhelmingly strong, have governed my life: the longing for love, the search for knowledge, and unbearable pity for the sufferings of mankind. These passions, like great winds, have blown me hither and thither, in a wayward course, over a deep ocean of anguish, reaching to the very verge of despair."

Oh, to be a person of passion—to care so deeply that you put all personal need aside in the pursuit of the goal you desire. The passionate way may not be easy or without inner pain, as Russell eloquently stated, but intense passion is rich in the intangible jewels of satisfaction, fulfillment, and deep joy.

What are you passionate about today?

Has GOD GIVEN ME A PASSION I'VE BEEN NEGLECTING?

Do in life what you would do even if no one paid you for it—do what you are passionate about. Soon men will pay almost anything for your services.

The Discovery of Comet Hale-Bopp

*We must give the more earnest
heed to the things we have heard,
lest we drift away.*

HEBREWS 2:1

Am I
ACTING ON
THE DREAMS
GOD HAS
LAID ON
MY HEART?

For astronomer Alan Hale, there's no line between vocation and avocation, between profession and passion. Astronomy is his life. "A lot of this is hobby," he has said. "I'm an amateur astronomer who also decided to make a professional career out of it."

Hale graduated from New Mexico State University with a doctorate in astronomy but then searched unsuccessfully for a research position. He finally formed the nonprofit Southwest Institute for Space Research, which does other research and education work as well as stargazing. Looking through his high-powered telescope continues to be Hale's great love, however. A concrete driveway doubles as his observatory and a basketball court.

Hale's approach is simple: "As long as the telescope is out, I might as well point it at something." One night while aiming at a cluster of stars known as M70, he saw a fuzzy blob where no fuzzy blob should have been. He checked his star charts, then sent an e-mail message to the International Astronomical Union. His find became known as the Hale-Bopp comet.

Discover what it is you love to do, and then do it with your whole heart. Who knows what you may find!

———

Nothing is impossible to the willing heart.

Are You a Spy?

Happy is the man who is always reverent, but he who hardens his heart will fall into calamity.

PROVERBS 28:14

For many years, it has been as common for Christians to give thanks before meals as it has been for them to eat.

During the Thirty Years' War, several Protestant officers were hiding together in a cave. Every day, a little girl from the nearest farm was sent to bring them provisions.

One day a stranger who happened to be walking through the woods joined the officers. Naturally, they were suspicious of him, but he talked so much like one of them that their doubts were overcome.

When the little farm girl came with their supplies, they offered to share their food with the stranger. To their surprise, he began to eat without giving thanks. That single omission revealed the true character of the man. He was what they had suspected at the first—a spy! They barely escaped from him and his comrades.

When we fail to pray, we cheat ourselves of our identity with Christ and deny ourselves the reputation of a faithful follower. A Christian who doesn't pray is like a spy who gets all his information secondhand rather than from the source—the commander in chief.

He who fails to pray does not cheat God. He cheats himself.

What AM I WILLING TO GIVE UP IN ORDER TO SPEND TIME WITH GOD IN PRAYER?

What Is Prayer For?

Let us therefore come boldly to the
throne of grace, that we may obtain mercy
and find grace to help in time of need.

HEBREWS 4:16

How DO
I RATE MY
RELATION-
SHIP WITH
JESUS?

A physician once went to the home of one of his patients who was dying of lung cancer. The doctor spent time sitting at the patient's bedside with the man's wife and children. The dying man knew that he had little time left, and he chose his words carefully, speaking to the physician in a hoarse whisper. Although he had not been a religious person, he revealed to his doctor that he had recently begun to pray frequently.

"What do you pray for?" the physician asked.

"I don't pray for anything," the dying man responded. "How would I know what to ask for?" The physician found this surprising. Surely this dying man could think of some request.

"If prayer is not for asking, what is it for?" the physician asked.

"It isn't for anything," the man said after a few moments of silent thought. "It mainly reminds me I am not alone."

God desires to have a relationship with each one of us. That relationship is the reason for our creation. Relationship with God is what gives our life meaning and purpose. Relationship is what Jesus embodied and what the Holy Spirit establishes. Relationship is why we pray and why we have the privilege of praying.

The greatest privilege God gives to you is
the freedom to approach Him at any time.

Knowing the Shepherd

I will lift up my eyes to the hills—from whence comes my help? My help comes from the LORD, who made heaven and earth.

PSALM 121:1-2

A house party once was held in an English manor. As was customary, the after-dinner entertainment featured recitations and songs from the guests. A famous actor was present, and when it came his turn to perform, he recited the Twenty-third Psalm. His rendition of the familiar psalm was magnificent and was received with much applause.

Later in the evening, the hostess noticed her little old great-aunt dozing in the corner of the room. She was almost completely deaf and had missed most of the evening's entertainment. Still, the other guests urged her to recite something. Since most people of that era knew many poems by memory, the hostess felt sure that her aunt would recite a poem. To everyone's surprise, the elderly woman stood up, her voice quivering, and recited the Twenty-third Psalm! When she finished, there were tears in most eyes, including those of the famous actor. One of the guests later approached the actor and said, "You recited that psalm absolutely superbly. It was incomparable. So why were we so moved by that funny, little old lady?"

He replied, "I know the psalm. She knows the Shepherd."

Prayer is our foremost way of getting better acquainted with Him.

—〇〇〇—

The first purpose of prayer is to know God.

IS THERE SOMETHING THAT KEEPS ME FROM FULLY KNOWING THE SHEPHERD?

A Better Recipe

*We desire that each one of you show
the same diligence to the full
assurance of hope until the end.*

HEBREWS 6:11

What

OPPORTUNI-
TIES HAS GOD
GIVEN ME
THAT WOULD
PROFIT FROM
HARD WORK?

During World War II, Marie Callender was making potato salad and coleslaw in a Los Angeles delicatessen. Then one day her boss asked her to make pies for the lunch crowd. It was the start of a new career!

At first she baked her pies at home, dragging hundred-pound flour sacks into her kitchen. Then in 1948, she and her husband sold their car and bought a Quonset hut, an oven, and a refrigerator—her first commercial kitchen.

She baked the pies; her husband delivered them to restaurants in the area. She began by baking about ten pies a day. Two years later, she was baking more than two hundred pies a day. Sixteen years later, several thousand were coming out of the oven each day.

Marie and her husband opened their first pie shop in Orange County in 1964. Over time, her husband, and later her son, guided the business to a soaring success. By 1986, Ramada Inns, Inc., bought the family business—115 restaurants at that time—from Marie and her son for $90 million.

If a young mother with a rolling pin and sack of flour could give rise to an empire, think what other opportunities await those who will respond with hard work and a "better recipe."

The recipe for successful achievement:
1. Enjoy your work. 2. Do your best.
3. Develop good working relationships.
4. Be open to opportunities.

The Source of Power

He is also able to save to the uttermost those who come to God through Him, since He always lives to make intercession for them.

HEBREWS 7:25

One day in Lucerne, Switzerland, a man rode to the summit of Mount Pilatus in a hydraulically powered cable car. As the car rose along the side of the mountain, he marveled at the wonders of modern engineering. A little more than halfway to the summit, he noticed a beautiful waterfall, splashing down the mountainside.

What a contrast! he thought. In one glance, he had a comparison of the primitive power of nature and the advanced power of technology. Then it occurred to him. The waterfall was not in contrast to the cable car. Rather, it was a complement—the source of the hydraulic power. It was the force of that water that was driving the cable car.

So it is with prayer. The power that takes us up to God is the same power that comes from God. He is the One who calls us to pray, enables us to pray, energizes our prayers with His Spirit, and gives us the capacity to receive His answers.

When we pray in the name of Jesus, the Lord is in our prayers as much as He is in the answers.

Our prayer and God's mercy are like two buckets in a well; while the one ascends, the other descends.

I HAVE FELT GOD TAKE ME UP TO HIS PRESENCE . . .

Going the Extra Mile

He who has a slack hand becomes poor,
but the hand of the diligent makes rich.

PROVERBS 10:4

Is THERE AN
"EXTRA MILE"
IN MY LIFE
I'VE NOT
WALKED
DOWN?

An insurance salesman in Nova Scotia was told by his boss that he and other agents were not assertive enough—that they were not as outgoing as they needed to be in order to score sales. Moments after this pep talk, when he returned to his office, the insurance salesman glanced out his window and had an idea.

Outside his seventeenth-floor window, he saw some window washers working from a scaffold. He quickly wrote a note and held it up to the window for them to see. The note asked if they'd be interested in life, accident, or disability insurance.

The men responded, jokingly, that they couldn't stop what they were doing to talk to him, but if he wanted to join them out on the scaffold, they'd be willing to listen to him while they worked. The insurance salesman took them up on their offer! Using an extra cable on the roof, he lowered himself onto their scaffold. During the course of their conversation, he sold one of the men fifty thousand dollars worth of life insurance!

Sometimes you have to go the extra mile to succeed. Challenge yourself today. Don't let a good opportunity pass you by, even if it seems extraordinarily difficult. With God, all things are possible!

It takes twenty years to make
an overnight success.

No One to Applaud

Children are a gift from God.
PSALM 127:3 TLB

Bill Galston was at the peak of his career when he resigned as a domestic policy adviser to President Clinton to return to teaching at the University of Maryland.

Galston had worked more than a decade on the ideas he hoped to see come to pass. At the White House, he helped in forming the National Campaign Against Teen Pregnancy, planning the National Service Program, and working on education reform and Head Start legislation. He consulted widely with administration officials, had an excellent reputation, and loved his job. He tried integrating time with his son, Ezra, into his schedule—even bringing him to his White House office in the evening—but Galston was continually hounded by the fact that he often came home too tired to spend quality time with his son. He struggled with the contradiction between his "Putting Children First" theme for welfare and the reality in his own home. What triggered his resignation? His son Ezra sent him a note: "Baseball's not fun when there's no one there to applaud you."

The choices you make not only impact your future, but the future of your children. Make sure you have their best in mind in your decisions today.

❦

The darn trouble with cleaning the house is it gets dirty the next day anyway, so skip a week if you have to. The children are the most important thing.

Is there someone in my life who could use a little extra attention today?

The Wind Beneath Their Wings

You, fathers . . . bring [your children]
up in the training and admonition
of the Lord.
EPHESIANS 6:4

What
BEAUTIES
HAS GOD
BLESSED ME
WITH AN
OPPORTUNITY
TO VIEW?

When John was just a boy, he journeyed with his family across the American continent. It took the Scottish family a full year to make their way from coast to coast. As each sunset and sunrise glorified the sky, the father would take his children out to show them the colorful wonder and speak to them about how the cloud formations were surely "the robes of God."

Who can fathom the full impact this trip had on young John? Or how deeply rooted became his reverence for nature on this year-long journey? What we do know is that John Muir became one of America's greatest naturalists. His love for nature led him to the mountains, the glacial meadows, and eventually to the icebound bays of Alaska. The lovely Muir Woods in northern California are named in his honor.

What are you showing your children today? What wind are you putting under their wings? What examples, what encouragement, what insights are you giving to your children?

As the song declares so poignantly, "You are the wind beneath my wings," so is a parent's influence upon a child.

Through the ages no nation has had
a better friend than the mother
who taught her child to pray.

Being Rooted

*Not forsaking the assembling of
ourselves together, as is the manner of some,
but exhorting one another, and so much
the more as you see the Day approaching.*

HEBREWS 10:25

The next time you visit a dense forest, try to imagine what is taking place under your feet. Scientists now know that when the roots of trees come into contact with one another, a substance is released that encourages the growth of a particular kind of fungus. This fungus helps link roots of different trees—even those of dissimilar species. If one tree has access to water, another to nutrients, and a third to sunlight, the fungus enables the transfer of these items to trees that may be in need. Thus, the trees have the means of sharing with one another to preserve them all.

Our culture today applauds individualism. However, it tends to isolate people from one another and cut them off from the mainstream of life. With more and more people working at home or in walled offices and with schedules crammed tighter than ever with work and activities, feelings of loneliness are more likely to increase than decrease. Don't allow isolation to overcome you!

Reach out to others. Give where you can. Learn to receive when others give to you. Build a network of friends, not just colleagues. And above all, root yourself into a group that nourishes and builds you up spiritually—your church.

Does MY CHURCH NOURISH ME?

*The church is like a bank—the more you
put into it, the more interest you have in it.*

Getting Your Z-z-z-z-zs

*It is vain for you to rise up early, to sit
up late, to eat the bread of sorrows;
for so He gives His beloved sleep.*

PSALM 127:2

What CAN I
GIVE UP IN
MY LIFE TO
MAKE TIME
TO RELAX
AND RENEW?

Medical researchers have come to what may seem to be a common-sense conclusion. A missing ingredient in many people's health may be "vitamin Z-z-z-z-z."

When participants in one study were cheated out of four hours of sleep for four consecutive nights, on average they had a 30 percent drop in their immune systems. Such a drop can tremendously increase a person's susceptibility to colds and flu and perhaps to other serious diseases. Says sleep researcher Michael Irwin, MD, "Many people just need a regular-length sleep to get their natural killer cells revved up again."

While a steady diet of sufficient sleep may not completely prevent disease, it can improve the body's defense system and help a person combat disease more efficiently and effectively.

Sleep is the cheapest health aid a person can "take." Sleep is God's own means of restoring health to the body, as well as providing rest to the mind. Often, after a good night's sleep, people report a new outlook on life or a change of heart.

Ask God to renew your strength as you sleep tonight. Then, get to bed on time so He can give you what you requested!

*When I come to the end of
my rope, God is there to take over.*

The Happiest People on Earth

*When you eat the labor of
your hands, you shall be happy,
and it shall be well with you.*

PSALM 128:2

A newspaper in England once asked this question of its readers: "Who are the happiest people on the earth?"

The four prize-winning answers were:

- A little child building sand castles.
- A craftsman or artist whistling over a job well done.
- A mother, bathing her baby after a busy day.
- A doctor who has finished a difficult and dangerous operation that saved a human life.

The newspaper's editors were surprised to find that no one submitted kings, emperors, millionaires, or others of wealth and rank as the happiest people on earth.

W. Beran Wolfe once said, "If you observe a really happy man, you will find him building a boat, writing a symphony, educating his son, growing double dahlias in his garden, or looking for dinosaur eggs in the Gobi desert. He will not be searching for happiness as if it were a collar button that has rolled under the radiator. He will not be striving for it as a goal in itself. He will have become aware that he is happy in the course of living life twenty-four crowded hours of the day."

Live your life to its fullest today.

———❦———

*Happiness not a state to arrive at,
but a manner of traveling.*

Am I
LOOKING AT
MY LIFE AS
EXCITING
OR BLAND?

Help of the Helpless

*Looking unto Jesus, the author and finisher of
our faith, who for the joy that was set before
Him endured the cross. . . . For consider
Him who endured . . . lest you become
weary and discouraged in your souls.*

HEBREWS 12:2-3

What

NEGATIVE

FORCES IN

MY LIFE HAVE

I TRUSTED

GOD TO

RESTRAIN?

After two long days of lying on the ocean floor in a disabled submarine, crewmembers received orders from their commanding officer to sing the following hymn:

*Abide with me! Fast falls the eventide.
The darkness deepens—Lord, with me abide!
When other helpers fail and comforts flee,
Help of the helpless, oh, abide with me!*

After the hymn had been sung, the commander explained to his men that the hymn was his prayer for them and that he hoped it would hold the same meaning for them as it did for him. He then explained that based upon the best information he had, they did not have long to live. There was little or no hope of outside aid, because any searchers who might be on the surface did not know the vessel's position.

Sedatives were distributed to the men to quiet their nerves. One sailor, overcome at the commander's news, fainted. As he swooned, he fell against a piece of equipment, setting in motion the surfacing mechanism that had been jammed! The submarine rose to the surface safely and soon made port.

When we hit bottom in life, prayer is our best resort, for only God knows how to constrain the forces that are keeping His blessings from reaching us!

———⊛⊛⊛———

*To look around is to be distressed.
To look within is to be depressed.
To look up is to be blessed.*

Become a World Traveler

*Pray for us; for we are confident that
we have a good conscience, in all
things desiring to live honorably.*

HEBREWS 13:18

In *Diamonds in the Dust,* Joni Eareckson Tada reveals that her bed is the place she prays best. Because of her paralysis, she is forced to lie down early each evening. Sometimes, a friend comes over to sit on the edge of her bed and pray with her. One night, her friend "sprang a surprise and brought a small short-wave radio. . . . She flicked it on and tuned in Trans World Radio from the Caribbean. Another jiggle of the knob and we picked up someone leading a Bible study over station HCJB in Ecuador. A little more fiddling and we pulled in the BBC from Hong Kong. Together, my friend and I tuned in to the world."

They used the radio as a springboard for prayer. Tada says, "We covered the planet, yet didn't budge beyond my bed. . . . Just as the voices of people around the world reached us through short wave, my prayers, immediate and instant, were touching others. That very second, godly grace was being applied as I prayed, and I didn't even have to leave my room."

Where will you travel in prayer today? What spiritual battles will you wage in faraway places? As you pray, remember these words of Bernard of Clairvaux: "However great may be the temptation, if we know how to use the weapon of prayer well we shall come off conquerors at last, for prayer is more powerful than all the devils."

IS MY PRAYER
LIST FAR-
REACHING?

*More can be done by prayer than anything
else. Prayer is our greatest weapon.*

A Pound of Prayer

*Out of the depths I have
cried to You, O LORD.*

PSALM 130:1

Do I TRUST
GOD TO MEET
MY NEEDS
WHEN ALL I
HAVE LEFT
IS PRAYER?

Many years ago, just after World War I, there was a grocer who tried to weigh a prayer. The week before Christmas, a woman came into his store and asked for food to make a Christmas dinner for her children. He asked her how much she had to spend. She answered, "My husband was killed in the war. I have nothing to offer but a prayer."

The grocer said gruffly, "Write it down," and turned to go about his business. To his surprise, however, the woman took a slip of paper from her purse and handed it to him. "I wrote it down during the night while I was watching over my sick baby," she said. The grocer took the paper and callously placed it on the weight side of his old-fashioned scales. He said, "I'll give you food equal to the weight of this prayer."

To his great astonishment, when he put a loaf of bread on the other side of the scale, it didn't budge. Startled, he added a brick of cheese, and then a turkey, but it still didn't move. Finally, he had loaded so much food on the scale it couldn't hold any more. He handed the woman a bag and said, "You'll have to sack it all yourself," then turned away. It was only after the woman left, tears of joy streaming down her face, that he discovered his scale had broken at the precise moment he placed her prayer on it. For the first time, he looked down to read what the woman had written: "Please, Lord, give us this day our daily bread" (Matthew 6:11).

*God's giving is inseparably
connected with our asking.*

In Need of Mercy

*Judgment is without mercy to
the one who has shown no mercy.
Mercy triumphs over judgment.*

JAMES 2:13

According to a traditional Hebrew legend, Abraham was sitting by his tent one evening when he saw an old man walking toward him. He could tell long before the man arrived that he was weary from age and travel. Abraham rushed out to greet him and then invited him into his tent. He washed the old man's feet and gave him something to eat and drink.

The old man immediately began eating without saying a prayer or invoking a blessing. Abraham asked him, "Don't you worship God?" The old traveler replied, "I worship fire only and reverence no other god." Upon hearing this, Abraham grabbed the old man by the shoulders and with indignation, threw him out of his tent into the cold night air.

The old man walked off into the night, and after he had gone, God called to His friend Abraham and asked where the stranger was. Abraham replied, "I forced him out of my tent because he did not worship You." The Lord responded, "I have suffered him these eighty years although he dishonors Me. Could you not endure him one night?"

Do you know someone who needs to experience your mercy as a tangible expression of God's grace? Don't turn away. Open the door of your heart.

Who HAS
GIVEN ME
THE MERCY
I NEEDED
IN LIFE?

*Mercy among the virtues is like the moon
among the stars. . . . It is the light that
hovers above the judgment seat.*

The River Flows to the Sea

Now the fruit of righteousness is sown
in peace by those who make peace.
JAMES 3:18

**How CAN
I BE A
PEACEMAKER
TODAY?**

Two men once made small talk at a party. "You and your wife seem to get along very well," one man said. "Don't you ever have differences?" "Sure," said the other. "We often have differences, but we get over them quickly."

"How do you do that?" the first man asked. "Simple," said the second. "I don't tell her we have them."

In *Letters to Philip,* Charles Shedd describes a slightly different situation—harmony that comes after love has conquered conflict. "In one town where I lived, two rivers met," he writes. "There was a bluff high above them where you could sit and watch their coming together. . . . Those two nice streams came at each other like fury. I have actually seen them on days when it was almost frightening to watch. They clashed in a wild commotion of frenzy and confusion. . . . Then, as you watched, you could almost see the angry white caps pair off, bow in respect to each other, and join forces as if to say, 'Let us get along now. Ahead of us there is something better.' Sure enough, on downstream, at some distance, the river swept steadily on once more."

Don't avoid the conflicts in your marriage. Choose to apply God's love in order to overcome them. Unresolved conflicts weaken a marriage, but conflicts resolved with love help make two small streams into one large river, flowing on to something better.

❧

Peace is not the absence of conflict
from life, but the ability to cope with it.

In the Blink of an Eye

Why, you do not even know what will happen
tomorrow. What is your life? You are a mist that
appears for a little while and then vanishes.

JAMES 4:14 NIV

We've only a moment here on earth. It just seems like a lifetime. Ask any ninety-year-old and she'll tell you, life flies by like a magic carpet.

Our lives are that moment when the perfume hangs in the air before dissipating. We've only a mist of a lifetime, and then it will be spent. While our souls will live eternally, our opportunities on this earth to love and laugh with people will be gone before we can fully appreciate it.

So we need to breathe deeply and live fully and thank wholeheartedly and kiss passionately and hug warmly and love without reserve. We need to have babies and train pets and smell good food and laugh with friends. We need to cry freely and dance sometimes and sing whenever we have the chance. We will only have a moment here, and then it will be gone. Looking ahead, it seems like a lifetime, but looking back, it's just the blink of an eye.

He who provides for this life, but takes no care for eternity, is wise for a moment, but a fool forever.

Is THERE SOMETHING KEEPING ME FROM LIVING MY LIFE TO THE FULLEST?

As White as Soapsuds

Confess your trespasses to one another, and pray for one another, that you may be healed. The effective, fervent prayer of a righteous man avails much.

JAMES 5:16

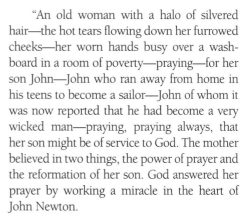

What MIRACLES AM I LOOKING TO GOD FOR?

"An old woman with a halo of silvered hair—the hot tears flowing down her furrowed cheeks—her worn hands busy over a washboard in a room of poverty—praying—for her son John—John who ran away from home in his teens to become a sailor—John of whom it was now reported that he had become a very wicked man—praying, praying always, that her son might be of service to God. The mother believed in two things, the power of prayer and the reformation of her son. God answered her prayer by working a miracle in the heart of John Newton.

"John Newton, the drunken sailor became John Newton, the sailor-preacher [who wrote the words to 'Amazing Grace']. Among the thousands of men and women he brought to Christ was Thomas Scott . . . [who] used both his pen and voice to lead thousands of unbelieving hearts to Christ, among them William Cowper . . . [who] in a moment of inspiration wrote 'There Is a Fountain Filled With Blood.' And this song has brought countless thousands to the Man who died on Calvary. All this resulted because a mother took God at His word and prayed that her son's heart might become as white as the soapsuds in the washtub."—from *Spring in the Valley* by Mrs. Charles E. Cowman.

When praying for your children, keep in mind that not only will your children's lives be changed, but they will change the lives of others.

───❊───

Many a man has kept straight because his mother bent her knees.

I Will Rejoice in the Lord

Though now you do not see Him,
yet believing, you rejoice with
joy inexpressible and full of glory.

1 PETER 1:8

A woman was fearful about the outcome of the surgery she faced. Doctors had not been able to discover the reason for her symptoms, and cancer seemed an undeniable possibility. To add to her concern, she had little in savings, and being self-employed, she had no insurance or paid sick leave.

As the day of her surgery drew closer, she found herself reading her Bible more and more frequently. A passage in Habakkuk puzzled her. The prophet obviously knew his nation was about to be invaded and ravaged, but he said, "Though the fig tree may not blossom, nor fruit be on the vines; though the labor of the olive may fail, and the fields yield no food; though the flock may be cut off from the fold, and there be no herd in the stalls—yet I will rejoice in the LORD" (Habakkuk 3:17-18). She began to reflect on the fact that God was always with her and always loved her. Instead of asking for healing, finances, or peace, her prayer became simply, "I love You, too! I love You, too!"

As it turned out, the surgeons removed a benign cyst. Her recovery passed quickly. Friends helped with meals, laundry, housecleaning, errands, and even a mortgage payment. She reflected later, "This experience made my love for God grow deeper. And that was far more meaningful than a good medical report."

If you are facing a burdensome situation today, reflect on God's love for you. Remember His faithfulness in the past. Then, with joy in your heart, tell God how much you love Him. As you express your love to Him, it will grow.

How HAS GOD BLESSED ME IN THE PAST?

No prayer of adoration will ever soar
higher than a simple cry: "I love You, God."

How to Fight Fair

Therefore, laying aside all malice,
all deceit, hypocrisy, envy, and
all evil speaking.
1 PETER 2:1

How WILL
I WORK
TOWARDS
A DEEPER
UNDER-
STANDING OF
SOMEONE IN
MY LIFE?

Author Charlie W. Shedd shares "Our Seven Official Rules for a Good, Clean Fight" in the book he wrote to his daughter, *Letters to Karen.* They are:

1. Before we begin we must both agree that the time is right.

2. We will remember that our only aim is deeper understanding.

3. We will check our weapons often to be sure they're not deadly.

4. We will lower our voices one notch instead of raising them two.

5. We will never quarrel or reveal private matters in public.

6. We will discuss an armistice whenever either of us calls "halt."

7. When we have come to terms, we will put it away till we both agree it needs more discussing.

"No small part of the zest in a good marriage comes from working through differences," Shedd says. "Learning to zig and zag with the entanglements; studying each other's reactions under pressure; handling one another's emotions intelligently—all these offer a challenge that simply can't be beat for sheer fun and excitement."

To handle yourself, use your head.
To handle others, use your heart.

Patience and Kindness

*Be completely humble and
gentle; be patient, bearing
with one another in love.*

EPHESIANS 4:2 NIV

Firmin Abautiz was known as a man of serene disposition. Nobody in his town could recall his having ever lost his temper during his eighty-seven years. One man, who doubted the possibility that a person could be so unflappable, made a deal with a housekeeper, offering her money if she could provoke him.

The housekeeper knew that Abautiz was fond of a comfortable, orderly bed, so she neglected to make his bed one day. The next morning, Abautiz kindly reminded her of the undone chore. The next night, Abautiz again found an unmade bed and the following morning, he again called it to her attention. She made a lame excuse, which he kindly accepted.

On the third morning, Abautiz said, "You still have not made my bed; it is evident you are determined not to do it. Well, I suppose you find the job troublesome; but it is of little consequence, for I begin to be used to it already." Moved by such kindness, the woman called off the deal and never again failed to make his bed as comfortable as possible!

Not everything can be the way we like it all the time, but criticism and harsh words rarely bring about a lasting and peaceful cooperation or fulfillment of our desires. Patience and kindness, on the other hand, do.

———∞———

*Living would be easier if men
showed as much patience at home
as they do when they're fishing.*

Whom IN
MY LIFE
CAN I GIVE
PATIENCE
AND KINDNESS
TO TODAY?

When the Shoe's on the Other Foot

Above all things have fervent love
for one another, for "love will
cover a multitude of sins."
1 PETER 4:8

How
DOES MY
PERCEPTION
OF MYSELF
AND OTHERS
NEED
ADJUSTING?

Have you ever noticed . . .

When others are set in their ways, they're obstinate—but you are firm and resolved.

When your neighbor doesn't like your friend, she's prejudiced—but when you don't like her friend, you're a good judge of character.

When she tries to treat someone especially well, she's buttering up the person—but when you do so, you're being thoughtful.

When she takes time to do things well, she's perfectionistic—but when you do so, you're striving for excellence.

When she spends a lot, she's a spend-thrift—but when you overdo, you're generous.

When she notices flaws in things, she's critical—but when you do, you are perceptive.

When she is mild-mannered, you call her weak—but when you are, you're gracious.

When she dresses well, she is extravagant—but when you do, you're tastefully in style.

When she says what she thinks, she's opinionated—but when you do, you're being honest.

When she takes great risks, she's foolhardy—but when you do, you're brave.

Faults are thick where love is thin.

Worry, Worry, Worry

*Casting all your care upon
Him, for He cares for you.*

1 PETER 5:7

People who continually worry about every detail of their lives are like this patient in a mental hospital who stood with her ear pressed against the wall:

"What are you doing?" asked a curious attendant.

"Shhhh," the woman whispered, beckoning to the attendant to join her at the wall.

The attendant pressed her ear to the wall and stood there for several moments listening intently. "I can't hear anything," she said.

"No," the patient replied with a furrowed brow. "It's been like that all day!"

Some worry about what might be said. Others worry about what hasn't been said. Some worry about what might happen. Others worry about what hasn't happened but should have happened by now. Others worry about their future while others fret over the consequences of their past.

We were created for abundant life—mind, body, and spirit. Like a flower, we were meant to blossom, not to wither on the vine. Turn your worries over to Jesus today and walk in peace—mind, body, and spirit.

What WORRIES DO I CONTINUE TO CARRY INSTEAD OF GIVING THEM TO GOD?

*Worry: the interest paid by
those who borrow trouble.*

343

Make an Honest Soap

For this very reason, giving all diligence, add to your faith virtue, to virtue knowledge, to knowledge self-control, to self-control perseverance, to perseverance godliness, to godliness brotherly kindness, and to brotherly kindness love. . . . Therefore, brethren, be even more diligent to make your call and election sure, for if you do these things you will never stumble.
2 PETER 1:5-7,10

I WILL ASK GOD FOR THE GIFTS OF HUMILITY AND GENEROSITY BECAUSE...

When William was only sixteen years old, he tied all his possessions into a small bundle and left home to seek his fortune. He told an old canal-boat captain that his father was too poor to keep him and the only trade he knew was soap and candle making.

The old captain knelt and earnestly prayed for the boy and then advised him, "Soon, someone will be the leading soap-maker in New York. It can be you as well as someone else. Be a good man, give your heart to Christ, pay the Lord all that belongs to Him, make an honest soap, give a full pound, and I'm certain you'll be a prosperous and rich man."

When he arrived in the city, William remembered the captain's words, and although poor and lonely, he joined a church and gave one-tenth of his first dollar, just as the captain had exhorted him. Once he gained regular employment, he soon became a partner in the business, then later, the sole owner. He made an honest soap, and as he became more successful, he increased his giving from 10 percent to 50 percent—eventually to 100 percent of his income. In all, William Colgate gave millions.

The marks of success are not only know-how and diligence, but also humility and generosity.

———— ✦ ————

Six essential qualities that are the key to success: sincerity, personal integrity, humility, courtesy, wisdom, charity.

Breathe without Ceasing

Now when Daniel knew that the writing was signed, he went home . . . knelt down on his knees three times that day, and prayed and gave thanks before his God, as was his custom since early days.

DANIEL 6:10

On a trip across the Atlantic, Dwight L. Moody had an opportunity to help the crew and other volunteers put out a fire in the hold of the ship. As they stood in the bucket brigade, a friend said to Moody, "Let's go up to the other end of the ship and pray."

Moody, an evangelist with a great deal of common sense, said, "No, sir, we will stand right here, pass buckets, and pray hard all the time we are doing so!"

To be a praying Christian does not mean we pray occasionally, but that we pray continually—wherever we are, whatever we are doing. We must put our faith into action. Just as . . .

- no one can live by taking a breath only once in awhile or survive by taking only a sip of water once a week

- no person can read by a light that flickers on and off

- no sailor can steer his course with only an occasional puff of wind.

So it is with prayer and the Christian life. We must pray always, in all things, and in spite of all circumstances.

Where DOES MY MIND AUTOMATICALLY TURN IN TIMES OF TROUBLE?

Pray devoutly, but hammer stoutly.

Grow in Grace

Grow in the grace and knowledge of our Lord and Savior Jesus Christ. To Him be the glory both now and forever. Amen.

2 PETER 3:18

What "SCRATCHES" IN MY LIFE WILL I CONSIDER IN A DIFFERENT LIGHT?

The story is told of a king who owned a valuable diamond, one of the most perfect and rare in the world. One day the diamond fell, and a deep scratch marred its face. The king summoned the best diamond experts in the land to correct the blemish, but they all agreed they could not remove the scratch without cutting away a good part of the surface, thus reducing the weight and value of the diamond.

Finally, one expert appeared and assured him that he could fix the diamond without reducing its value. His confidence was convincing, and the king gave the diamond to the man. In a few days, the artisan returned the diamond to the king, who was amazed to find that the ugly scratch was gone, and in its place, a beautiful rose was etched. The former scratch had become the stem of an exquisite flower!

Any mistake we make in life may temporarily mar our reputation. But if we stick to what we know is right and continue to conform our will to that of God's, we can trust Him to turn the "scratches" on our souls into part of His signature. That's what it means to grow in God's grace.

❦

Success in life is a matter not so much of talent or opportunity as of concentration and perseverance.

Wholeness

*If we confess our sins, He is faithful
and just to forgive us our sins and to
cleanse us from all unrighteousness.*

1 JOHN 1:9

When Helen Keller was about six years old, her aunt made her a doll out of towels. It was a gangly, misshapen creation. The first thing Helen noticed when she picked up the doll, however, was not its shape, but that it had no eyes. She tugged at a string of beads her aunt was wearing and placed them approximately where the doll's eyes should have been. Her aunt touched Helen's eyes and then with Helen's hand in hers, touched the doll's head. Helen nodded, "Yes!"

Immediately, her aunt found two buttons and sewed them onto the doll. Not being able to see herself, Helen insisted that her aunt make her doll better than she was. She wanted her doll to be whole.

Each of us instinctively desires to be whole. In the recesses of our hearts, we know that we are not complete, in spite of what others tell us or what we try to tell ourselves. True wholeness comes when our entire identity is with the Lord. He alone is complete.

Our prayers take on new intensity and meaning when we have a hunger to become like Christ. It is then that prayer becomes a path to genuine health and wholeness. In becoming like Christ, we become whole.

How WILL
I STRIVE
TO BECOME
CHRIST-LIKE
TODAY?

*Do not our prayers for help mean: Help
me to be better than I know myself to be.*

Down in the Mire

*If anyone sins, we have an
Advocate with the Father,
Jesus Christ the righteous.*

1 JOHN 2:1

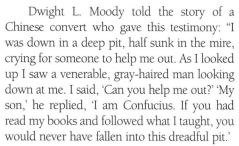

Am I
DEPENDING
ON CHRIST
TO
INTERCEDE
FOR ME WITH
THE FATHER?

*If we could hear Christ praying
for us in the next room, we would
have no fear. Yet distance makes no
difference. He is praying for us.*

Dwight L. Moody told the story of a Chinese convert who gave this testimony: "I was down in a deep pit, half sunk in the mire, crying for someone to help me out. As I looked up I saw a venerable, gray-haired man looking down at me. I said, 'Can you help me out?' 'My son,' he replied, 'I am Confucius. If you had read my books and followed what I taught, you would never have fallen into this dreadful pit.'

"Then he was gone. Soon I saw another man coming. He bent over me with closed eyes and folded arms. 'My son,' Buddha said, 'forget about yourself. Get into a state of rest. Then, my child, you will be in a delicious state just as I am.' 'Yes,' I said, 'I will do that when I am above this mire. Can you help me out?' I looked and he was gone.

"I was beginning to sink into despair when I saw another figure above me. There were marks of suffering on His face. 'My child,' He said, 'what is the matter?' But before I could reply, He was down in the mire by my side. He folded His arms about me and lifted me up and then fed and rested me. When I was well He did not say, 'Shame on you for falling into that pit.' Instead He said, 'We will walk on together now.' And we have been walking together until this day."

No one can pray for you with greater insight or compassion than Jesus. The Bible says He is continually making intercession to the Father on your behalf. He doesn't condemn you when you fail; He climbs right into your failure with you and pulls you out. He is the friend who sticks closer than a brother.

Small Deeds

My little children, let us
not love in word or in tongue,
but in deed and in truth.
1 JOHN 3:18

A missionary was sailing home on furlough when she heard a cry one night—a cry that is perhaps the most frightening to hear when at sea: "Man overboard!" She quickly arose from her berth, lit her cabin lamp, and then held it at the window of her cabin in hopes of seeing some sign of life in the murky waters outside.

Seeing nothing, she hung the lamp back on its bracket, snuffed it out, and returned to her berth to pray for the man lost at sea. In the morning, she discovered the man had been rescued. Not only that, but she learned it was the flash of her lamp through the porthole that showed the rescuers the location of the missing man, who was desperately clinging to a rope still attached to the deck. He was pulled from the cold waters in the nick of time. Her small deed of shining a lamp at the right time had saved a man's life.

It isn't the size of the deeds you do that counts. It's the fact that you do them for good and not for evil, trusting that God can take every deed you perform and use it for His purpose—in your life and in the lives of others.

The smallest deed is better
than the greatest intention!

How AM I LOOKING FOR GOD TO WORK THROUGH MY ACTIONS?

Only Temporary

*The God of all grace, who called you to his
eternal glory in Christ, after you have suffered
a little while, will himself restore you and
make you strong, firm and steadfast.*

1 PETER 5:10 NIV

What CIRCUM-
STANCES IN
MY LIFE
WOULD
CHANGE IF I
VIEWED THEM
AS ONLY
TEMPORARY?

In *My Mother Worked and I Turned Out
Okay*, Katherine Wyse Goldman tells about
Margaret, one of five children in a family during
the 1930s and 1940s.

Margaret's mother left her alcoholic
husband and took her children to live in a
three-room apartment, which was all she could
afford. To make ends meet, she worked two
jobs. Her night job, from 10 P.M. to 7:30 A.M.,
was editing the company newspaper for the
Pennsylvania Railroad. The children would
greet their mother by the curb when her trolley
pulled up in the morning, and she'd get them
ready for school. After only a couple of hours of
sleep, she'd go to her day job at 10 A.M. A little
after 4 P.M., her children would greet her at the
same curb. After a light supper, the children did
their homework as quietly as possible so their
mother could get a few more hours of sleep.
Margaret said of her mother: "Mother never had
a day off both jobs at the same time. My grandmother wanted to put us in foster homes, but
my mother said no, that she could do it. She'd
tell us the way we lived was temporary."

What wonderful wisdom to apply to any
of the hardships we experience as mothers!
Remember that this, too, is only temporary.

❈

*Think of the sacrifice your mother had
to make in order that you might live.
Think of the sacrifice God had to make
that you and your mother might live.*

Nobody's Perfect

*Now this is the confidence that we have in Him,
that if we ask anything according to His will,
He hears us. And if we know that He hears us,
whatever we ask, we know that we have
the petitions that we have asked of Him.*

1 JOHN 5:14-15

While teaching a Bible class, a woman lost her place in her notes as she was speaking. As she continued to speak, she tried to find where she had gotten off course, but when she realized she was hopelessly lost in her own muddle of words, she apologized to the group and paused to search for the missing page. The pause grew agonizingly long and at last, she gave up the search and ad-libbed her way through the rest of the lesson. She couldn't remember the applications she had planned to make, forgot part of her main illustration, and knew her conclusion was weak. As she left the lectern, she was on the verge of tears, feeling like an abysmal failure.

To her great surprise, a woman came to her to say that she thought this had been the best Bible class so far. Later, another woman called to thank her for a specific word that was just what she needed to hear.

The teacher called a friend and said, "I don't understand what happened. I had prepared the best I could." Her friend laughed and said, "Do you remember what you said last week—that you were praying these women would be able to relate to you and you to them? Perhaps that's precisely what happened. They aren't perfect, either!"

God's answers to prayer may not always be what we expect, but they are always fruitful.

Does
ANYTHING
KEEP ME FROM
LOOKING
FOR GOD'S
ANSWERS TO
MY PRAYERS?

———❦———

*Good prayers never come creeping home.
I am sure I shall receive either
what I ask, or what I should ask.*

351

Simple Decision Making

Do you see a man hasty in his words?
There is more hope for
a fool than for him.
PROVERBS 29:20

Have I PUT
MY ENTIRE
BEING INTO
THE HANDS
OF THE ALL-
KNOWING
GOD?

When reporters bombarded Cardinal Francis Spellman with a barrage of questions during a surprise interview, he finally pointed to a mounted fish on the wall behind his desk. Under the fish was inscribed: "If I had kept my mouth shut, I wouldn't be here."

Perhaps the most potent words in any language are a simple yes or no, without explanation or elaboration. Most decisions eventually become that simple.

To reach the point of answering yes or no, we do well to ask ourselves these questions:

1. *Is there anyone else who must take part in this decision?* If you are either the sole decision maker or the final decision maker, then you alone must make a decision!

2. *What will happen if I wait?* In most cases, things will either get better or worse. Weigh your decision in the balances, realizing that your decision is likely to lean in favor of the heavier weight of the argument, then decide.

3. *Does the decision have a moral dimension?* If so, hold to your values and make your decision based upon them.

In every decision, lean on the One who knows the beginning from the end of every situation—God!

Just when I need Him, He is my all,
answering when upon Him I call;
tenderly watching lest I should fall.

Lord, Be My Strength

But you, beloved, building yourselves
up on your most holy faith,
praying in the Holy Spirit.

JUDE 20

Dr. A. B. Simpson, a New York preacher, was plagued by poor health. Two nervous breakdowns and a heart condition led a well-known New York physician to tell him—at the age of thirty-eight—that he would never live to be forty. The physician's diagnosis was no surprise to Simpson. Preaching was agonizing for him; even climbing a slight elevation left him breathless.

In desperation, Simpson went to the Bible to find out what Jesus had to say about disease. He became convinced that Jesus always meant for healing to be a part of redemption. One Friday afternoon shortly after Simpson came to this conclusion, he went for a walk in the country. Coming to a pine woods, he sat down on a log to rest and pray. He asked Christ to enter him and to become his physical strength until his life's work was accomplished. He later said, "Every fiber in me was tingling with the sense of God's presence."

Days later, Simpson climbed a three-thousand-foot mountain. He said, "When I reached the top, the world of weakness and fear was lying at my feet. From that time on I literally had a new heart." He went on to preach three thousand sermons in the next three years, holding as many as twenty meetings a week. He amassed an amazing volume of work before he died—at the age of seventy-six.

Whatever you may be facing that leaves you feeling weak and fearful—illness, injury, stress, or anxiety—God will take your strength, which is weakness, and replace it with His strength. His strength is more than enough to see you through every trial or temptation, and it's always available. All you need to do is ask.

IS THERE SOMETHING THAT KEEPS ME FROM COMPLETELY TRUSTING IN GOD'S STRENGTH?

Those who quietly, through prayer,
used God's power, were the ones
who made the world move forward.

Overflowing Blessings

*A man's pride will bring him low, but
the humble in spirit will retain honor.*

PROVERBS 29:23

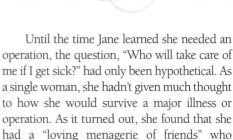

Where AM
I SEEKING
GOD'S
PROVISION?

Until the time Jane learned she needed an operation, the question, "Who will take care of me if I get sick?" had only been hypothetical. As a single woman, she hadn't given much thought to how she would survive a major illness or operation. As it turned out, she found that she had a "loving menagerie of friends" who "cobbled together a schedule of ministry and then passed the baton from one to the next" while she marveled at her blessing.

Stephanie was the ringmaster, the one by her side at the hospital, who also helped her check her incision and take showers. Bob drove up from Los Angeles with his dog to stay for a few days after she returned home. Peggy brought over Thai take-out food. Ann arrived with a bread machine and bags of groceries. She also made soup, mopped the kitchen floor, and did the laundry. Michelle brought mail from the office and drove her to doctors' appointments.

It was amazing to Jane that these various people hardly knew each other when they first began helping her, but by the time she recovered, they had all become friends.

God's provision in your life is always beneficial for you. However, He often provides in such wonderful abundance that even those who carry the blessing to you are blessed themselves.

---

*The branches that bear
the most fruit hang the lowest.*

Reaping a Harvest

*Remember this: Whoever sows sparingly
will also reap sparingly, and whoever
sows generously will also reap generously.*

2 CORINTHIANS 9:6 NIV

Whose LIFE
CAN I INVEST
IN TODAY?

The late Spencer Penrose, whose brother was a major political leader in Philadelphia in the late nineteenth century, was considered the black sheep of the family. He chose to live in the West, instead of the East. In 1891, fresh out of Harvard, he made his way to Colorado Springs. Not long after his move, he wired his brother for $1,500 so that he might go into a mining venture. His brother telegraphed him $150 instead—enough for train fare home—and warned him against the deal.

Years later, Spencer returned to Philadelphia and handed his brother $75,000 in gold coins—payment, he said, for his investment in his mining operation. His brother was stunned. He had qualms about accepting the money, however, and reminded his brother that he had advised against the venture and had only given him $150. "That," replied Spencer, "is why I'm only giving you $75,000. If you had sent me the full $1,500 I requested, I would be giving you three-quarters of a million dollars."

Nothing invested; nothing gained. Every harvest requires an initial seed. Be generous in your seed sowing. Plant into good ground, and you can anticipate a good return.

—∞∞—

*He that would have fruit
must climb the tree.*

Starve Your Anger

Set a guard, O LORD, over my mouth;
keep watch over the door of my lips.
PSALM 141:3

Have THERE
BEEN WORDS
I'VE SPOKEN
TO SOMEONE
THAT
SHOULD BE
REGRETTED?

General Horace Porter once wrote about a conversation he had with General Ulysses Grant one evening while they were sitting by a campfire. Porter noted, "General, it seems singular that you should have gone through all the rough and tumble of army service and frontier life and have never been provoked into swearing. I have never heard you utter an oath."

Grant replied, "Well, somehow or other, I never learned to swear. When a boy, I seemed to have an aversion to it, and when I became a man I saw the folly of it. I have always noticed, too, that swearing helps to arouse a man's anger; and when a man flies into a passion his adversary who keeps cool always gets the better of him. In fact, I could never see the value of swearing. I think it is the case with many people who swear excessively that it is a mere habit . . . they do not mean to be profane; to say the least, it is a great waste of time."

Not only does anger give rise to harsh words, but also harsh words feed anger. The seething soul uses up valuable inner energy, leaving far less for the normal healthy functioning of spirit, mind, and body. To rid yourself of feelings of anger and frustration, perhaps the first step is to watch your tongue!

If you feel "dog tired" at night, maybe it's
because you "growled" all day.

Twelve Dollars and Eighty-two Cents

O LORD, how manifold are thy works!
in wisdom hast thou made them all:
the earth is full of thy riches.

PSALM 104:24 KJV

A young boy was walking along a road one day when he spotted a copper penny shining in the dust. He picked it up and clutched it with excitement. The penny was his, and it had cost him nothing!

From that day on, wherever he walked, he kept his head down and his eyes closely surveying the ground for more pennies—and perhaps even greater treasure. During his lifetime, he found more money to be sure. In fact, he collected 302 pennies, 24 nickels, 41 dimes, 8 quarters, 3 half-dollar pieces, and 1 worn-out paper dollar—a total of $12.82. He kept his treasure safe, protecting it as a legacy of free wealth. He delighted in the fact that the money had cost him nothing.

Or had it? In the course of scouting out his treasure, he had missed seeing the full beauty of 35,127 sunsets, the splendor of 327 rainbows, the beauty of white clouds floating overhead in crystal blue skies, birds soaring, squirrels hopping from branch to branch in the trees above the paths on which he walked, and the brilliance of autumn leaves fluttering against a backdrop of autumn sunshine.

What he had acquired—all $12.82—certainly wasn't equal to what he had missed.

Have I BECOME SO FOCUSED ON SMALL THINGS THAT I'M MISSING THE BEAUTY GOD HAS PLACED AROUND ME?

No one ever said on their deathbed: I wish I would have spent more time at work!

Finding Yourself

You created my inmost being; you knit me together in my mother's womb. I praise you because I am fearfully and wonderfully made; your works are wonderful.

PSALM 139:13-14 NIV

What KIND OF PERSON HAS GOD REVEALED HE CREATED ME TO BE?

One of the central characters of the 1960s TV show, *Dobie Gillis*, was Maynard, a beatnik with beads, sandals, and goatee who avoided work at all cost. He was more comical than intelligent. In one show, Maynard informed Dobie that he was planning to do what many rock stars were doing during that era—make a pilgrimage to the Far East to consult with a guru about the meaning of life. Maynard did his best to explain to Dobie why he felt he needed to speak with an ancient wise man and find out who he really was.

Dobie finally said to him with candor, "Maynard, you will never find yourself on a mountain in Tibet."

"Why not?" Maynard asked.

"Because you didn't lose yourself on a mountain in Tibet!"

The real you cannot be found on a mountain somewhere or in any other change of physical location. You find yourself, not by searching outside, but through the Spirit of God within you. When you ask God to reveal who He created you to be, you can rejoice in His loving grace and mercy. He will gently point out your weaknesses and failings and graciously forgive you when you ask. The One who created you is the One who knows you. You will only find yourself in Him.

God reveals Himself unfailingly to the thoughtful seeker.

More Than Enough

*Beloved, I pray that you may prosper
in all things and be in health,
just as your soul prospers.*

3 JOHN 2

One day a poor young artist called her aunt to let her know that she was leaving on a trip. She was going to try to sell her wood carvings of sea birds to the owner of the gift shop at a fashionable resort. She asked her aunt to pray that her venture would be successful. Her aunt assured her that she would pray for the largest order she had ever received!

That evening, the young artist called her aunt back. With great exuberance, she told her aunt what had happened. Not only had the gift-shop owner purchased all of her carvings, but also the owner of a chain of gift shops had ordered as many carvings as she could make! She was filled with wonder at how abundantly God had answered prayer. "Now," she said to her aunt, "pray that I can fill his order!"

Her aunt wisely replied, "The Lord doesn't open a door for us unless He expects us to walk through it successfully. When you pray for rain, don't be surprised when you get a cloudburst!"

Are you praying for God to meet a need in your life today? Are you expecting a bare-minimum, meager-but-satisfactory answer? Or, are you expecting an abundant, more-than-enough supply? Our God is a generous giver!

How HAS GOD PROVEN HIMSELF TO ME IN THE PAST AS THE GENEROUS GIVER?

*Prayer is not overcoming God's reluctance;
it is laying hold of His highest willingness.*

359

Find No Excuse for Mediocrity

We pray this in order that you may live a life worthy of the Lord and may please him in every way: bearing fruit in every good work, growing in the knowledge of God.

COLOSSIANS 1:10 NIV

How HAS A SITUATION CHANGED IN MY LIFE WHEN I PUT MY ALL INTO THE EFFORT?

Someone once asked Al Jolson, a popular musical comedy star of the twenties, what he did to warm up a cold audience. Jolson answered, "Whenever I go out before an audience and don't get the response I feel that I ought to get . . . I don't go back behind the scenes and say to myself, 'That audience is dead from the neck up—it's a bunch of wooden nutmegs.' No, instead I say to myself, 'Look here, Al, what is wrong with you tonight? The audience is all right, but you're all wrong, Al.'"

Many a performer has blamed a poor showing on an audience. Al Jolson took a different approach. He tried to give the best performance of his career to his coldest, most unresponsive audiences, and the result was that before an evening was over, he had them applauding and begging for more.

You'll always be able to find excuses for mediocrity. In fact, a person intent on justifying a bad performance usually has their excuses lined up before the final curtain falls. Choose instead to put your full energy into your performance. Your extra effort will turn an average performance into something outstanding.

⸺⸺⸺

Every job is a self-portrait of the person who does it. Autograph your work with excellence.

Giving Up Control

*I cried out to the LORD because of my affliction,
and He answered me. Out of the belly of
Sheol I cried, and You heard my voice.*

JONAH 2:2

After two failed attempts at landing, the balloonist panicked. He frantically searched for a third spot to attempt a touchdown, but all he could see for miles was thick woods. He had only half of one tank of fuel left. Nevertheless, he felt his only option was to hit the burners and try to find a clearing. Nearly paralyzed with fear, he cried out to God, "Help me. Take control of this situation. Lord, find me a safe place to land!" With that prayer, a feeling of calm came over him. His fists unclenched, and he felt a wave of peace.

Even so, the landscape below sped by, and he had no idea where his ground crew might be. Then he spotted a small clearing directly ahead—and in it, two of the biggest bulls he had ever seen. "Lord, I trusted You to find me a safe place to land, and I trust You completely with those bulls!" He held on tightly as the basket roughly hit the ground, tipped over, and was dragged along the ground for about fifty yards.

To his amazement, the bulls seemed oblivious to all the commotion. Almost instantly, his ground crew came racing toward him. One of them said, "You got caught in some nasty wind shear. It's a miracle you kept control." The balloonist knew the true miracle. The true miracle was that he had given up control.

God may not always answer our prayers the way we think they ought to be answered. When we give up all control, and simply trust Him, He will handle any obstacle that gets in our way.

What AREA OF MY LIFE DO I NEED TO GIVE UP CONTROL IN?

*Prayer always gets through to God
no matter where a person might be.*

Pray Without Ceasing

*My voice you shall hear in the
morning, O LORD; in the morning I
will direct it to You, and I will look up.*

PSALM 5:3

IS ANYTHING
STOPPING
ME FROM
BEGINNING
EACH DAY
WITH
PRAYER?

The wife of a dairy farmer habitually rose at four-thirty each morning to milk the cows. When she recognized the need to begin each morning with prayer, she began rising thirty minutes earlier to pray before going to the barn. "Just made a startling discovery!" she wrote in her journal shortly after starting this practice. "The time on my knees each morning is the preparation for prayer. The rest of the day then becomes the prayer."

The great Christian doctor Paul Tournier had a similar experience with prayer. Determined to have a time of prayer before his early rounds, he went to his study, took out his pocket watch, and sat down. He planned to commit an hour to prayer. After a few minutes, he opened his eyes and discovered only a few minutes had elapsed! The next time he looked at his watch, it had been only a few more minutes.

Finally, the hour was over. He was disappointed that he had felt nothing during his prayer time. As he prepared to rise from his desk, he had an impulse to remain seated for a few more moments. He said it was in those moments that God visited his heart. He was convinced that God had used the hour to test his obedience; the reward came in the brief time that followed.

The Bible tells us to "pray without ceasing" (1 Thessalonians 5:17). On the surface, that admonition seems impossible. How can we carry out our responsibilities if we are locked in a prayer closet? However, if you begin the day in prayer and maintain the attitude of prayer in your heart, your entire day can be spent in communion with God, dwelling in His presence.

*He who runs from God in the morning will
scarcely find Him the rest of the day.*

Look for the Beauty

Happy are the people who are in such a state; happy are the people whose God is the LORD!

PSALM 144:15

One rainy day a woman overheard someone say, "What miserable weather!" She looked out her office window to see a big fat robin using a nearby puddle of water for a bathtub. He was splashing and fluttering, thoroughly enjoying himself. She couldn't help but think, *Miserable for whom? It's all a matter of perspective.*

That's a lesson that Lincoln Steffens learned as a young boy. He was watching an artist paint a picture of a muddy river. He told the artist he didn't like the picture because there was so much mud in it. The artist admitted there was mud in the picture, but what he saw was the beautiful colors and contrasts of the light against the dark.

Steffens later preached in a sermon, "Mud or beauty—which do we look for as we journey through life? If we look for mud and ugliness, we find them—they are there. Just as the artist found beauty in the muddy river, because that is what he was looking for, we will find, in the stream of life, those things which we desire to see. To look for the best and see the beautiful is the way to get the best out of life each day."

No one ever developed eyestrain from looking on the bright side.

Do I HAVE A PERSPECTIVE THAT NEEDS CHANGING?

It's All about Relationship

I will extol You, my God . . . I will bless You,
and I will praise Your name forever and ever.
Great is the LORD, and greatly to be praised.

PSALM 145:1-3

What
BLESSINGS
CAN I THANK
GOD FOR
TODAY?

Imagine for a moment that someone you love comes to you and asks to borrow a small sum of money. You no doubt would lend it gladly, in part because of the close relationship you share.

Now imagine that this same person continues to come to you, asking for loans, food, clothing, the use of your car, a place to stay, and to borrow tools and appliances. While you do love this person, you would probably begin to feel that something was wrong. It's not the asking, but the attitude.

What causes the dilemma in this type of situation? The person who is coming with requests no longer sees his friend as someone with thoughts and feelings, but as a source of goods and services. From the perspective of the one who is giving, the friend with whom dreams and innermost thoughts have been shared is now perceived as being concerned only with getting his own needs met.

So often we come to God in prayer with our request list in hand—"God, please do this," or "God, I want that." We are wise to reconsider our relationship with God in prayer. Who is this One to whom we pray? How good has He been to us? Doesn't He deserve our thankful heart?

We are missing out on the incredible benefits of an intimate relationship with God when we always come to Him with an empty hand, instead of a heart full of praise and thanksgiving.

Prayer crowns God with the honor and
glory due to His name, and God crowns
prayer with assurance and comfort.

Safe in His Arms

He shall cover you with His feathers,
and under His wings you shall take refuge;
His truth shall be your shield and buckler.
You shall not be afraid of the terror by night.

PSALM 91:4-5

One night, just days before Christmas, a fire broke out in the home of a family as they slept. One of the girls, Carolyn, who was eight years old at the time, woke up to a popping sound. She knew it wasn't a sound that she was accustomed to hearing at night, so she slipped out of bed to find the source of the strange noise. As she dashed down the hall, she saw swirls of smoke. Carolyn raced to the bedrooms of her parents and siblings.

"Fire!" she screamed. "There's a fire in our house! We've got to get out!"

Immediately, her parents and sister woke up, jumped from their beds, and ran out of the house. But her brother, four-year-old Jason, remained fast asleep. Outside, his parents noticed that their only son was missing. They were panic stricken.

Fearing the boy was still inside, his father headed for the porch as flames whirled up to ten feet in front of him. Before he opened the door, Carolyn burst out the front door, firmly holding Jason's hand. Braving dense smoke, she had gone back inside to find her little brother.

When the news media asked the girl why she had gone back into the burning house for her brother, she simply smiled and said, "Because I love him." Even in the midst of a fiery trial, God is with you. And He just doesn't offer protection during the day; His protection extends into the night as well. Relax, knowing that you're safe in God's arms.

IS THERE A REASON I DON'T FEEL SAFE IN THE ARMS OF GOD?

_____

God plus one is always a majority!

Propelled by a Dream

*God also bearing witness both with signs and
wonders, with various miracles, and gifts of
the Holy Spirit, according to His own will?*
HEBREWS 2:4

What IS
MY ONE
OBJECTIVE
IN LIFE?

At the age of sixteen, Romana was desert-
ed by her husband and left to raise her two children alone. Living in Mexico, she was poverty
stricken, untrained, and unable to speak
English, but she dreamed of a better life. With
only a few dollars to fuel that dream, she
headed for Los Angeles, where she used her last
seven dollars to take a taxi to the home of a
distant relative.

Romana refused to live on the charity of
others. She immediately found a job washing
dishes, followed by a job making tortillas from
midnight to 6 A.M. From her two jobs she was
able to save $500, which she used to invest in
her own tortilla machine. Over time, and with
a great deal of hard work, Romana became the
manager of the largest Mexican wholesale food
business in the world.

Eventually, Romana Banuelos was hand-
picked by Dwight D. Eisenhower to become
the thirty-seventh United States Treasurer. She
exemplified what Eisenhower proclaimed
about dreams propelling our future: "We
succeed only as we identify in life, or in war, or
in anything else, a single overriding objective,
and make all other considerations bend to that
one objective."

---

*Too many people quit looking for
work when they find a job.*

The Art of Listening

*Be silent in the presence
of the Lord GOD; for the
day of the LORD is at hand.*

ZEPHANIAH 1:7

A woman complained that she was coming down with the flu, so her husband took her to the doctor. Immediately, the doctor thrust a thermometer in her mouth and said, "Sit there quietly for five minutes." The woman did as she was told.

The husband was astonished and fascinated. When the doctor returned to the examining room, he pointed with enthusiasm to the thermometer and said, "Doc, how much will you take for that thing?"

Listening is truly a fine art—a great personal trait to cultivate. Those who have the ability to listen are truly valuable.

A man was considered an expert in staging sales seminars. As his new assistant was helping him set up the stage for a presentation, he gave him this advice: "One temptation I must warn you against is this: As you are conducting a meeting, you will often find people disagree with some of your ideas. You may see someone shaking his head negatively as you speak. Now, the natural thing for you to do is to take out after that person and try to convince him further that you are right. Don't do it. The chances are he is the only person listening to you!"

*A good listener is not only popular
everywhere, but after
awhile he knows something.*

How CAN I PRACTICE THE ART OF LISTENING TO THOSE AROUND ME?

Only Love Lasts

He does not delight in the strength of the horse;
He takes no pleasure in the legs of a man.
The Lord takes pleasure in those who fear
Him, in those who hope in His mercy.

PSALM 147:10-11

How CAN I FOCUS MORE ON PEOPLE THAN ON THINGS?

H. Ross Perot, internationally famous billionaire, entrepreneur, and politician, was once quoted as saying, "Guys, just remember, if you get real lucky, if you make a lot of money, if you go out and buy a lot of stuff—it's gonna break. You got your biggest, fanciest mansion in the world. It has air-conditioning. It's got a pool. Just think of all the pumps that are going to go out. Or go to a yacht basin any place in the world. Nobody is smiling, and I'll tell you why. Something broke that morning. The generator's out; the microwave oven doesn't work. . . . Things just don't mean happiness."

When you look around today at the things you possess, ask yourself a question, "What is likely to be in existence two hundred years from now?"

Very likely, nothing you currently own, occupy, or consider to be yours will still have any value, and virtually everything you have may be considered garbage one day. The things of life simply aren't permanent. What is lasting is the love we share and pass on to the next generation.

Success is getting what you want;
happiness is wanting what you get.

Straight Talk about Spending Time with Your Kids

*He has blessed your
children within you.*

PSALM 147:13

Lee Iacocca, former president of Ford Motor Company and former CEO of the Chrysler Corporation, writes in his book, *Straight Talk:*

"My parents spent a lot of time with me, and I wanted my kids to be treated with as much love and care as I got. Well, that's a noble objective . . . but to translate it into daily life, you really have to work at it.

"I spent all my weekends with the kids and all my vacations. Kathi was on the swim team for seven years, and I never missed a meet. Then there were tennis matches . . . and piano recitals. I made all of them too. I was always afraid that if I missed one, Kathi might finish first or finish last and I would . . . not be there to congratulate—or console—her.

"The same with Lia. . . . Once I picked up Lia at Brownie camp. She was six years old and came running out to the car in her new khaki uniform with an orange bandana around her neck and a little beanie on her head. She had just made it into the Potawatami Tribe. She had hoped to join the Navajoes, as she called them, but she was turned down. Still, she was excited, and so was I. Funny thing, I missed an important meeting that day, but for the life of me I have no recollection of what it was."

*A man wrapped up in himself
makes a very small package.*

How CAN I PLAN MY LIFE AROUND SPENDING TIME WITH THE PEOPLE IMPORTANT TO ME?

Family Traditions

*Having a form of godliness
but denying its power.*
2 TIMOTHY 3:5

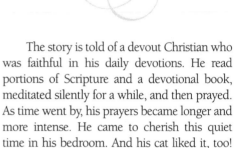

What

RITUALS DO I
HAVE IN MY
LIFE I WOULD
LIKE TO
PASS ON TO
THE NEXT
GENERATION?

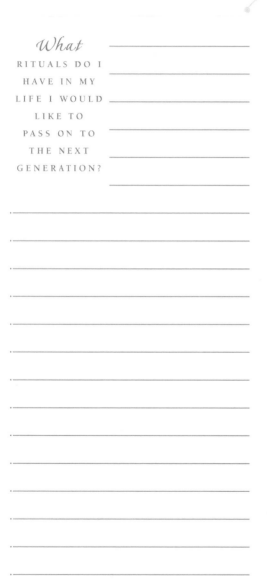

The story is told of a devout Christian who was faithful in his daily devotions. He read portions of Scripture and a devotional book, meditated silently for a while, and then prayed. As time went by, his prayers became longer and more intense. He came to cherish this quiet time in his bedroom. And his cat liked it, too! She would snuggle against him, purring loudly. This interrupted the man, so he put a collar around the cat's neck and tied her to the bedpost whenever he wanted undisturbed devotional time.

The daughter of this man noticed how much his devotional time meant to him, and she adopted the practice. She dutifully tied her cat to the bedpost and proceeded to read and pray. Her prayer time was shorter, however. The day came when her son grew up. He desired also to keep some of the family traditions, but by his generation, the pace of life had quickened greatly. He felt he had no time for elaborate devotions, so he eliminated the time for meditation, Bible reading, and prayer. Still, in order to carry on the tradition, while dressing each morning, he tied his cat to the bedpost!

Explain to your children why you keep certain rituals, lest they follow them blindly, without meaning or purpose.

---

*Children have never been very good at
listening to their elders, but they have
never failed to imitate them.*

Honest Communication

*Husbands, likewise, dwell with them with
understanding, giving honor to the wife,
as to the weaker vessel, and as being
heirs together of the grace of life, that
your prayers may not be hindered.*

1 PETER 3:7

Bill and Lynne Hybels write in *Fit to Be
Tied*, "Picture this: It is midnight. The full moon
is postcard perfect and the breeze is warm.
Lynne and I are sitting on a park bench at a
wooded camp in Wisconsin. Twenty years old.
Dating seriously. No one around . . . I wrap my
arms around her. This is what it's all about, I
think. Lynne lifts her head and looks deeply
into my eyes. 'Bill, I just don't feel close to you
right now.' . . . 'For heaven's sake, honey, what
do you want?' I hug her a little tighter, laugh off
her comment, and dismiss it from my mind.

"Big mistake! If I could play that scene
over, I would do it this way. I would take her
hands off my shoulders, slide about a foot away,
look her straight in the eye and say, 'Why don't
you feel close to me? . . . If you don't know
exactly why you said it, just start talking about
how you feel. Maybe we can figure it out.'

"A response like that would have set a
precedent for honest communication that
could have made our marriage much easier.
Instead we set a precedent for evasiveness, for
burying feelings, for dismissing uncomfortable thoughts."

Never dismiss what your spouse says.
There's a grain of truth in every joke, every sigh,
and every whim. Don't let those opportunities
for honest communication pass you by. Seize
the moment to grow closer to one another.

How WOULD
I RATE THE
LEVEL OF
HONEST
COMMUNI-
CATION WITH
THOSE
CLOSEST
TO ME?

*Communication is depositing a
part of yourself in another person.*

371

Good Humor

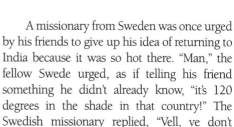

Let Israel rejoice in their Maker; let the children of Zion be joyful in their King.

PSALM 149:2

Have I BEEN ASKING GOD TO KEEP ME CHEERFUL NO MATTER WHAT THE SITUATION?

A missionary from Sweden was once urged by his friends to give up his idea of returning to India because it was so hot there. "Man," the fellow Swede urged, as if telling his friend something he didn't already know, "it's 120 degrees in the shade in that country!" The Swedish missionary replied, "Vell, ve don't always have to stay in the shade, do ve?"

Humor is not a sin. It is a God-given escape hatch. Being able to see the lighter side of life is a virtue. And indeed, every vocation and behavior in life has a lighter side, if we are only willing to see it. Wholesome humor can do a great deal to help defuse a tense, heated situation.

In developing a good sense of humor, we need to be able to laugh at our own mistakes; accept justified criticism—and recover from it; and learn to avoid using statements that are unsuitable—even though they may be funny.

James M. Gray and William Houghton—two godly men—were praying together one day, and the elderly Dr. Gray concluded his prayer by saying, "Lord, keep me cheerful. Keep me from becoming a cranky, old man." Keeping a sense of humor is a great way to avoid becoming a bitter, impatient, critical person.

It isn't your position that makes you happy or unhappy, it's your disposition.

Gossip Golden?

Let your speech always be with grace,
seasoned with salt, that you may know
how you ought to answer each one.

COLOSSIANS 4:6

Laura Ingalls Wilder writes in *Little House in the Ozarks:* "I know a little band of friends that calls itself a women's club. The avowed purpose of this club is study, but there is an undercurrent of deeper, truer things than even culture and self-improvement. There is no obligation, and there are no promises; but in forming the club and in selecting new members, only those are chosen who are kind-hearted and dependable as well as the possessors of a certain degree of intelligence and a small amount of that genius which is the capacity for careful work. In short, those who are taken into membership are those who will make good friends, and so they are a little band who are each for all and all for each. . . .

"They are getting so in the habit of speaking good words that I expect to see them all develop into Golden Gossips.

"Ever hear of golden gossip? I read of it some years ago. A woman who was always talking about her friends and neighbors made it her business to talk of them, in fact, never said anything but good of them. She was a gossip, but it was 'golden gossip.' This women's club seems to be working in the same way."

Who wouldn't enjoy belonging to such a club?

———❦———

Whoever gossips to you
will be a gossip of you.

Am I A "GOLDEN GOSSIP?"

I Think You Are Wonderful

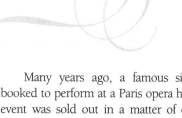

She opens her mouth with wisdom, and
on her tongue is the law of kindness.
PROVERBS 31:26

Who IN MY
LIFE HAS
GIVEN ME A
WORD OF
ENCOURAGE-
MENT WHEN
I NEEDED IT?

Many years ago, a famous singer was booked to perform at a Paris opera house. The event was sold out in a matter of days. The entire city was abuzz with anticipation. The night of the performance, the hall was packed with stately dressed men and women eager to hear the much-admired musician. The house manager took the stage and announced, "Ladies and gentlemen, thank you for your enthusiastic support. I am afraid that due to illness, the woman whom you've all come to hear will not be performing tonight. However, we have found a suitable substitute we hope will provide you with comparable entertainment."

The crowd groaned so loudly in its disappointment that few heard the singer's name. Their excitement fizzled into frustration. The stand-in singer gave everything she had, but when her performance was over, she was met with an uncomfortable silence rather than applause. Then, from the balcony, a child stood up and shouted, "Mommy, I think you are wonderful!"

The crowd instantly responded with a thunderous ovation.

Once in awhile we all need to hear someone say, "I think you are wonderful." Today, be the person who gives a kind word of encouragement to someone in need. God will reward you.

A good word costs no more than a bad one.

Reflections

Reflections

Reflections

Acknowledgments

We acknowledge and thank the following people for the quotes used in this book: George Herbert Palmer (9), Glen Wheeler (10, 217, 328, 338, 350), Henri Nouwen (11), Baron Pierre de Coubertin (12), Ralph Waldo Emerson (14, 86, 88, 163), Herbert Bayard Swope (16), Peter Drucker (18), Robert South (19), Robert Freeman (20), Mahalia Jackson (21), G. Ashton Oldham (22), Martin Luther (24, 318), Jonathan Winters (25), Mary Cholmondeley (26), Hannah More (33, 35), Ann Taylor (34), Joseph Fort Newton (36), Giuseppe Garibaldi (39), Ron Dentinger (40), Larry Eisenberg (45), Arnold Glasgow (47, 141), Jeremy Taylor (48), John Greenleaf Whittier (49), Thomas Paine (50), Julian of Norwich (51), Ole Hallesby (54), Sir James Mackintosh (56), Archbishop Robert Leighton (59), attributed to Saint Patrick (61), Henry Ward Beecher (62), Abraham Joshua Heschel (63), Cyrus (66), Sydney J. Harris (67), Jonathan Swift (68), Arabian Proverb (69), Julius Hare (72), Richard Exley (74), Dorothy Bernard (75), C. H. Spurgeon (77), Mark Twain (78, 287, 292), Sophocles (79), Mother Teresa (80, 118, 127, 166), Charlotte Elliott (81), Herman Melville (82), Bernard (83), Dr. Anthony P. Witham (84, 254), Pendar (85), John Stevenson (87), James Dobson (91, 126), C. Everett Koop (92), Josh Billings (94, 259), William Makepeace Thackeray (95), Bob Brown (101), Gotthold Ephraim Lessing (102), Abraham Lincoln (103, 189), Charles Colson (104, 206), Jack Hayford (108), Michel de Montaigne (110), Dwight L. Moody (111, 262), Farmer's Almanac (115), Henry Wadsworth Longfellow (116), John Aikman Wallace (124), George M. Adams (125), A. T. Mercie (129), Frederick Buechner (130), Betty Mills (132), William J. H. Boetcker (135), Edward George Bulwer-Lytton (136), Albert Einstein (137), H. M. Field (138), Johann Wolfgang von Goethe (142, 310), Victor Hugo (143), George Sand (144), Lawrence D. Bell (146), George F. Tilton (149), Joanna Baillie (150), Shannon Fife (152, 300), Jim Elliot (155, 187), Corrie ten Boom (156, 270), Bruce Larson (157), T. J. Bach (158), Mort Walker (159), Janette Oke (160), Dante Gabriel Rossetti (161), Zig Ziglar (167, 188), Dr. Ronald Levant and John Kelly (168), Charles "Tremendous" Jones (169, 293), Dietrich Bonhoeffer (172), Horace Greeley (174), George Appleton (175), Leonard Ravenhill (177), Thomas Fuller (178, 355), William James (179, 312), James Russell Lowell (182), Thomas Brooks (183, 288, 364), Wofford B. Camp (185), Galileo (186), Walt Disney (190), Saint Basil (191), Merlin R. Carothers (193), Teresa of Avila (194), June Henderson (197), Jean Jacques Rousseau (198), Herbert Hoover (199), Homer (200), Charles Habib Malik (201), Helen Keller (203), Jackie Sherrill (205), Thomas Carlyle (209), Joseph Addison (210), Doug Larson (211), H. G. Wells (212), William A. Ward (215), Sidlow Baxter (218), Amelia Edith Barr (220), Helen Pearson (221), Alexander Whyte (223), Anna Pavlova (224), Erwin W. Lutzer (226), William Shakespeare (227), Joseph P. Dooley (228), Olin Miller (229), Eliza M. Hickok (230), Arthur Schopenhauer (231), Ann Landers (233), Oswald Chambers (234), Lady Bird Johnson (236), French Proverb (239), Reginald Johnson (246), Saint Ambrose (247), Margaret Thatcher (248), John Mason (249), James Robertson (250), Wilson Mizner (251, 367), Mary Pickford (253), Marcus Aurelius Antoninus (255), William McGill (257), David Wilkerson (258), Søren Kierkegaard (263), George Herbert (265), William Poole (269, 352), Edward I. Koch (272), J. R. Miller (274), Joyce Heinrich and Annette LaPlaca (275), Phillips Brooks (276), Francois de La Rochefoucauld (279), Sally Berger (283), Hubert van Zeller (284), Alphonse Karr (285), Mark Steele (289), Charles Buxton (290), W. D. Gough (291), Jakob Böhme (295), Ben Sweetland (298), C. Raymond Beran (299), C. W. Wendte (302, 346), Joseph Joubert (308), Earline Steelburg (311), Arthur Ashe (313), Edwin Markham (314), Booker T. Washington (315), William Arthur Ward (317), Thomas Heywood (320), George Failing (321), Wesley L. Duewel (322), Charles L. Allen (323), Denis Waitley and Reni Witt (324), Mark Hopkins (325), Eddie Cantor (326), Barbara Bush (327), Margaret Lee Runbeck (331), Billy Graham (333), Edwin Hubbel Chapin (335), Tillotson (337), Louis Cassels (339), Donald Laird (340), James Howell (342), George W. Lyon (343), William Menninger (344), Sir William Gurney Benham (345), Dorothy Thompson (347), Joseph Hall (351), Edward P. Roe (353), Honoré de Balzac (358), Richard C. Trench (359), James Montgomery (361), James Baldwin (370), English Proverb (374).

References

Unless otherwise indicated, all Scripture quotations are taken from *The New King James Version* of the Bible. Copyright © 1979, 1980, 1982, 1988, 1994, Thomas Nelson, Inc.

Scripture quotations marked NIV are taken from the *Holy Bible, New International Version®*. NIV®. Copyright © 1973, 1978, 1984 by International Bible Society. Used by permission of Zondervan Publishing House. All rights reserved.

Verses marked TLB are taken from *The Living Bible* © 1971. Used by permission of Tyndale House Publishers, Inc., Wheaton, Illinois 60189. All rights reserved.

Scripture quotations marked KJV are taken from the *King James Version* of the Bible.

If you have enjoyed this book, or if it has
impacted your life, we would like to hear from you.
Please contact us at:

Honor Books
Department E
P.O. Box 55388
Tulsa, Oklahoma 74155
Or by e-mail at info@honorbooks.com

Additional copies of this book and other titles
in our Devotional Series are available
from your local bookstore.

God's Little Devotional Journal
God's Little Devotional Book
God's Little Devotional Book, II
God's Little Devotional Book for Moms
God's Little Devotional Book for Dads
God's Little Devotional Book for Students
God's Little Devotional Book on Prayer
God's Little Devotional Book on Success

Honor Books
Tulsa, Oklahoma